Public Culture

Institute for Public Knowledge

Editor
Shamus Khan

Senior Editors
John Jackson
Andrew Lakoff
Sharon Marcus
Fred Turner
Caitlin Zaloom

Executive Editor
Eric Klinenberg

Editorial Committee
Nadia Abu El-Haj
Craig Calhoun
Neve Gordon
Manu Goswami
Greg Grandin
Bruce Grant
Josh Kun
Johan Lindquist
Alondra Nelson
Eyal Press
Erica Robles-Anderson
Josef Sorett
Marita Sturken
Sudhir Venkatesh
Andrea Voyer
Guobin Yang

Founding Editors
‡Carol A. Breckenridge
Arjun Appadurai

Managing Editor
Stephen Twilley

Assistant Editor
Samuel Kellogg

T0313436

Public Culture

Institute for Public Knowledge

Volume 31, Number 3
September 2019

Violence and Policing

POLICING THE POLICE

Coming Attractions

Call for Contributions

Public Culture aims to publish original research of the highest caliber, and we welcome your submissions. We value strong writing, clear argumentation, imaginative theory, and an engaging prose style. *Public Culture* reaches an audience that transcends scholarly disciplines and extends beyond the academy. We seek work that persuades through evidence, logic, and analysis and that presumes no shared theoretical proclivities, political values, or specialized vocabularies.

Brief opinion-oriented pieces (of 500–3,000 words) run at the front of each issue in the Forum section. Full-length articles (of 6,000–9,000 words) based on original research are at the core. We also feature in-depth discussions with leading contemporary thinkers. Typically, we are familiar only with scholarly labor's final results, published books and articles, or occasional lectures. The interviews we publish call attention to the backstage of intellectual practice. In addition to original research essays, opinion pieces, and conversations, *Public Culture* welcomes translations of previously published, groundbreaking essays.

Our sister publication, *Public Books* (www.publicbooks.org), welcomes proposals for review essays about books (fiction or nonfiction), films, exhibitions, or plays, as well as profiles of intellectuals or literary scenes, visual essays, and multimedia work. Authors interested in submitting to *Public Books* should send proposals of 500 words or fewer to editorial@publicbooks.org.

Public Culture, 20 Cooper Square, Suite 517, New York, NY 10003; phone: 212-998-7866; fax: 212-998-8468; email: info@publicculture.org; web: www.publicculture.org.

Violence Work and the Police Order

Madiha Tahir

In Fall 2011, an American marine—who was involved in the brutal 2004 assault on Fallujah, Iraq—excoriated the NYPD for getting rough with Occupy protesters in Times Square, New York City. Standing in his fatigues and occasionally pointing at the medals pinned to his chest, Sergeant Shamar Thomas chided the police repeatedly, "This is not a war zone!" He paced back and forth in front of a cluster of police officers. "If you want to go kill and hurt people," Thomas screamed at the cops, "go to Iraq! Why are you hurting US citizens?"

Classically, the *state* is understood as a monopoly on violence, or the legitimate use of force over a given territory. In this sense, the state does not minimize force, and its agents—the police—do not eliminate violence. Instead, it legitimates violence through its monopolization of "legitimate" policing. To put it in David Correia and Tyler Wall's (2018: 6) apt and blunt phrasing, "police are violence workers." As violence work, policing exceeds the institution of the police. Indeed, the latest bout of American invasions that cluster under the label "global war on terror" have been framed as a policing operation by American officials as well as several scholars. The latter have argued that there has been a convergence between policing and the military apparatus along with a recent conceptual collapse between the "enemy" (war) and the "criminal" (policing) (Hardt and Negri 2001; Peter Andreas and Richard Price 2001; Virilio quoted in Neocleous 2014; Kahn 2013).

Thomas's castigation of the police can be understood as reestablishing that distinction, and with it, he demarcates an "inside" territory of the nation-state where violence must be regulated, and an "outside"—Iraq, Afghanistan, Yemen, Somalia, Pakistan, and elsewhere—where overwhelming violence can be enacted and justified. Thinking with Rancière (2010) we may say that Thomas urges a particular distribution of the sensible; by partitioning the world into "here" and "there,"

Public Culture 31:3 DOI 10.1215/08992363-7532643
Copyright 2019 by Duke University Press

he polices and reaffirms the current social order that calls for a redistribution of violence away from the inside and toward that which is construed as the outside. What, then, is the relationship between these two violence workers, the soldier and the police officer? Should we characterize violence work, from Ferguson to Fallujah, as policing? And if so, how? What productive analytics, politics, and solidarities can such a framing underwrite? Equally important, what significant inequalities in the global regimes of power does such an analytic obscure?

The essays in this special issue of *Public Culture* do not converge upon a singular understanding. Rather, this issue leverages the strengths of an interdisciplinary conversation—the authors of these papers met and engaged each other at a workshop hosted by Columbia University, generously sponsored by the Institute for Social and Economic Research and Policy—drawing upon a range of empirically grounded and analytically rigorous papers that examine the discourses and practices of policing as a concept. These papers open up our understanding, providing critical insights into the transformation of the relations policing produces, and the order it develops and sustains.

Police Order

In his influential work on the nexus between war power and police power, Mark Neocleous (2011, 2014) has argued that the police ought to be thought of less as an institution (the police), and more as a broad range of powers concerned with constructing a specific social order, an understanding that draws upon and echoes Foucault's (1972: 170) analysis of the police as the "ensemble of mechanisms serving to ensure order." Indeed, this in part explains why the present wars have been termed "policing" operations, although the phenomena may not at all be new. Colonial wars, the most prevalent form of warfare, were often conceived of as "small wars," or "imperial policing" operations, where overwhelming bouts of militarist violence worked in tandem with colonial civil administration to construct a colonial social order (Neocleous 2014; Moyn 2013; Khalili 2012).

Several papers in this issue explore the construction of the contemporary police order and its genealogical and material antecedents. Caren Kaplan and Andrea Miller situate contemporary police technologies, including drones, alongside longer histories of colonial aerial policing and use of civil air power as a technique for controlling populations. They refuse easy distinctions between military and police violence, and shift us away from the techno-fetishism that has often plagued analyses of military and police technologies. Their paper draws our attention to the everydayness of violence work by the police, which, they argue, appears obscure and unremarkable when set against the spectacle of war. Drawing on examples from policing by the Los Angeles Police Department as well as aerial patrol at the US-Mexico border, Kaplan and Miller show how policing reorganizes spatial arrangements by constructing and maintaining boundary lines through checkpoints, raids, aerial patrols, and predictive policing technologies. Their paper enriches our understanding of policing as boundary work.

Rivke Jaffe examines the temporal dimension of the police order through her account of "speculative policing," a future-oriented policing that navigates between calculable (risky) and incalculable (uncertain) futures. Jaffe develops her analysis through ethnographic fieldwork in Jamaica, where the government initiated and used a state of emergency to establish and expand a host of securitization measures including curfews, checkpoints, detention, and data collection of residents in inner-city neighborhoods. These policing practices combined the "risk management of future-oriented policing," writes Jaffe, "with an interest in unlocking the potential of real estate." Thus, future-oriented crime management strategies that anticipate citizens as potential future criminals occurred in tandem with a crackdown on informal economic activities aimed at increasing the potential for real estate redevelopment. Jaffe carefully unpacks these parallel and linked processes to develop a probing inquiry into the techniques and logics of speculative policing as it attempts to control not only the present but also uncertain futures.

The spatial and temporal construction of the police order also arranges social relations as boundaries that partition and sort not only spaces but bodies. Andrew Carruthers ably explores questions of relationality and migrant journeys in the Indonesia-Malaysia borderlands, where ethnic Bugis migrants from Indonesia attempt to pass as Bugis-Malaysians in order to cross the border. Bugis resemble local Malay in speech, and this similitude constructs a productive space for police work, which attempts to establish thresholds of detection. Policing, Carruthers argues, is better understood as the processes of establishing thresholds of sensible intensity, thresholds that in turn underwrite an array of activities and behaviors as Bugis work to regulate their intensities in order to pass. These thresholds thus emerge as critical to establishing forms of relationships; whether one is able to be "more or less" establishes relations to the state, police, and community, and even to one's own identity.

Where Carruthers focuses on relations as the strategic and delicate art of modulating verbal and corporeal cues, Fatima Mojaddedi's finely wrought ethnographic account of the experiences of one Afghan translator, Matin, illuminates how war can "make strange the familiar." Matin, who translates for American forces as they occupy and patrol various parts of his country, speaks of feeling *dil tang*—as though his heart is tight or closed—a sense that, as Mojaddedi shows, redoubles his alienation from the rural countryside that he is asked to translate. As Afghans bootstrap tactics to survive, endure, and, hopefully, outlive the war, Matin experiences the scene of his translation work as unruly and irrepressible, rife with disguises, masks, and double-talk, and immune to an intelligible translation. That which normative theory would hold as a medium of relationality, speech in a war zone, instead becomes volatile. It is, as Mojaddedi writes, both a "medium of persuasion and . . . an uncontrollable instrument of war that proceeds alongside the translator." Finally, the scale of violence that Matin must navigate—beheaded bodies, ambushes, improvised explosives and mine blasts—provides a critical and necessary vantage point to think through the implications of boundaries. Analytical inquiry into the links between police power and war power must also contend with the material distinctions evident in the violence waged "here" and "not here."

"Hey You There!"

What is it to be interpellated as a subject of the law? How does this relate to the construction of subjectivity? Critical Black studies scholarship has especially taken up this question and analyzed the formation of Black subjectivity and its relationship to racialized violence (Hartman 1997; Sexton 2008; Sharpe 2016; Weheliye 2014). These investigations have revealed not only the paucity of the categories of Man but, relatedly, the inextricable relation between anti-Blackness and the violence of the law. In this issue, Jesse Goldberg thinks alongside James Baldwin to further inquire into the racial politics of the law, specifically anti-Blackness as the very condition of possibility of American law itself. Goldberg follows Baldwin as the latter reflects upon his experiences with the violent force of the law through the figure of the policeman, a rumination that severs the normative relationship between the law and justice. In so doing, Baldwin, Goldberg argues, foreshadows the work of Jared Sexton (2007), who has outlined the dependence of the law on that which it polices. Thus, Goldberg writes, "to extricate Blackness from law is to tear apart the fabric of law."

There are resonances of this argument in Didier Fassin's rich ethnographic analysis of French policing of ethno-racial minorities. Fassin asserts that it is not the task of the social scientist to furnish analyses that assist the police in legitimizing their use of force. In keeping with that view, Fassin characterizes the use of overwhelming force as a form of retributive punishment, contra analysts and normative theorists who dismiss the use of violence by police officers as merely deviant or "excessive." Fassin argues, in effect, that the police are violence workers that function as part of a broader punitive apparatus that metes out individual, random, and collective punishment to menace and terrorize racialized communities. "Remarkably, whether it is targeted on a suspect, random or collective," writes Fassin, "such retribution selectively concerns youth from the working class belonging to ethno-racial minorities and living in public housing." Finally, he also attends to the colonial genealogy of these policing practices, tracing patterns and resonances with the development of special police units meant to surveil Algerians in the metropole during the Algerian struggle for independence.

Ilana Feldman's historically informed work in this issue tracks colonial attempts to eliminate the native (Wolfe 2006) in occupied Palestine by legally defining away Palestinian political personhood and political community. Feldman notes that the denial of Palestinian *political* status is critical to Israel's claim that the territories are not occupied. Consequently, a range of actors, from British colonial officials during the Mandate period to the ICRC, to Israel, have attempted to adjudicate just what kind of subjects Palestinians are and ought to be before the law. Feldman focuses specifically on the criminalization of Palestinian political community and the proliferation of categories of crime and prisoners that denied the possibility of a collective Palestinian politics. Provocatively, Feldman argues that while policing is a work of sorting, it also "operates through indistinction . . . by making it difficult for people to know precisely where they stand in relation to the line of illegality, guilt, and, even, proper politics."

What is it to defy this order in the most intimate sphere of the self, the body? Michelle Velasquez-Potts's paper—a necessary and alarming read for its spare descriptions of the force-feeding of Guantánamo prison hunger strikers—tackles this question through the torturous vicissitudes of the body subjected to the biopolitics of the carceral empire. She asks us to consider seriously former Guantánamo prisoner Samir Naji al Hasan Moqbel's call to "look to Guantánamo" in light of the pain that he and his fellow hunger strikers endured. Looking, in this instance, is not merely a visual task, but an ethical witnessing that exceeds the disinterested visual gaze. Velasquez-Potts centers the relational capacities of pain and the embodied, corporeal, fleshly responses of the hunger strikers, from their refusal of the feeding tube by biting down on it to the tormented misery of repeated insertions, to vomiting and losing consciousness. It is these moans, utterances, and gastric expulsions that reveal what the politics of care are really about in this carceral scene—the elimination of political opposition through the medicalized surveillance of the captive body. While in Mojaddedi's ethnography, even the communicative encounter loses its capacity for relationality, Velasquez-Potts opens the possibility of considering the relational nature of pain when understood less as a private event than as a social relationship that calls forth an ethical obligation to respond.

Policing the Police

Finally, several papers in this issue inquire into the internal politics of the police as an institution. Stuart Schrader looks historically at the role of police in US politics since the 1960s. He shows how police have pivoted from being the subject of state policy, as constructed by politicians, to something more powerful and independent—placing politicians under their thumb. Schrader's work initiates a history we know little about, an organizational and institutional history of the police themselves, and how such organizational emergence (and power) are fundamentally changing the capacity for policing—both what it can do, and what can constrain it. That the police now make explicit and implicit demands by, for instance, turning their back to Mayor De Blasio as a rebuke for his remarks on the failed indictment of the police officer who murdered Eric Garner, are the result of the history that Schrader traces, one is that is critical for both scholars and activists as we assess the structural and systemic issues with policing.

This is in part what makes reform so impossible. Indeed, organizer, educator, and prison abolitionist Mariame Kaba (Kaba and Duda 2017) is blunt in her assessment that the "the system—the prison industrial complex—isn't broken." Its function is to maintain and reproduce white supremacy—a project that has been in place since well before the election of Donald Trump. Kaba has argued that the response to the current juncture is a transformational politics that strategically exploits opportunities in order to wage a resistance against a capitalist, white supremacist, and colonial system. In this issue, Kim Shayo Buchanan and Phillip Atiba Goff take a targeted approach at one aspect of the policing and prison system—the relationship between police body cameras and gender equity. While the debates around body cameras have centered on questions of racial injustice, Buchanan and Goff show that the policies that govern body cams also have the effect of reproducing gender inequity against women, sex workers, trans people, and gender-nonconforming individuals. Moreover, they tackle the thorny issue of reform, arguing that body cameras can only improve the current situation if a shift toward more gender-equitable body camera policies is "accompanied by a systematic institutional commitment to just and ethical policing." Buchanan and Goff thus provide a productive juxtaposition to Goldberg's analysis—via Baldwin—of the inherently unjust nature of police power.

Samira Bueno and Graham Denyer Willis continue this theme of studying the police themselves by looking at an "exceptional prison" in Brazil, which is to say a prison where the inmates are not "criminals" but instead police who have broken the law. We see, here, both the possibilities of what prisons could be and a reflection of the privilege of nonaccountability. Bueno and Willis's ethnographically informed paper can usefully be read in light of Fassin's demonstration that police officials and societal expectations legitimate police violence as retribution. The exceptional prison allows us to ask about the partition between forms of tolerable violence committed by the police and that violence which is deemed punishable. Bueno and Willis also find that speaking of police violence as excessive or "unjust" obscures the dynamics of violence work. The officers in the exceptional prison are not there because they have killed; they are there because they have committed a kind of border-crossing. "They were arrested," the authors write, "for crossing the fungible but observable line between what is constructed as permissible and not." From the vantage point of the exception, Bueno and Willis deliver an intriguing and unsettling analytical investigation into the workings of the police order.

Emerging Solidarities

Violence workers punish (Fassin, Goldberg), regulate our capacity to relate as communities, individuals, and political subjects (Carruthers, Mojaddedi, Feldman, Velasquez-Potts); securitize sites, temporality, and bodies (Kaplan and Miller, Jaffe, Velasquez-Potts), and manipulate the visual field (Goff, Velasquez-Potts), while demanding and receiving privileges (Schrader, Bueno and Willis). Yet, against these inordinate obstacles, solidarities persist. In August 2014, police, outfitted in riot gear, unleashed rubber bullets and tear gas on protesters in Ferguson, Missouri, who were demonstrating against the murder of Michael Brown, an eighteen-year-old Black man, by a police officer, Darren Wilson. As photos of the attack circulated, Palestinian social media users expressed their solidarity by tweeting advice on how to handle tear gas; one Twitter user also posted a photo of a tear gas canister with its Pennsylvania production address evident and noted, "Made in USA teargas canister was shot at us a few days ago in #Palestine by Israel, now they are used in #Ferguson," highlighting the centrality of the United States in the global reproduction of racialized violence (Molloy 2014). Engagements and solidarity also quickly emerged offline. A Palestine contingent was present at the 2014 "Ferguson October" National Weekend of Resistance. Palestinian students from Birzeit University in occupied West Bank traveled to St. Louis and Ferguson to meet with anti-racist and anti–police brutality activists.

Subsequently, fourteen Black, Arab, and Latina activists traveled to Palestine with a delegation from Dream Defenders, a social justice organization founded after Trayvon Martin's murder that voted to endorse the Boycott, Divestment, Sanctions movement (Bailey 2015). These actions build on a longer history of Black radical solidarity with the Palestinian liberation movement since at least 1967 (Kelley 2015; Lubin 2014, 2016; Feldman 2015).

There are, of course, critical distinctions between Gaza and Ferguson. Gaza is an open-air prison subjected to a severe economic and food blockade where Israel has used a caloric intake measure to limit food to Gazans (Associated Press 2012). And, as commentator Mychal Denzel Smith expressed, "The people of Ferguson aren't being treated like a foreign army. They're being treated like Black people in America" (quoted in Bailey 2015: 1019). While Marine Sergeant Thomas's partitioning of the world obscures and renders banal the function of US policing as already a system of racialized violence (Kaplan and Miller), Smith's observation pivots toward an interrogation of the longer history of US militarized policing. It refuses to exceptionalize American police violence by comparison with Israel; rather, it reveals the persistent and systematic violence to which Black Americans have long been subject. That history is critical to understanding how US policing tactics have been globalized, even as counter-insurgency strategies from Vietnam to the "war on terror" have been circulated back to the United States (Schrader, Goldberg; see LeVine 2014).

Yet, drawing studied connections between the two sites has not only provided the grounds for solidarity, it also sustains the potential for a more capacious transnational Left politics in an era where such solidarities have suffered breakdown even in light of multiple American invasions, the continued sprawl of the military-industrial complex, the mounting visual evidence of Black death at the hands of the police within the United States, and the continuation of the American colonial-settler project evidenced by the assault on Dakota pipeline protesters at Standing Rock.

These political engagements have produced a sophisticated and rich scholarly, activist, and public conversation on the politics of race formation, settler-colonialism, and the obligations that solidarity entails (Bailey 2015; Kelley 2015, 2016). It is here that a transformative resistance to policing may be located—in an analytics and a politics that negotiate the material distinctions of disparate sites alongside our capacity to establish relational solidarities and make possible human flourishing, despite—and against—the macabre labor of violence workers.

Andreas, Peter, and Richard Price. 2001. "From War Fighting to Crime Fighting: Transforming the American National Security State." *International Studies Review* 3, no. 3: 31–52.

Associated Press. 2012. "Israel Used 'Calorie Count' to Limit Gaza Food During Blockade, Critics Claim." *The Guardian*. October 17. https://www.theguardian.com/world/2012/oct/17/israeli-military-calorie-limit-gaza.

Bailey, Kristian Davis. 2015. "Black–Palestinian Solidarity in the Ferguson–Gaza Era." *American Quarterly* 67, no. 4: 1017–26.

Correia, David, and Tyler Wall. 2018. *Police: A Field Guide*. New York: Verso Books.

Hardt, Michael, and Antonio Negri. 2001. *Empire*. Cambridge: Harvard University Press.

Feldman, Keith P. 2015. *A Shadow over Palestine: The Imperial Life of Race in America*. Minneapolis: University of Minnesota Press.

Foucault, Michel. 1980. *Power/Knowledge: Selected Interviews and Other Writings, 1972–1977*. New York: Pantheon.

Hartman, Saidiya V. 1997. *Scenes of Subjection: Terror, Slavery, and Self-making in Nineteenth-Century America*. Oxford University Press on Demand.

Kaba, Mariame, and John Duda. 2017. "Towards the Horizon of Abolition: A Conversation with Mariame Kaba." *The Next System Project*. November 9. https://thenextsystem.org/learn/stories/towards-horizon-abolition-conversation-mariame-kaba.

Kahn, Paul W. 2013. "Imagining Warfare." *European Journal of International Law* 24, no. 1: 199–226.

Kelley, Robin D. G. 2015. Comments made during the "Roundtable on Anti-Blackness and Black-Palestinian Solidarity," moderated by Noura Erakat, June 3. http://www.jadaliyya.com/Details/32145.

Kelley, Robin D. G. 2016. "Thug Nation." In *Policing the Planet: Why the Policing Crisis Led to Black Lives Matter*, edited by Jordan T. Camp and Christina Heatherton. New York: Verso Books.

Khalili, Laleh. 2012. *Time in the Shadows: Confinement in Counterinsurgencies*. Stanford, CA: Stanford University Press.

LeVine, Mark. 2014. "Ferguson Is Not Gaza . . . Yet." *Al-Jazeera*. August 18. http://america.aljazeera.com/opinions/2014/8/ferguson-police-violenceisraeli andusmilitarizedpolicies.html.

Lubin, Alex. 2014. *Geographies of Liberation: The Making of an Afro-Arab Political Imaginary.* Chapel Hill: University of North Carolina Press.

Lubin, Alex. 2016. "Black Panther Palestine." *Studies in American Jewish Literature* 35, no. 1: 77–97.

Molloy, Mark. 2014. "Palestinians Tweet Tear Gas Advice to Protesters in Ferguson." *The Telegraph.* August 15. https://www.telegraph.co.uk/news/worldnews/northamerica/usa/11036190/Palestinians-tweet-tear-gas-advice-to-protesters-in-Ferguson.html.

Moyn, Samuel. 2013. "Drones and Imagination: A Response to Paul Kahn." *European Journal of International Law* 24, no. 1: 227–33.

Neocleous, Mark. 2011. "The Police of Civilization: The War on Terror as Civilizing Offensive." *International Political Sociology* 5, no. 2: 144–59.

Neocleous, Mark. 2014. *War Power, Police Power.* Edinburgh: Edinburgh University Press.

Rancière, Jacques. 2010. *Dissensus: On Politics and Aesthetics.* New York: Bloomsbury Academic.

Sexton, Jared. 2007. "Racial Profiling and the Societies of Control." In *Warfare in the American Homeland: Policing and Prison in a Penal Democracy*, edited by Joy James, 197–218. Durham, NC: Duke University Press.

Sexton, Jared. 2008. *Amalgamation Schemes: Antiblackness and the Critique of Multiracialism.* Minneapolis: University of Minnesota.

Sharpe, Christina. 2016. *In the Wake: On Blackness and Being.* Durham, NC: Duke University Press.

Weheliye, Alexander G. 2014. *Habeas Viscus: Racializing Assemblages, Biopolitics, and Black Feminist Theories of the Human.* Durham, NC: Duke University Press.

Madiha Tahir is a doctoral candidate at Columbia University researching the spatial and surveillance politics of (semi)autonomous warfare. She is the recipient of the Wenner-Gren dissertation fieldwork grant. Tahir is the director of *Wounds of Waziristan* (2013), an essay film on survivors of drone attacks and the coeditor of an edited volume of essays, *Dispatches from Pakistan* (2012). She cofounded Tanqeed (www.tanqeed.org), a bilingual digital journal that publishes critical essays by scholars and journalists, with Mahvish Ahmad.

Drones as "Atmospheric Policing": From US Border Enforcement to the LAPD

Caren Kaplan and Andrea Miller

In the space of less than twenty years, drones have become ubiquitous components of the security infrastructures that produce and police territories and borders of all kinds—from national dividing lines to the more scattered or almost imperceptible spatial relations that have come to characterize an era of globalized conflicts. Most often associated with the sensing and "signature strike" operations inherited from the Bush administration and perfected under the aegis of the Obama administration in Iraq and Afghanistan, drones (unmanned aerial vehicles, or UAVs) are now in use "at home" in many countries including the United States. The rapid incorporation of UAVs into conventional battlefield arenas as well as zones considered to be far distant from war suggests that, regardless of size or range, these aerial vehicles and associated systems are believed to offer significant benefits to national governments, municipalities, institutions, and various organizations and interest groups. The use of unmanned aerial systems (UAS) to supplement and operationalize US border enforcement and municipal policing disturbs the supposed boundary between military and civilian or battleground and home front. Indeed, rather than simply "blurring" the line between these hallmark components of the liberal state, the integration of UAS into border enforcement and civil policing supports Tyler Wall's (2013: 38) contention that the "security state and security industries" are "virtually indistinguishable."

We would like to thank Madiha Tahir, Shamus Khan, Ilana Feldman, Fatima Mojaddedi, and the other participants in a *Public Culture* workshop for insightful comments and suggestions. We would also like to thank Javier Arbona, Jennifer Greenburg, Laleh Khalili, Ingrid Lagos, Anjali Nath, Lisa Parks, Stuart Schrader, Eric Smoodin, and Tyler Wall.

Public Culture 31:3   DOI 10.1215/08992363-7532679
Copyright 2019 by Duke University Press
419

How can we understand the growing reliance on drones across political and cultural sectors as guarantors of defense and security beyond oppositional terminologies and concepts? The movement between "military" and "civilian" drone applications cannot be characterized so much as a "trickle down" from military research and development to nonmartial applications than as part of the infrastructure of an "ecology of power" that extends beyond the traditional battlefield (see Bélanger and Arroyo 2016: 17). Mark Neocleous (2013: 580) has argued that we need to think of "war power" and "police power" as a "nexus"—co-constituting and mutually engaged. Thus, it is not simply that a previously neutral or benevolent police become corrupted through "militarization" or that the military safeguards only through "policing." Rather, our understanding of "war power as police power" (Neocleous 2014) underscores that the nation-state operationalizes its authority through deployments of weaponized force including air power to manage, control, and punish populations and to secure territory (see also Kaplan 2018). The modern military has always included policing functions, and modern police forces have always drawn on military surplus equipment and military practices, procedures, and personnel (see Neocleous 2014; Wall 2016; Seigel 2015; Schrader 2014; Miller 2019). The difference between the military and the police is one of the core structuring elements of the liberal nation-state—yet this separation is aporetic. As Micol Seigel (2018: 54) points out, this divide endures "only because people work hard to make it do so. . . . The dedicated ideological labor required to shore up the bounds of the civilian-military distinction is serious violence work." This perceived gap between the military and the police, then, creates and maintain notions of interiority and exteriority for the nation-state. It evacuates everyday manifestations of power and renders banal the persistent violence of policing, in favor of the spectacularization of war at a distance.

Situating drones in an expanded field of a war power–police power nexus draws together histories of so-called small wars, insurgencies, civil rebellions, labor strikes, prison uprisings, and practices of resistance at various scales that have responded and continue to respond to colonial occupation and racial capitalism. The rise of air power as an operation of state control on behalf of industrialized nations throughout the twentieth century helps us understand how things like drones are activated and mobilized across various scales of time and space in the context of the security state. This long arc of air power and colonial and civil policing contributes to the emergence of what Anna Feigenbaum and Anja Kanngieser (2015: 81) have called "atmospheric policing": "those technologies and techniques for controlling populations that are fundamentally predicated on their relationship with air" and that "colonize space in ways that other weapons do not." Once we situate drones as a technology of atmospheric policing, we develop a better understanding of the ways these assemblages converge with other forms of atmospheric violence, including the toxic afterlives of warfare that permeate the air (as well as bodies, soil, water, and memory) (see Lindqvist 2001; Sloterdijk 2009; Arbona 2010; Feigenbaum 2017; Lambert 2017; Kechavarzi-Tehrani 2017; Shapiro and Kirksey 2017; Simmons 2017).

As Peter Sloterdijk (2009: 47–48) has argued, "being-in-the-breathable" has been at risk since the onset of chemical warfare in World War I. The "colonial present" (Gregory 2004) of atmospheric policing includes the deployment of chemical and sonic weaponry and all manner of attacks on the environments and resources required to support life, inflicting affective and sensorial terror (see Schrader 2018; Nieuwenhuis 2016, 2017; McCormack 2010). The "combat breathing" that Frantz Fanon (1965: 65) linked to resistance and resilience in the face of colonial occupation and terror reminds us that, as Léopold Lambert (2017: 15) puts it, "colonial domination" does not just take place "at the surface of cartographic territories" but "through the (attempted) atmospheric control of every aspect of life." Understanding atmospheric policing as a key mode of operation in the war power–police power nexus links decolonial struggles with protest activism like the Movement for Black Lives (see Márquez and Rana 2017). As Kristen Simmons (2017) writes, echoing Eric Garner's last words: "Breathing in a settler atmosphere is taxing. Some of us can't breathe" (see also Dillon and Sze 2016; Camp and Heatherton 2016: 1–2; Heatherton 2016). Thus, the use of drone technologies to police and manage all manner of perceived crises and threats simultaneously participates in and revivifies an emergency logic of the state through which drone violence, surveillance, and humanitarian interventions operate routinely even as they emerge as exceptional within popular technocultural imaginaries.

The co-constituting convergence of war power and police power through atmospheric policing persists and intensifies in the colonial present of expansive state violence across a range of practices and deployments. Lisa Parks (2018: 14) links the atmospheric to her theorization of "vertical mediation" in the era of drone warfare, arguing that innumerable cultural practices "move through (or beyond) the atmosphere" as they are produced, distributed, and received, and thereby generate "affects and sensations, modulate moods, reorder lifeworlds, and alter everyday spaces." Similarly attuned to the affective as well as the material effects of contemporary securitization, Peter Adey (2014: 841) has explored "security atmospheres" as fundamentally immersive and dynamic, such that the "everyday is policed as if the worst case was always possible." Drones operate aerially, but they produce atmospheric policing through their mediation of grounded, material elements. As Parks puts it (2018: 146–47), as drones move through air space, they not only alter the "chemical composition of the air" or affect the "thought or behavior" of those who operate them or are subject to their sensing operations: drones "shape where people move and how they communicate, which buildings stand and which are destroyed, who shall live and who shall die." The pervasive integration of drones into atmospheric policing does not reduce all operations to the same intensity of violence. The atmospheric policing of drones is augmented by their asymmetric deployment of power, particularly their relatively inconspicuous presence (both audibly and visibly—although their targets on the ground can become adept at hearing and seeing them) (see Bracken-Roche 2016: 169; Hussain 2013). As Madiha Tahir (2012: 110) reminds us, the deployment of weaponized drones in Pakistan (and elsewhere) places entire populations "under conditions of terror" so that the United States "can hunt for terrorists," constituting tacit justification and approval for material injuries and deaths as national policy under the sign of atmospheric policing.

Despite their mediation of everyday life over a *longue durée*, the dynamic, atmospheric properties of the complex assemblage that we refer to colloquially as the "drone" can tilt discussion toward its newness and exceptionality. It is important to remember that, as Katherine Chandler (2017) and Katherine Hall Kindervater (2017) have established, "unmanned" aerial vehicles have been developed by the military since the inception of aviation. Moreover, while the more spectacular lethal effects of drone weaponization preoccupy both celebratory and critical discussions, the rapid integration of the technology into civil society challenges the exceptionality of the technology. Particularly over the last ten years, the drone's more transparently military applications—such as aerial surveillance and "signature strikes" that lead to large-scale civilian casualties—have come to coexist with the brisk development of humanitarian nongovernmental, business, and recreational automated aerial technologies (see Sandvik and Jumbert 2017; Klauser and Pedrozo 2017). Even as public awareness of the pervasive military use of drones has steadily increased, a veritable boom in civilian and commercial applications of the technology has taken place. The justification of the "good drone" in civil society assumes a neutral benevolence to algorithmically driven technologies (see Crampton 2016). Both government and industry advertise drone capacities as the apotheosis of technological mastery thanks to a "digital sublime" that mythologizes artificial intelligence (AI) and algorithmic processes as seemingly unfailable (see Boucher 2015; Burgess 2015; Bolman 2017).

While drones are highly complex technological assemblages that mobilize innumerable industries, technologies, and human actors to produce sophisticated data used not only by militaries but also by municipalities, nongovernmental organizations, industries, and recreational users, they have limits (see Parks 2018). Although drones are popularly perceived to operate in air space at a vast distance from a singular human operator and even semiautonomously, as "quasi-human bod[ies]," drones still work with and through an interface devised by human beings that is, therefore, subject to all manner of "failure" as well as "success" (see Kaufmann 2017: 174; see also Gregory 2011; Chandler 2017; Kindervater 2017; Tahir 2017; Parks 2018). As Mareile Kaufmann (2017: 174) argues, drones create "new forms of presence and absence" through the "technological limits" of their design. In the emergency situations that Kaufmann examines in her work, the drone's sensing and perceptual limitations not only impact the outcome of humanitarian rescue operations but also generate and inflect the very ways that "emergencies" come to be known and understood as such (186). Drone sensing and "unsensing" participates in and fortifies perceived divisions of all kinds, including the commonsense distinction between military and civilian realms (even as the drone's histories and applications exemplify the practices of policing that co-constitute both).

In this way, as Tyler Wall (2016: 1136) has pointed out, the drone works in the service of producing, containing, and managing what he describes as "the ordinary emergency logic of police power." This "globalizing of police logics around the world" includes the "broad discretionary powers, executive decisions, institutional impunity, legal unaccountability, and necropolitics" that are usually imputed to weaponized drones in battle zones (1137). Thus those activities that generate the most public outrage in relation to drone operations at war are themselves an intrinsic part of "the most banal operations of police power" (1136–37), the everyday violence of atmospheric policing (see also Hussain 2003). Maintaining an attention to the everyday "violence work" (Seigel 2018: 12–13) of atmospheric policing by drones refuses the exceptional and spectacular attachments to a digital sublime and the reification of the supposed separation of war power and police power. Rather than reproduce narratives of "dronification" (Shaw and Akhter 2014; Shaw 2016), we argue that drones become intelligible as technologies of atmospheric policing when they are situated in relation to numerous histories and materialities: most specifically, the history of air power not only vis-à-vis war power but also *as* police power (see Satia 2014; Neocleous 2013). The drone, then, is but one (albeit significant) technology of everyday policing practices that can be traced through genealogies of colonial violence and population management.

Atmospheric Policing as Border Enforcement

One pervasive application of atmospheric policing takes place through US border enforcement, in which sensing and surveillance operations proceed almost unremarked until moments of perceived crisis attract public and media attention. The hallmarks of the Obama-era drone program—network-centric distance warfare, around-the-clock "situational awareness," supposedly precise targeted assassinations, and an inverse ratio of mortality of military personnel to local population (with a lethal lack of distinction between combatants and civilians)—underscore the appeal of drones to US police departments and US Customs and Border Protection (CBP). In the post-9/11 era, as the Department of Homeland Security (DHS) has expanded its organizational and legal reach to incorporate the CBP, the technologies of border enforcement have come to include a growing reliance on UAS that include ground and aerial vehicles and sensors, ground stations, communications systems, databases, pilots, analysts, and so forth. Keeping in mind Christine Agius's (2017: 370) caution that "more than demarcations," borders are "constitutive," the installation and operation of UAS in the United States is part of the "violence work" (Seigel 2018: 12–13) of nation-state geographies as they emerge in the era of the "war on terror."

Justifications for funding atmospheric UAS (and several decades of previous "high-tech" surveillance programs) are often premised on the argument that the nonurban zones of the border are so vast that they are difficult, if not almost impossible, to police by any other means—a border geography created by the policies and practices of the CBP itself. While the CBP was established as far back as 1924, "modern" US boundary enforcement in this zone began in 1994 when the CBP attempted to shift immigration from metropolitan "corridors" to more rural areas in an effort to both discourage and channel border crossings (see Boyce 2016). While it was hoped that the rigors of traversing harsh terrain that included deserts and mountains would diminish the number of people making unauthorized attempts to enter the United States, CBP assumed that pushing such migration away from cities and into the countryside would isolate and, in effect, overtly criminalize migrants, making it easier to identify and remove border crossers (248). Therefore, from the 1990s onward, border enforcement operations drew on what Mathew Coleman (2007: 56) refers to as the "criminalization of immigration law." These practices, routinized in ways reminiscent of earlier periods of immigration policing in the 1930s and 1950s, increasingly produced immigrants as subjects of policing and criminalization without options for legal recourse or recognition (see Coleman 2012: 424–25). Yet, the effort to push border crossers into dangerous stretches of uninhabited territory as criminalized subjects produced mixed results. As Geoffrey Boyce points out (2016: 249), unauthorized entry ballooned even as the hazards of such crossings greatly increased. Agence France-Presse (2018) reports that just in the last year as border crossings decreased "dramatically" by 44 percent from 611,689 to 341,084, the number of people who died attempting to cross the border rose significantly to 412. A report issued by the International Organization for Migration (2018), a United Nations nongovernmental organization, noted that even the number of these deaths, which overwhelmingly occurred because of "prolonged exposure to the extreme environments" as well as to drownings during river crossings, must be assumed to be an underestimation. If more people are choosing to avoid undocumented border crossing, those that do make the attempt face intensified atmospheric policing and encounters with other technologies that augment the violence work of border surveillance and enforcement.

In this moment of greater focus on the inherent violence of the "hardened" US-Mexico border, it is easy to forget that, back in the late 1980s and 1990s, there was avid discussion of an increasingly "borderless" world brought about by globalization and the mobility of transnational corporations and capital (see Rivera 2012; King 1991; Ohmae 1999). Even as, because of the so-called war on drugs, the US-Mexico border was increasingly constituted through militarized policing, free-market advocates, transnational corporations, and liberal politicians were calling for a relaxation of border enforcement. Thanks to NAFTA and other such initiatives throughout the period, although the US-Mexico border became "impressively policed," it also became "busier and more business friendly" (Andreas 2003: 6), leading to greater flows of people, goods, and services between the two nations. It is generally agreed that the September 11, 2001, attacks abruptly put an end to such open border movements, as securitization became not only an increasing political requirement but a burgeoning business opportunity in and of itself as surveillance and sensing operations attracted DHS funding (Nevins 2010; Coleman 2007, 2012).

Throughout the 1990s and into the next century, attempts to secure the enormous 8,878-mile perimeter of the continental United States prioritized areas of perceived greater risk to the defense of the nation-state. The two great land mass borders have presented securitization with a formidable task even without taking the coastlines into account. The uneven application of UAS between the northern boundary line with Canada (which extends for 3,283 miles) and the southern boundary with Mexico (which is measured at 1,954 miles) demonstrates the ways that geographical borders are constituted through differing intensities of violence (see Andreas 2003; Coleman 2012; MacDonald 2018). There is widespread acknowledgment that the US-Mexico border is one of the most "militarized" in the world (see Pompa 2018).[1] Donald Trump's bombastic threats to completely wall off almost two thousand miles of territory accompanied by a marked increase in detentions and deportations of undocumented persons has generated a spectacle of crisis. Trump's relentless demand for a physical barrier that will inscribe a geographical boundary in three dimensions coexists with the efforts to implement UAS and other atmospheric policing operations in the border zone that have been underway for several decades. As Alex Rivera (2012: 10) has pointed out in this regard, "The new systems don't replace the pre-existing ones—they exist in parallel and intermingle."

Nevertheless, the aporetic divide separating war power and police power, especially in relation to drones, reconstitutes itself as the news media seems to be able to concentrate on only one term of the binary at a time. Thus, during the Obama presidency, while whatever slim outrage was increasingly directed against drone operations, particularly in the border zone between Afghanistan and Pakistan, "situational awareness" and other sensing operations in the US-Mexico border zone were largely ignored and underreported in the mainstream press. Meanwhile, although the Trump administration has greatly increased drone attacks overseas,[2] there is little comment on this violent development, while racist discourse and policies directed against asylum seekers and border crossers who gather at southern checkpoints have, at the very least, garnered media attention (see Ackerman 2018; Axe 2018; Rosenthal and Schulman 2018). When we critique the deployment of drone technologies by the CBP, we disturb the spectacularization of a unifocal media gaze on a narrow conception of border zone geography that also occludes any recognition of more dispersed border policing along with colonial histories and continuities.

Atmospheric policing of undocumented border crossings from the south, then, operates in several dimensions—constituting a geographical zone across the boundary of Mexico and the United States while simultaneously operating through

---

1. As the ACLU (Pompa 2018) reports, the "number of Border Patrol agents more than doubled between fiscal year 2000 and 2011." By 2016, CBP officers numbered 19,437 in the field nationwide, augmented by significant numbers of personnel from other agencies and the National Guard and US military.

2. As Lisa Parks (2018: 191) notes, "Within his first 100 days of office, Trump authorized almost 100 drone strikes in Yemen alone, making vertical violence a defining characteristic of his Presidency." Spencer Ackerman (2018) reports that Trump "launched 238 drone strikes in his first two years in office."

scattered practices of locating, identifying, criminalizing, and detaining subjects. Indisputably, after the attacks of September 11, 2001, and the accompanying rapid escalation of militarized security, the US-Mexico territorial border has become more intensely policed and surveilled. Until the adoption of UAS, CBP aerial vehicles included helicopters, light airplanes, and aerostats. Aerostats that are part of the Tethered Aerostat Radar System (TARS) have been used by the Department of Defense in the Middle East and South Asia and by DHS in the Florida Straits and parts of the Caribbean as well as the borders with Canada and Mexico (see Longmire 2014: 71–73). With border enforcement placed under the aegis of the newly formed DHS, advocacy increased for "high-tech" approaches including "sensors, light towers, mobile night vision scopes, remote video surveillance systems, directional listening devices, [and] various database systems," as well as drones (Haddal and Gertler 2010: 1). The large-scale Predator B made by General Atomics was put into use at the US-Mexico border by the CBP in 2005, and a version adapted for use by the Coast Guard, nicknamed the "Guardian," was deployed in 2008 (see Longmire 2014: 76). In September 2017, CBP announced that it would begin to test a small unmanned aerial systems (sUAS) program. Now supplementing the larger and much more expensive Predator B drones, which cost upward of $16.9 million per unit and weigh forty-nine hundred pounds, are smaller, less expensive UAVs, such as AeroVironment's RQ-20B Puma (fourteen pounds) and RQ-11B Raven (just over four pounds), as well as InstantEye quadcopters (CBP 2017). In an April 2018 report (DHS 2018b: 3), the DHS argued that because sUAS "are highly portable and can be rapidly deployed to high-risk areas," incorporating these technologies into existing border surveillance will allow "CBP to reduce surveillance and situational awareness gaps."

The expansion of the CBP's drone program to include sUAS must be considered in conjunction with the network of digital and human surveillance practices that identify undocumented immigrants as criminal subjects both at official US national borders and throughout the internal territories of the United States. As Coleman suggests (2012), placing violence at the US-Mexico border in relation to internal immigration policing makes it possible to draw deeper connections between these and other counterinsurgency practices that animate racialized US policing. For example, as Coleman (2012, 2007) and Joseph Nevins (2018, 2012) point out, undocumented immigrants are, in fact, more likely to be apprehended in transit at a distance from actual borders, whether traveling to work, school, or other daily activities that simply require movement, as well as at places of work or during migrations across and through border zones (see also Amoore 2013: 79–104). In addition to the use of more conventional forms of apprehension by police, such as the traffic stop or checkpoint, as of January 2018, Immigration and Customs Enforcement (ICE) has gained access to Vigilant Solutions' national database of more than 6.5 billion license plate scans, supplemented by license plate reader data provided by other police agencies throughout the United States (Maas 2018; Farivar 2018). License plate readers, or LPRs, are often positioned atop stop lights or police patrol vehicles and can scan up to sixty license plates per second. LPR data is then stored in large, interoperable databases at the local, regional, and national levels and can be queried to generate intimate snapshots about drivers' routes, homes, workplaces, and other areas where they travel (Farivar 2015).

Creating data mosaics such as these to identify and predict criminality, in this case the criminality associated with undocumented border crossing, is not disconnected from the proliferation of surveillance technologies such as drone imagery, ground sensors, and aerostatic imagery throughout the US-Mexico border region, as well as what is referred to as "pattern-of-life" analysis in US drone warfare and its broader war on terror. Within this framework of counterinsurgency, the accretion of data points, when placed in relation with each other, generate predictive patterns of mobility and partial subjects as either threatening or nonthreatening, criminal or lawful (see also Amoore 2013; Chamayou 2015, 2014; Miller 2017). While the scale and applications of these policing practices should not be oversimplified or conflated, algorithmically driven forms of surveillance, exemplified by but not limited to drone surveillance, work in concert with rather than supersede other more conventional forms of US counterinsurgency and policing practices. Together, these digital, and nonetheless deeply human, policing practices are purported to enhance perceived situational awareness and to generate threatening and criminal subjects.

The "virtual wall" that atmospheric policing is presumed to offer border surveillance has many documented limitations.[3] Congressional Research Service

3. The term *virtual fence* was first applied to the SBI*net* program, inaugurated in 2006 and touted by DHS (2009: 2) as the best way to protect the United States "from dangerous people" and to achieve "effective control of U.S. borders." Despite the $8 billion poured into SBI*net*, by 2010 the DHS admitted that the program was a failure, with cost overruns, "poor oversight," lack of a "clear focus," and poor communications with the program's primary developer (Boeing) (see *Homeland Security Newswire* 2010). SBI*net* was preceded by the project launched in 1989 as the Intelligent Computer-Aided Detection System (ICAD), which became upgraded and transformed into the Integrated Surveillance Intelligence System (ISIS) in 1998. Although a 2005 Office of Inspector General audit of ISIS revealed "dubious contracting practices, inadequate equipment and misuse of operations support centers," the technology platform was folded into a newer program, the America's Shield Initiative (ASI) (see National Immigration Forum 2014). By 2005, approximately $340 million

(CRS) reports and an audit by the DHS Office of Inspector General found both benefits and limitations in the deployment of UAVs in border zones. Benefits listed in the CRS report include "improving coverage" in remote sectors, greater length of time in the air (over conventional helicopters), more "sustained coverage," greater range, personnel safety, and precise and real-time imagery (Haddal and Gertler 2010: 3). Limitations of UAVs in use along the border have been reported to include a high accident rate (with at least two crashes), inability to fly or provide useful data because of bad weather, and much higher costs than manned aviation along with shifting and complex regulations and policies related to integrating into civilian airspace (4–5). CBP drones cannot fly in restricted airspace or anywhere near commercial flight zones (which precludes operations in and around key regions such as San Diego, California, and Yuma, Arizona) (Bier and Feeney 2018: 2). A CATO Institute report pessimistically noted that in 2013 drones regularly patrolled only "about 170 miles of the 2,000 southern land border" (Bier and Feeney 2018: 2). Moreover, a recent DHS audit found that surveillance and reconnaissance systems used by the CBP did not institute effective safeguards for UAV images and video, placing border surveillance operations at "increased risk of compromise" (DHS 2018a: 2).[4]

After decades of layered "high" and "low-tech" border enforcement tactics and strategies, the most recent implementation of sUAS, utilizing much smaller, consumer-grade drones, brings a variety of users to the border zone, producing new subjects of atmospheric policing. As one UAS industry news service (UAS Vision 2018) has pointed out, small unmanned aircraft systems are piloted by "drug traffickers looking for a way into the country, the U.S. government trying to keep them out, and even journalists hoping to get a new point of view." The small size and light weight of the aircraft make them very difficult for any targeted or interested individual or group to detect. With the CBP move to incorporate sUAS

---

had been allocated to ISIS and AI, yet both programs failed to perform meaningfully. Nevertheless, SBI*net* was funded, implemented, and discontinued—all within five years at an even greater cost than its predecessors.

4. The finances of the alluring capacities of the UAS "virtual wall" are sobering. According to the libertarian CATO Institute (funded by the Koch brothers): "Each Predator B drone costs $17 million to purchase and $12,255 per flight hour to operate. Thus, CBP's drone program cost a grand total of $225 million from 2013 to 2016. These figures likely understate the cost of the system's depreciation because they assume a 20-year lifespan, but 18 percent of CBP drones crashed in their first 10 years. For comparison, manned aircraft with surveillance capabilities similar to the Predator B cost only $1,500 to $2,000 per flight hour. Each drone apprehension costs the federal government $32,000. This cost of drone apprehension compares with the average cost of apprehension of less than $9,000" (Bier and Feeney 2018: 3).

along with the growing ubiquity of similar aircraft deployed by many different groups with any number of interests and intents, the atmosphere of the US-Mexico border will become a much more crowded and complex space. The extremist vigilante group, the American Border Patrol (ABP), which operates its three aircraft as well as foot patrols from a ranch in southeastern Arizona, recently demonstrated a stand-alone seismic detection and ranging mechanism (SEIDARM) that would be used to detect sUAS as well as "persons and/or vehicles" at the border (see Waitt 2018). ABP, described by the Southern Poverty Law Center (SPLC) as "one of the most virulent anti-immigrant groups" in the United States, believes that "terrorist groups" will use sUAS to launch attacks on US territory from Mexico (SPLC 2018; Waitt 2018). Former DHS Security Chief Kirstjen M. Nielsen (2018) believed that sUAS "can be used to spy on us, to threaten our critical infrastructure, or to attack crowds and public places." Warning of a "spike in the use of drones at our borders," Nielsen cautioned that "drones will soon become a part of everyday life" and, therefore, investment in "drone-defense technologies" must be implemented as soon as possible.

The spectacular panic of the threatening drone swarms notwithstanding, sUAS at the US-Mexico border exemplify the "ordinary emergency logic of police power" (Wall 2016: 1136). If the larger UAVs were too distant and rarified to fully replace the finely tuned capacities of the human border patrol (whether CBP or ABP) to read signs left by border crossers on the ground in order to track and hunt them down (referred to as "sign cutting"),[5] then the smaller aircraft offer new, if less spectacular, opportunities for atmospheric policing (see Longmire 2014: 83). This rearticulation and reimagination of indigenous ways of knowing place may be transposed to the sUAS to enhance situational awareness in the everyday routine of border enforcement. The war power–police power nexus ensures that the latest instantiation of drone systems will create new avenues for profiteering, regenerate racialized border spectacles, and reanimate and transform atmospheric policing. The movement of small aircraft—more silent and mobile if less able to achieve greater heights and less directly weaponized than their larger military counterparts—in the zone we know as the US-Mexico border will make a difference in the air space, certainly. Lockheed Martin, Boeing, and other aerospace contractors and researchers are betting that the next iteration of sUAS will operate more autonomously, in coordinated "swarms," changing "movements on the ground," "affecting thought and behavior," altering conditions in the air (see

---

5. We thank Christina Jo Pérez for drawing our attention to the way that CBP "sign cutting" practices rely on and generate mythologies around Indigenous modes of reading the environment.

Parks 2018: 146–47). Situating CBP sUAS in the atmospheric dynamics of the war power–police power nexus requires new understandings of those borders "on the inside of the U.S. state" as well as the geopolitical national boundary line and of policing as it is operationalized across multiplicities of authorities and scales (see Coleman 2012: 420).

Atmospheric Policing and SWAT in the Los Angeles Police Department

"Modern policing," as Joshua Reeves and Jeremy Packer (2013: 360) have argued, involves more than "just cops walking (or driving their beat)." Reeves and Packer remind us that media, including police intelligence and logistical communications, have been "central to the fledgling liberal police project" since the late eighteenth and nineteenth centuries, linked to anthropometric science and rogue's galleries, as well as twentieth-century automobility and digital technologies (361). More recently, a "digital ideal" that promotes "rapid and flawless storage, translation, and dissemination of evidence and other data" has "preoccupied the police imagination" (361). Policing in the United States has not only emulated military forms of organization from its inception as a professionalized force but also adopted operational practices and technologies for information gathering and population control from the military as well (see Correia and Wall 2018: 149–50). Just as air power has been crucial for the military throughout the twentieth century and into the twenty-first, control and deterrence via atmospheric policing have been foundational components of modern police forces.

Given the rise of a formidable war power–police power nexus since the nineteenth century at the very least, technology transfers between the military and the police are not a new phenomenon. Police in the United States have drawn on military concepts, modes of organization, and equipment (including, from the era of World War I, aerial vehicles)[6] from their inception. In a report published in 2014, the American Civil Liberties Union (ACLU) charged that police in the United States have become dangerously militarized with almost no oversight or official restraint. In an exhaustive study, they conclude that US policing, especially via paramilitary teams like SWAT, has become "excessively militarized," largely owing to federal programs like the US 1033 Program that "create incentives" for state and local police to acquire and use weapons that would otherwise be used

6. One of the first recorded deployments of an aerial vehicle by police took place in 1914 in Miami when a Curtiss F-type seaplane was used to capture an escaped prisoner. By 1918, the New York Police Department had formed its volunteer air section using surplus decommissioned Navy planes.

only on battlefields. As a consequence, the ACLU found that, while the justification for the acquisition of aggressive weaponry was often linked to incidents of hostage, active shooter, or barricade scenarios, the majority of deployments of paramilitary weapons were used to execute search warrants in "low-level drug investigations." Further, the ACLU (2014: 5–6) concluded that the use of aggressive tactics and weaponry "primarily impacted people of color," revealing "stark, often extreme racial disparities" in the use of SWAT teams and in the deployment of aggressive weaponry, leading to a marked increase in the "risk of bodily harm and property damage."

In focusing on the most recent, egregious flow of weaponry from offshore battlefields to municipalities in the United States, the ACLU rightfully draws our attention to urgent matters that require all manner of redress. Yet, the history of flows of military equipment, weaponry, procedures, and organizational structures stretches back much farther than the 1033 Program cited in the ACLU study. Here, once again, "militarization" is a less efficacious concept, since it constructs a more benign police force in an idealized past that is only recently linked to the military. Without reducing significant distinctions in levels of violence and harm to banal equalizations, greater attention to the continuities of colonial policing practices across time and space makes possible a much richer, more complex set of histories of state violence and population control. How, then, to account for the kinds of intensification in aggressive policing and the more recent racialized geographies of cities like Los Angeles where SWAT teams deploy paramilitary weaponry for routine "emergencies" without resorting to simplistic constructs of "militarization"?

We can link the scattered border zones that the CBP instantiates "on the inside" of the United States through conventional physical checkpoints and raids as well as through situational awareness systems to the predictive policing technologies and paramilitary weaponry deployed by the Los Angeles Police Department (LAPD) SWAT as a war power–police power nexus with deep roots in a specific place. Los Angeles is known to be a city forged through aggressive policing and containment. While the entire state of California plays a significant role in this history of genocide, carcerality, and racial violence (see Gilmore 2007; Cuevas 2012), Los Angeles has constituted itself paradoxically as a city of immigrants that works to pacify and expel those who challenge the emergency logic of nation-state borders. Incarceration and policing play a key role in this history. As Kelly Lytle Hernández (2017: 2) argues, despite the fact that levels of incarceration in Los Angeles have surpassed those of counterpart urban areas at least since the 1980s, what is remarkable is that "the rate of incarceration during the 1930s in Los

Angeles was no different than it is today." Even before a formalized legal structure governed practices of confinement in Los Angeles, one of the first structures erected by Spanish colonists in 1781 was a jail used to imprison the Native Tongva people (4, 29). By 1910, Los Angeles "operated one of the largest jail systems in the country" (2). Additionally, Hernández rightfully demonstrates that the LAPD has functioned as a counterinsurgency force, describing Los Angeles as a nodal point in the cross-border *magonista* movement that led up to the Mexican Revolution (92–130). Through a joint counterinsurgency program undertaken by Mexico and the United States, thousands of magonistas were arrested and imprisoned, including political leader Ricardo Flores Magón, who spent a total of three years in US prisons, nineteen months of that time in the Los Angeles County Jail (93). Hernández (96) draws on the cross-border policing of the magonista movement to demonstrate that incarceration did not contain magonista insurgency but, rather, fomented it.

Notably, these cross-border counterinsurgency operations took place just after the first wave of professionalization swept through the LAPD under Chief John M. Glass at the turn of the twentieth century. The magonista counterinsurgency described by Hernández, then, poses a significant challenge to the mythology of police professionalization, particularly as it has been narrated through the history of the LAPD (Herbert 1996, 1997), in which emphases on individual officer conduct and technologization were meant to dispel growing concerns with police violence. As "a story about the reform of the police into the force of progress" (Correia and Wall 2018: 123), the nineteenth and twentieth-century reimagination of policing as not simply a profession but a science also positioned individual police as experts in a technology-driven field (122–26). The mythology of professionalization has created further perceptual difference between the tenuously bifurcated war power and police power, eliding the function of police as a counterinsurgency force (see Schrader 2017). However, as the story of the magonistas forcefully demonstrates, the LAPD has continued to perform the violence work of pacification under the sanitizing sign of professionalization and technologization.

In this context, the adoption of sUAS by the LAPD is not an aberration; rather, it demonstrates the consonance between forms of atmospheric policing by and for the colonial settler state—working to consolidate both its territorial expansionist and racial projects (see also Wall 2016; Neocleous 2013; Satia 2006). Thus, the addition of drones to supplement SWAT operations is in keeping with, rather than a departure from, a history of atmospheric policing within the LAPD. While LAPD SWAT has become infamous for its disproportionate policing of Los Angeles's Black and brown communities, aerial surveillance of racialized communities

433

has been endemic to the LAPD since it acquired air power. As Mike Davis (1990: 251–52) describes, the LAPD's effort to achieve "ground-air synchronization" following the 1965 Watts Rebellion grew to such intensity that so-called high-crime areas were under nineteen-hour-per-day surveillance and exceeded "even the British Army's aerial surveillance of Belfast." As the first of its kind, LAPD SWAT has from its inception included the use of air power and aerial surveillance to supplement its ground operations and to contain racialized threat (see Davis 1990; Adey 2010; Singh 2014; Wagner 2009). Notably, the LAPD's first SWAT operation on December 6, 1969—a raid on the Los Angeles headquarters of the Black Panthers—included aerial support provided by a helicopter (Davis 1990: 298; Balko 2014: 76–78).

As air support became a prime feature of LAPD policing throughout the late twentieth century, some neighborhoods of Los Angeles became subject to the loud, thumping noise of the police helicopter rotors—a nocturnal sonic signature that has evoked comparisons to war zones.[7] Once again in the forefront, the LAPD began to integrate conventional helicopters in predictive policing practices in the early years of the current decade. The "everyday emergency" atmospherics produced by routine police operations that include predictive procedures focuses scrutiny of specific populations in minutely granulated ways. As the Stop LAPD Spying Coalition (2018: 1) reported recently, predictive policing can be situated "within the broader creep of data-intensive surveillance." Operation LASER was launched by the LAPD in 2011, using a predictive policing system developed by PredPol Inc. to "develop hotspots in neighborhoods" and to create a list of targeted individuals (3). Individuals who are identified through predictive features and data collected from patrol and parole officers are placed into a chronic offender bulletin (COB) and ranked via a point system. Those individuals with the most points become "primary targets" for policing (3). LASER and PredPol coordinate with atmospheric policing, emulating the utopian "system of systems" made infamous during the so-called digital revolution in military affairs of the 1990s and reflect the use of predictive analytics as a key feature of the US war on terror (see Miller 2019). Indeed, PredPol emerged from "military-funded university research based on statistics from the 2003 Iraq insurgency," while LASER is based on technology created by Palantir, a "big data company" that "mines government and corporate

---

7. The Los Angeles Police Department (LAPD) Air Support Division was inaugurated in 1956 with a single helicopter and is currently the largest municipal police aviation department in the United States, featuring helicopters, fixed-wing aircraft, and, now, drones (see Correia and Wall 2018: 69).

databases for signs of criminal and or international terrorist activity" (6).[8] Drawing on Palantir and PredPol informatics, LAPD helicopters fly over "hot spots" as a mode of deterrence as well as pursuit (see Mather and Winton 2015), creating new articulations of much older understandings of particular spaces as criminogenic (Jefferson 2017).

The noisy drawbacks of helicopter flyovers in densely populated areas may be partially alleviated by the partial rollout of sUAS in LAPD atmospheric policing. The LAPD acquired its first two small drones in 2014, discarded from Seattle following a public outcry over their proposed implementation in that city. The two 3.5-pound Draganflyer X6 drones caused controversy in Los Angeles as well. As the *Los Angeles Weekly* (Anderson 2014) reported at the time, then-LAPD Chief Charlie Beck "made the rounds" of newspaper editorial boards and television stations in an attempt to gain public trust. Privacy concerns and Federal Aviation Administration (FAA) regulations at the time that prevented drone flights above four hundred feet kept the Draganflyers in storage. The 2017 LAPD SWAT sUAS pilot program aims to assuage public concerns by emphasizing search and rescue. Their guidelines and procedures document (LAPD 2017) clearly specifies, however, that SWAT seeks to learn whether sUAS will "enhance" their ability to "safely resolve dangerous, high-risk tactical situations and improve situational awareness capabilities during natural disasters and catastrophic incidents."

Converging initiatives by the aerospace industry, research universities, government departments, and consumers have led to a sharp uptick in interest in UAVs and sUAS (see Kaplan 2017). According to a recent study conducted by the Center for the Study of the Drone (2017: 1), as of April 2017, more than 347 police departments and emergency management units have acquired UAVs, primarily in the form of consumer-grade drones. Aiding in this development, the US Department of Transportation opened a pilot program of their own in May 2018 aimed at "opening the skies to advanced drone operations in regions across the nation" (see McNeal 2018). In response to increasing industry pressure, the Integration Pilot Program (IPP) allows for operations otherwise prohibited by FAA regulations, such as "flight over people, at night, and beyond the line of sight" (McNeal 2018). Deviating from the top-down practices of FAA regulation, the IPP will give participating communities latitude in testing drones for their own purposes and in their own ways (although while coordinating with state and local government, departments of transportation, zoning boards, etc.).

---

8. It is worth noting that Palantir was founded by Peter Thiel, "a prominent advisor to and supporter of Donald Trump" (see STOP LAPD Spying Coalition 2018: 6).

Nearly coterminous with the rollout of the US Customs and Border Protection (CBP) sUAS program, in early October 2017 the LAPD posted its suggested guidelines for implementing an sUAS pilot program to supplement its current SWAT operations (LAPD 2017). These guidelines, approved for adoption by the Los Angeles Police Commission on October 17, 2017 (see also Meredith 2017), describe that "sUAS may be deployed to provide enhanced *situational awareness*" in cases of "barricaded suspects; active shooter incidents; assessments of explosive devices and explosions; hostage situations; natural disasters; hazardous materials incidents; search and rescue operations; and perimeter searches of armed suspects with superior firepower, an extraordinary tactical advantage, or who are wanted for assault with a firearm against a police officer" (LAPD 2017; emphasis added). In addition to the wide range of events and situations for which drones are imagined to be of particular use for LAPD SWAT, it is noteworthy that they are explicitly identified as enhancing situational awareness in police operations. Here, civil police forces do not simply rely on military terminology to describe the environmental attunement of police personnel; these proposed guidelines demonstrate the powerful association of drone sensing with a perceived ability to radically extend the police sensorium beyond human capabilities. The logic presented by the LAPD indicates that situational awareness is rendered more complete and the propensity for human error is all but eliminated through the technological precision attributed to the drone. Further, by using the language of situational awareness, the proposed guidelines imply that drone sensing is much more than visual, where the sensory capabilities that the drone affords presumably outweigh the potential invasiveness of drone surveillance. These twinned justifications accrue added significance given the violent histories of racialized policing associated with the Los Angeles Police Department and, not least of all, LAPD SWAT.

Conclusion

Atmospheres are not stationary containers of the air we breathe. Atmospheres are dynamic constructs—elements of mobility as well as containment, joyful pleasure as well as weaponization, enduring as well as vulnerable to extinction. If atmospheres are potentially multiple, the relatively recent history of the occupation of air space for policing offers a potential entry into critical engagements with the colonial present of violence work. The advent of air power in the twentieth century inaugurated what Sloterdijk (2009: 29) has described as "atmoterrorism," "an assault on the enemy's acute environmental living conditions, starting with a poison attack on the human organism's most immediate environmental resource: the air he breathes," and what Feigenbaum and Kanngieser (2015) have called "atmospheric policing." Drawing on Feigenbaum and Kanngieser's term, we have attempted to create a space for understanding the specificity of drones in operation in the air over nation-state border zones as well as interior metropolitan areas without losing historical connections to other atmospheric modes of terror, such as the deployment of the lethalized form of tear gas directed against asylum seekers at the US-Mexico border in November 2018 (and that is regularly used to attack civilians in sites ranging from Gaza to the streets of Paris and cities throughout the United States). Sonic weaponry such as the long range acoustic device (LRAD) and tear gas work with drone systems, large and small, to isolate populations and deprive them of freedom of movement, the right to work, to protest, and to inhabit space, as well as the right to breathe.

This violence work of atmospheric policing in the colonial present writ large operates specifically in the case of drones. UAVs and UAS at every scale and range change and interact with the atmospheres through which they move and mediate relations with the ground. The relentless processes of colonialism that require dedicated practices of territorial occupation and aerial patrol and attack have brought fear into the lives of those who must look skyward before they dare to move or even breathe, changing their "patterns of life" or risk death. The routinization of atmospheric policing does not diminish its harrowing effects on those who are constituted as its target subjects. Yet, the war power–police power nexus strives to maintain a division between state violence that is directed "overseas" against purportedly deserving targets and the control and interdiction of criminalized populations "at home." These sensing operations, increasingly operated at smaller scales and with more layers of data mining and situational awareness, alter and produce identities, influence behavior, and restructure perceptions of locative life. In this way, situating the drone as a significant iteration of atmospheric policing requires attending to its densely political complexities, such that its past as well as its potential must be historically grounded rather than contextually unmoored.

References

Ackerman, Spencer. 2018. "Trump Ramped Up Drone Strikes in America's Shadow Wars." *Daily Beast*, November 25. www.thedailybeast.com/trump-ramped-up -drone-strikes-in-americas-shadow-wars.

ACLU (American Civil Liberties Union). 2014. *War Comes Home: The Excessive Militarization of American Policing*. New York: American Civil Liberties Union.

Adey, Peter. 2010. "Vertical Security in the Megacity: Legibility, Mobility, and Aerial Politics." *Theory, Culture & Society* 27, no. 6: 51–67.

Adey, Peter. 2014. "Security Atmospheres or the Crystallization of Worlds." *Environment and Planning D: Society and Space* 32, no. 5: 834–51.

Agence France-Presse. 2018. "US-Mexico Border Migrant Deaths Rose in 2017 Even as Crossings Fell, UN Says." *The Guardian*. February 6. www.theguardian .com/us-news/2018/feb/06/us-mexico-border-migrant-deaths-rose-2017.

Agius, Christine. 2017. "Ordering without Bordering: Drones, the Unbordering of Late Modern Warfare and Ontological Insecurity." *Postcolonial Studies* 20, no. 3: 370–86.

Amoore, Louise. 2013. *The Politics of Possibility: Risk and Security beyond Probability*. Durham, NC: Duke University Press.

Anderson, Rick. 2014. "Game of Drones: How LAPD Quietly Acquired the Spy Birds Shunned by Seattle." *Los Angeles Weekly*, June 19. www.laweekly.com /news/game-of-drones-how-lapd-quietly-acquired-the-spy-birds-shunned-by -seattle-4794894.

Andreas, Peter. 2003. "A Tale of Two Borders: The U.S.-Canada and U.S.-Mexico Lines after 9-11: Integration and Exclusion in a New Security Context." In *The Rebordering of North America*, edited by Peter Andreas and Thomas J. Biersteker, 1–23. London: Routledge.

Arbona, Javier. 2010. "Dangers in the Air." *Places Journal*, October. placesjournal. org/article/dangers-in-the-air-aerosol-architecture-and-invisible-landscapes/.

Axe, David. 2018. "While No One Is Looking, Trump Is Escalating America's Drone War." *Motherboard*, June 22. motherboard.vice.com/en_us/article /7xmadd/trump-escalating-americas-drone-war.

Balko, Radley. 2014. *Rise of the Warrior Cop: The Militarization of America's Police Forces*. New York: Public Affairs.

Bélanger, Pierre, and Alexander S. Arroyo. 2016. *Ecologies of Power: Countermapping the Logistical Landscapes and Military Geographies of the US Department of Defense*. Cambridge, MA: MIT Press.

Bier, David J., and Matthew Feeney. 2018. "Drones on the Border: Efficacy and Privacy Implications." Immigration Research and Policy Brief No. 5. Washington, DC: CATO Institute.

Bolman, Brad. 2017. "A Revolution in Agricultural Affairs: Dronoculture, Precision, Capital." In *The Good Drone*, edited by Kristin Bergtora Sandvik and Maria Gabrielsen Jumbert, 129–52. London: Routledge.

Boucher, Philip. 2015. "Domesticating the Drone: The Demilitarisation of

Unmanned Aircraft for Civil Markets." *Science and Engineering Ethics* 21, no. 6: 1393–1412.

Boyce, Geoffrey A. 2016. "The Rugged Border: Surveillance, Policing, and the Dynamic Materiality of the US/Mexico Frontier." *Environment and Planning D: Society and Space* 34, no. 2: 245–62.

Bracken-Roche, Ciara. 2016. "Domestic Drones: The Politics of Verticality and the Surveillance Industrial Complex." *Geographica Helvetica* 71, no. 3: 167–72.

Burgess, Matt. 2015. "Drones Will Make It Easier to Park Your Car, Says Orbital Insight." *Wired*, November 27. www.wired.co.uk/article/james-crawford-orbital -insight-wired-retail-2015.

Camp, Jordan T., and Christina Heatherton. 2016. "Introduction: Policing the Planet." In *Policing the Planet: Why the Policing Crisis Led to Black Lives Matter*, edited by Jordan T. Camp and Christina Heatherton, 1–11. London: Verso.

Center for the Study of the Drone. 2017. "Public Safety Drones." dronecenter. bard.edu/files/2017/04/CSD-Public-Safety-Drones-Web.pdf.

Chamayou, Grégoire. 2014. "Patterns of Life: A Very Short History of Schematic Bodies by Grégoire Chamayou." *Funambulist: Bodies, Designs, and Politics* (blog), December 14. thefunambulist.net/2014/12/04/the-funambulist-papers -57-schematic-bodies-notes-on-a-patterns-genealogy-by-gregoire-chamayou/.

Chamayou, Grégoire. 2015. *A Theory of the Drone*, translated by Janet Lloyd. New York: The New Press.

Chandler, Katherine. 2017. "American Kamikaze: Television-Guided Assault Drones in World War II." In *Life in the Age of Drone Warfare*, edited by Lisa Parks and Caren Kaplan, 89–111. Durham, NC: Duke University Press.

Coleman, Mathew. 2007. "Immigration Geopolitics beyond the Mexico-US Border." *Antipode* 39, no. 1: 54–76.

Coleman, Mathew. 2012. "From Border Policing to Internal Immigration Control in the United States." In *A Companion to Border Studies*, edited by Thomas M. Wilson and Hastings Donnan, 419–37. Malden, MA: Wiley-Blackwell.

Correia, David, and Tyler Wall. 2018. *Police: A Field Guide*. London: Verso.

Crampton, Jeremy. 2016. "Assemblage of the Vertical: Commercial Drones and Algorithmic Life." *Geographica Helvetica* 71: 137–46.

Cuevas, Ofelia. 2012. "Welcome to My Cell: Housing and Race in the Mirror of American Democracy." *American Quarterly* 64, no. 3: 605–24.

CBP (Customs and Border Protection). 2017. "CBP to Test the Operational Use of Small Unmanned Aircraft Systems in 3 U.S. Border Patrol Sectors." Press release, September 14. www.cbp.gov/newsroom/national-media-release/cbp-test-operational-use-small-unmanned-aircraft-systems-3-us-border.

Davis, Mike. 1990. *City of Quartz: Excavating the Future in Los Angeles.* New York: Verso.

DHS (Department of Homeland Security). 2009. *SBInet Program: Program-Specific Recovery Act Plan.* May 15. www.dhs.gov/xlibrary/assets/recovery/CBP_SBInet_Program_Final_2009-05-15.pdf.

DHS (Department of Homeland Security). 2018a. *CBP Has Not Ensured Safeguards for Data Collected Using Unmanned Aircraft Systems.* September 21. www.oig.dhs.gov/sites/default/files/assets/2018-09/OIG-18-79-Sep18.pdf.

DHS (Department of Homeland Security). 2018b. *Privacy Impact Assessment Update for the Aircraft Systems.* April 6. www.dhs.gov/sites/default/files/publications/privacy-pia-cbp018a-aircraftsystems-april2018.pdf.

Dillon, Lindsey, and Julie Sze. 2016. "Police Power and Particulate Matters: Environmental Justice and the Spatialities of In/securities in U.S. Cities." *English Language Notes* 54, no. 2: 13–23.

Fanon, Frantz. 1965. *A Dying Colonialism.* New York: Grove.

Farivar, Cyrus. 2015. "We Know Where You've Been: Ars Acquires 4.6M License Plate Scans from the Cops." *Ars Technica*, March 24. arstechnica.com/tech-policy/2015/03/we-know-where-youve-been-ars-acquires-4–6m-license-plate-scans-from-the-cops/.

Farivar, Cyrus. 2017. "In 3-1 Vote, LA Police Commission Approves Drones for LAPD." *Ars Technica*, October 17. arstechnica.com/tech-policy/2017/10/los-angeles-set-to-be-largest-us-police-force-with-drones/.

Farivar, Cyrus. 2018. "Technology Turns Our Cities into Spies for ICE, Whether We Like It or Not." *Los Angeles Times*, May 2. www.latimes.com/opinion/op-ed/la-oe-farivar-surveillance-tech-20180502-story.html.

Feigenbaum, Anna. 2017. *Tear Gas: From the Battlefields of World War I to the Streets of Today.* London: Verso.

Feigenbaum, Anna, and Anja Kanngieser. 2015. "For a Politics of Atmospheric Governance." *Dialogues in Human Geography* 5, no. 1: 80–84.

Gilmore, Ruth Wilson. 2007. *Golden Gulag: Prisons, Surplus, Crisis, and Opposition in Globalizing California.* Berkeley: University of California Press.

Gregory, Derek. 2004. *The Colonial Present.* Malden, MA: Blackwell.

Gregory, Derek. 2011. "From a View to a Kill: Drones and Late Modern War." *Theory, Culture & Society* 28, nos. 7–8: 188–215.

Haddal, Chad. C., and Jeremiah Gertler. 2010. "Homeland Security: Unmanned

Aerial Vehicles and Border Surveillance." Congressional Research Service Report. Washington, DC: Library of Congress, 1–7.

Heatherton, Christina. 2016. "#BlackLivesMatter and Global Visions of Abolition: An Interview with Patrisse Cullors." In *Policing the Planet: Why the Policing Crisis Led to Black Lives Matter*, edited by Jordan T. Camp and Christina Heatherton, 35–40. New York: Verso.

Herbert, Steve. 1996. "The Geopolitics of the Police: Foucault, Disciplinary Power, and the Tactics of the Los Angeles Police Department." *Political Geography* 15, no. 1: 47–57.

Herbert, Steve. 1997. *Policing Space: Territoriality and the Los Angeles Police Department*. Minneapolis: University of Minnesota Press.

Hernández, Kelly Lytle. 2017. *City of Inmates: Conquest, Rebellion, and the Rise of Human Caging in Los Angeles, 1771–1965*. Chapel Hill: University of North Carolina Press.

Homeland Security News Wire. 2010. "Why SBInet Has Failed." May 19. www .homelandsecuritynewswire.com/why-sbinet-has-failed.

Hussain, Nasser. 2003. *The Jurisprudence of Emergency: Colonialism and the Rule of Law*. Ann Arbor: University of Michigan Press.

Hussain, Nasser. 2013. "The Sound of Terror: Phenomenology of a Drone Strike." *Boston Review*, October 16. bostonreview.net/world/hussain-drone-phenomenology.

International Organization for Migration. 2018. "Migrant Deaths Remain High Despite Sharp Fall in US-Mexico Border Crossings in 2017." Press release, February 6. www.iom.int/news/migrant-deaths-remain-high-despite-sharp-fall -us-mexico-border-crossings-2017.

Jefferson, Brian Jordan. 2017. "Predictable Policing: Predictive Crime Mapping and Geographies of Policing and Race." *Annals of the American Association of Geographers* 1, no. 108: 1–16.

Kaplan, Caren. 2017. "Drone-o-Rama: Troubling the Temporal and Spatial Logics of Distance Warfare." In *Life in the Age of Drone Warfare*, edited by Lisa Parks and Caren Kaplan, 161–78. Durham, NC: Duke University Press.

Kaplan, Caren. 2018. *Aerial Aftermaths: Wartime from Above*. Durham, NC: Duke University Press.

Kaufmann, Mareile. 2017. "Drone/Body: The Drone's Power to Sense and Construct Emergencies." In *The Good Drone*, edited by Kristin Bergtora Sandvik and Maria Gabrielsen Jumbert, 168–94. London: Routledge.

Kechavarzi-Tehrani, Dariouche. 2017. "The Colonial Gas Machine: Teargas Grenades, Secular Humanist Police, and the Intoxification of Racialized Lives." *Funambulist*, Nov./Dec.: 16–21.

Kindervater, Katherine Hall. 2017. "The Technological Rationality of the Drone Strike." *Critical Studies on Security* 5, no. 1: 28–44.

King, Anthony D. 1991. *Culture, Globalization, and the World System*. Minneapolis: University of Minnesota Press.

Klauser, Francisco, and Silvana Pedrozo. 2017. "Introduction: Power and Space in the Drone Age." *Geographica Helvetica* 72: 409–10.

Lambert, Léopold. 2017. "Introduction: A 'Breathing Combat' against the Toxicity of the Colonial/Racist State." *Funambulist*, Nov./Dec.: 12–15.

LAPD (Los Angeles Police Department). 2017. *Los Angeles Police Department Small Unmanned Aerial System Pilot Program Deployment Guidelines and Procedures*. October 17. assets.lapdonline.org/assets/pdf/2017.10.17%20-%20 APPROVED%20FINAL%20-%20sUAS%20Guidelines.pdf.

Lindqvist, Sven. 2001. *A History of Bombing*. New York: The New Press.

Longmire, Sylvia. 2014. *Border Security: Why Big Money, Fences, and Drones Aren't Making Us Safer*. New York: Palgrave MacMillan.

Maass, Dave. 2018. "ICE Accesses a Massive Amount of License Plate Data: Will California Take Action?" Electronic Frontier Foundation. January 29. www.eff .org/deeplinks/2018/01/ice-accesses-massive-amount-license-plate-data-will -california-take-action.

MacDonald, Thomas. 2018. "The Shocking Difference between the Canadian and American Border Patrol Agencies." *MTL Blog*. www.mtlblog.com/news /the-shocking-difference-between-the-canadian-and-american-border-patrol -agencies-photos.

Márquez, John D., and Junaid Rana. 2017. "Black Radical Possibility and the Decolonial International." *South Atlantic Quarterly* 116, no. 3: 505–28.

Mather, Kate, and Richard Winton. 2015. "LAPD Uses Its Helicopters to Stop Crimes before They Start." *Los Angeles Times*, March 7. www.latimes.com/local /crime/la-me-lapd-helicopter-20150308-story.html.

McCormack, Derek P. 2010. "Remotely Sensing Affective Afterlives: The Spectral Geographies of Material Remains." *Annals of the Association of American Geographers* 100, no. 3: 640–54.

McNeal, Gregory S. 2018. "New Program Will Help Spark an Era of Drone Innovation." *Real Clear Policy*, May 24. www.realclearpolicy.com/articles/2018 /05/24/new_program_will_help_spark_an_era_of_drone_innovation_110646 .html.

Meredith, Sam. 2017. "Drones Set to Be Deployed by Los Angeles Police Department." *CNBC*, October 18. www.cnbc.com/2017/10/18/lapd-drones-set-to-be -deployed-by-los-angeles-police-department.html.

Miller, Andrea. 2017. "(Im)Material Terror: Incitement to Violence Discourse as Racializing Technology in the War on Terror." In *Life in the Age of Drone Warfare*, edited by Lisa Parks and Caren Kaplan, 112–33. Durham, NC: Duke University Press.

Miller, Andrea. 2019. "Shadows of War, Traces of Policing: The Weaponization of Space and the Sensible in Preemption." In *Captivating Technology: Race, Carceral Technoscience, and Liberatory Imagination in Everyday Life*, edited by Ruha Benjamin, 108–36. Durham, NC: Duke University Press.

National Immigration Forum. 2014. "Integrated Fixed Towers, the Waste Continues." April 2. immigrationforum.org/article/integrated-fixed-towers-waste -continues/.

Neocleous, Mark. 2013. "Air Power as Police Power." *Environment and Planning D: Society and Space* 31, no. 4: 578–93.

Neocleous, Mark. 2014. *War Power, Police Power.* Edinburgh: Edinburgh University Press.

Nevins, Joseph. 2010. *Operation Gatekeeper and Beyond: The War on "Illegals" and the Remaking of the U.S.-Mexico Boundary.* New York: Routledge.

Nevins, Joseph. 2012. "Policing Mobility, Maintaining Global Apartheid—From South Africa to the United States." In *Beyond Walls and Cages: Bridging Immigrant Justice and Anti-prison Organizing in the United States*, edited by Jenna M. Loyd, Matt Mitchelson, and Andrew Burridge, 19–26. Athens: University of Georgia Press.

Nevins, Joseph. 2018. "The Speed of Life and Death: Migrant Fatalities, Territorial Boundaries, and Energy Consumption." *Mobilities* 13, no. 1: 29–44.

Nielsen, Kirstjen M. 2018. "The U.S. Isn't Prepared for the Growing Threat of Drones." *Washington Post*, July 4. www.washingtonpost.com/opinions/the-us -isnt-prepared-for-the-growing-threat-of-drones/2018/07/04/30cc2a76-7eef -11e8-b9f0-61b08cdd0ea1_story.html?utm_term=.fc63ff6564ea.

Nieuwenhuis, Marjin. 2016. "Breathing Materiality: Aerial Violence at a Time of Atmospheric Politics." *Critical Studies on Terrorism* 9, no. 3: 499–521.

Nieuwenhuis, Marijn. 2017. "Atmospheric Governance: Gassing as Law for the Protection and Killing of Life." *Environment and Planning D: Society and Space*, August 31. doi.org/10.1177/0263775817729378.

Ohmae, Kenichi. 1999. *The Borderless World: Power and Strategy in the Interlinked Economy.* New York: Harper Collins.

Parks, Lisa. 2018. *Rethinking Media Coverage: Vertical Mediation and the War on Terror.* New York: Routledge.

Pompa, Cynthia. 2018. "President Trump Is Accelerating the Militarization of the

Southwest Border." American Civil Liberties Union, December 5. www.aclu.org /blog/immigrants-rights/president-trump-accelerating-militarization-southwest -border.

Reeves, Joshua, and Jeremy Packer. 2013. "Police Media: The Governance of Territory, Speed, and Communication." *Communication and Critical/Cultural Studies* 10, no. 4: 359–84.

Rivera, Alex. 2012. "Border Control: Malcolm Harris Interviewing Alex Rivera." *New Inquiry* 6: 5–20.

Rosenthal, Daniel J., and Loren Dejonge Schulman. 2018. "Trump's Secret War on Terror." *Atlantic*, August 10. www.theatlantic.com/international/archive /2018/08/trump-war-terror-drones/567218/.

Sandvik, Kristin Bergtora, and Maria Gabrielsen Jumbert. 2017. *The Good Drone*. London: Routledge.

Satia, Priya. 2006. "The Defense of Inhumanity: Air Control and the British Idea of Arabia." *American Historical Review* 3, no. 1: 16–51.

Satia, Priya. 2014. "Drones: A History from the British Middle East." *Humanity* 5, no. 1: 1–31.

Schrader, Stuart. 2014. "Policing Empire." *Jacobin*, September 5. www.jacobinmag .com/2014/09/policing-empire/.

Schrader, Stuart. 2017. "More than Cosmetic Changes: The Challenges of Experiments with Police Demilitarization in the 1960s and 1970s." *Journal of Urban History*, April 28: 1–24.

Schrader, Stuart. 2018. "Tear Gas and the U.S. Border." *Process* (blog), December 6. www.processhistory.org/schrader-teargas-border/.

Seigel, Micol. 2015. "Objects of Police History." *Journal of American History* 102, no. 1: 152–61.

Seigel, Micol. 2018. *Violence Work: State Power and the Limits of Police*. Durham, NC: Duke University Press.

Shapiro, Nicholas, and Eben Kirksey. 2017. "Chemo-Ethnography: An Introduction." *Cultural Anthropology* 32, no. 4: 481–93.

Shaw, Ian. 2016. "The Urbanization of Drone Warfare: Policing Surplus Populations in the Dronepolis." *Geographica Helvetica* 17: 19–28.

Shaw, Ian, and Majed Akhter. 2014. "The Dronification of State Violence." *Critical Asian Studies* 46, no. 2: 211–34.

Simmons, Kristen. 2017. "Settler Atmospherics." *Cultural Anthropology* 32, no. 4. culanth.org/fieldsights/1221-settler-atmospherics.

Singh, Nikhil Pal. 2014. "The Whiteness of Police." *American Quarterly* 66, no. 4: 1091–99.

Sloterdijk, Peter. 2009. *Terror from the Air*. Los Angeles: Semiotext(e).

SPLC (Southern Poverty Law Center). 2018. "American Border Patrol/American Patrol." www.splcenter.org/fighting-hate/extremist-files/group/american-border -patrolamerican-patrol.

Stop LAPD Spying Coalition. 2018. "Dismantling Predictive Policing in Los Angeles: May 8th Report Summary." stoplapdspying.org/wp-content/uploads /2018/05/Before-the-Bullet-Hits-the-Body-Report-Summary.pdf.

Tahir, Madiha. 2012. "Louder than Bombs." *New Inquiry* 6: 100–110.

Tahir, Madiha. 2017. "The Containment Zone." In *Life in the Age of Drone Warfare*, edited by Lisa Parks and Caren Kaplan, 220–40. Durham, NC: Duke University Press.

UAS Vision. 2018. "Drone Activity Soaring at US-Mexico Border." www.uas vision.com/2018/07/09/drone-activity-soaring-at-us-mexico-border/.

Wagner, Bryan. 2009. *Disturbing the Peace: Black Culture and the Police Power after Slavery*. Cambridge, MA: Harvard University Press.

Waitt, Tammy. 2018. "US Not Prepared for Growing Border Drone Threats." *American Security Today*, July 10. americansecuritytoday.com/us-not-prepared -growing-border-drone-threats-learn-videos/.

Wall, Tyler. 2013. "Unmanning the Police Manhunt: Vertical Security as Pacification." *Socialist Studies* 9, no. 2: 32–56.

Wall, Tyler. 2016. "Ordinary Emergency: Drones, Police, and Geographies of Legal Terror." *Antipode* 48, no. 4: 1122–39.

Caren Kaplan is professor of American studies at the University of California, Davis. She is the author of *Questions of Travel* (1996) and *Aerial Aftermaths: Wartime from Above* (2018), among other works.

Andrea Miller is a PhD candidate in the Cultural Studies Graduate Group at the University of California, Davis.

Speculative Policing

Rivke Jaffe

On Sunday, May 23, 2010, Jamaica's Prime Minister Bruce Golding declared a state of emergency. His government sought to arrest and extradite Christopher "Dudus" Coke, the country's most notorious criminal "don." Soldiers and police forced their way into Tivoli Gardens, the Kingston neighborhood where the don's headquarters were located, killing sixty-nine people in what became known as the "Tivoli incursion." Dudus was not caught until a month after the security operation and was immediately extradited to the United States, where he is currently in federal prison serving a twenty-three-year sentence for arms and drugs trafficking. After having "recaptured" Tivoli, the government established a military presence in the neighborhood that lasted over a year, posting soldiers in Dudus's former office. The security forces installed military checkpoints at all of the entrances to the neighborhood and implemented a 6:00 p.m. curfew that lasted over a month; nobody could leave after 6:00 p.m. unless they received a police permit to do so. The state of emergency was extended, and similar military curfews and a range of other "antigang" measures were rolled out in adjacent neighborhoods in West and Central Kingston, inner-city neighborhoods in the historic downtown area of Jamaica's capital. In the months and years that

I am very grateful to Shamus Khan and Madiha Tahir for their editorial support in developing the special issue on violence and policing that this article forms a part of, and for their feedback and that of the other authors featured in this issue during Columbia University's workshop on the topic. I am also indebted to Anthony Harriott, Anouk de Koning, Wayne Modest, and members of the Securcit+ reading group for their helpful comments on earlier versions of this article. Thanks also to audiences at the University of Florida, the University of Pennsylvania, Utrecht University, and the London School of Economics and Political Science for their responses to presentations of earlier versions, and to Ieva Jusionyte, Deborah Thomas, Jolle Demmers, and Austin Zeiderman for facilitating these events. The article draws on research funded by the European Research Council (ERC) under the European Union's Horizon 2020 research and innovation program (grant agreement no. 337974, SECURCIT), and by the Netherlands Organisation for Scientific Research (NWO, grant nos. W01.70.100.001 and 452-12-013).

Public Culture 31:3   DOI 10.1215/08992363-7532751
Copyright 2019 by Duke University Press

followed, politicians, government officials, and a range of commentators increasingly connected these policing measures to the possibility of fashioning a new urban future. New forms of urban intervention, they suggested, would summon a crime-free and prosperous Kingston into being.

Jamaica's recent policing strategies resonate with urban regeneration policies across the world, where new forms of crime prevention intersect with real-estate speculation. In this article I scrutinize such strategies to develop a theorization of what I call "speculative policing": an experimental, future-oriented form of policing that connects crime prevention to other forms of negotiating urban risk and uncertainty.[1] Not coincidentally, these modes of policing are applied primarily in areas of the city seen as having most potential for commercial redevelopment. Speculative policing works to establish a specific sociopolitical order, while rendering economically productive the differentiated and dynamic value of urban spaces and populations. In Kingston as elsewhere, the logic underlying this form of security governance is to make urban space safe for profit and investment. Yet the political process of implementing this mode of urban policing is itself quite uncertain, or even risky. It involves flexible, provisional forms of policy making and intervention that anticipate failure and that themselves skirt the edges of the law.

Speculative policing combines three future-oriented phenomena that engage with risk and uncertainty in different ways: preventive policing, real-estate speculation, and experimental modes of governance. These phenomena are in themselves not necessarily new, and each has developed an orientation toward the future according to what is largely an internal logic: preventing crime, capturing the rent gap, and innovating urban planning and policy. The specificity of speculative policing, I suggest, lies in the conjunction of these three phenomena in contemporary cities. Their combination implies the emergence of a new mode of urban security governance, a form of political and economic rationality that is speculative both in its underlying logic and in its everyday implementation.

1. Following the economist Frank Knight ([1921] 2006: 19–20), risk is often understood as a quantifiable, calculable form of uncertainty, while true uncertainty cannot be measured or rationalized. However, as Caitlin Zaloom (2004: 384) points out, "the analytic distinction between risk and uncertainty does not hold up under a consideration of speculation as a practice." The practices of speculative policing involve navigating and mitigating the gap between calculable and incalculable futures, between risk and uncertainty, to render it politically and economically productive. For distinct but related approaches to security and the calculation of the incalculable, see de Goede 2012 and Amoore 2014.

Speculative policing has much in common with what Neil Smith (1996) described as revanchist urbanism, a repressive, exclusionary form of urban governance aimed at restoring a bourgeois sociopolitical order. In Jamaica, such revanchism is evident in the desire expressed by nostalgic upper-middle classes to reclaim a downtown Kingston they feel they lost to poverty, crime, and squalor (see, e.g., Dodman 2007), and the punitive interventions broadly seen as necessary to achieve this. However, whereas the temporality of revanchism is largely oriented toward the past, speculative policing has the future as its point of reference. It is aimed not so much at restoring a previous era as managing the uncertain futures that present a challenge to municipal governments everywhere (see Zeiderman et al. 2015).

A first element of speculative policing is its emphasis on "preventive" and "proactive" approaches, aimed at crime prevention and future offenders. While preventive policing is by no means new (see, e.g., Browne 2015; Dodsworth 2016), the current popularity of such approaches has been read as signaling a temporal shift in policing, characterized by an orientation toward the future and a move away from post hoc crime solving toward the prevention of criminal acts (Zedner 2007). Rather than necessarily engaging with actual perpetrators or victims, such a preemptive form of policing is aimed at crime prevention and future offenders. This privileging of a biopolitical logic of population management, over sovereign or disciplinary approaches to criminal justice, entails a conceptualization of crime as a risk that can be understood and managed through actuarial calculations, similar to those that insurance companies make. This logic of actuarialism is accompanied by a prioritization of mitigating loss over punishing wrongdoing. In addition, the production of security involves a broad range of state and nonstate actors, from the police to private security companies and voluntary groups (Zedner 2007).

This temporal orientation of much contemporary policing can be understood as part of a broader turn toward governing through the management of risk. Beyond managing risk, however, speculative policing seeks to render it economically productive. As studies of cities from Rio de Janeiro to Mexico City to Amsterdam suggest, the most repressive forms of crime prevention take place in precisely those areas that have the highest potential for urban regeneration and real-estate development (e.g., Freeman 2012; Davis 2013; Wright 2013; de Koning 2015). Speculative policing combines the risk management of future-oriented policing with an interest in unlocking the potential of real estate. As security forces target crime threats, property owners and corporate investors feel more comfortable taking financial risks. The potential for economic profit lies in the contrast between the future economic value of real estate and the social value and crime risk associated with current residents. Politicians, bureaucrats, and developers estimate the economic potential of urban place through calculations that combine location, architecture, and reputation, in relation to the addition or subtraction of specific urban populations (low-income residents vs. office workers, criminals vs. artists). Beyond the value of land and housing, in cities such as Rio de Janeiro the regularization of water and electricity consumption concurrent with the "pacification" of low-income areas indicates a recognition of the consumer potential that can similarly be unlocked for corporate investors, if security risks are managed strategically (e.g., Pilo' 2017).

A third element is the exploratory, experimental nature of the urban security governance strategies themselves. New policing policies are developed and implemented not so much in a linear fashion, according to a blueprint logic. Rather, the high-crime, high-value zones where speculative policing is rolled out from Kingston to Rio de Janeiro might best be seen as sociospatial prototypes. Public policy making increasingly follows a practice of prototyping previously associated with design; characterized by flexibility, provisionality, and anticipation; and understood as "creative, contingent and emergent [rather than] rational, linear and reproducible" (Kimbell and Bailey 2017: 218). Speculative policing involves prefigurative experiments that urban governance actors hope will generate a new and improved city of the future, even as they anticipate their failure. As Alberto Corsín Jiménez (2014: 381, emphasis in original) suggests, "An important feature of prototyping . . . is the incorporation of *failure* as a legitimate and very often empirical realisation." Failure and success become blurred in this context: rather than being conceived in terms of delivering measurable outcomes or meeting preset targets, policy "success" may be reframed as having gained increased learning opportunities, or the habituation and support of various constituencies. This resonates with what Oren Halpert et al. (2013: 275) call "test-bed urbanism," a "perpetually provisional" form of city making that involves a "tense relation between performance and aspiration." Yet despite its nonlinear nature, what appears more stable in the context of policing is that these experimental techniques are generally tested on impoverished, racialized spaces and populations. In their discussion of the test-bed city, Halpert et al. (275) note that it is both "a rehearsal of our future and an archive of our past." This archival feature is certainly evident in a postcolonial city such as Kingston, where colonial genealogies of differentiated policing inform the deployment of security policies (see Harriott 2000; Campbell 2015).

In this article, I develop an elaboration of speculative policing through an analysis of urban development in "post-Dudus" Jamaica. My analysis draws on a total of sixteen months of ethnographic research conducted during the period 2008–18 on donmanship and on new modes of security governance. This research included participant observation in a West Kingston neighborhood I call Brick Town, which had previously been under the leadership of an influential don I call the General. In addition, I conducted interviews with a range of actors throughout the city, including dons and their seconds-in-command, politicians, senior officers in the police and military, private security company owners and managers, and representatives of local and international development agencies and nongovernmental organizations.

The 2010 state of emergency presented a disruption to an established sociopolitical order in which dons such as Dudus colluded with politicians, bureaucrats, and police to cogovern urban territories and populations. In the next section, I provide a background to this system of donmanship. Then I discuss attempts by Jamaica's security forces and political and business elites to capitalize on the moment of rupture to recalibrate the previous don-based urban order. I outline how a loose alliance sought to shift control to state actors while simultaneously mobilizing downtown Kingston's potential for economic regeneration. Starting in 2010, the Jamaican security forces organized curfews in allegedly criminogenic inner-city neighborhoods, which involved the detention and "processing" of male residents. In addition, they compiled and publicized lists of "persons of interest," alleged dons, who were summoned to police stations. These technologies of data collection and listing tended to concentrate on specific areas within the Kingston Metropolitan Region and involved various forms of legal exceptionalism. I show how these same areas were the focus of real-estate development and broader urban regeneration strategies that included the initiation of a major commercial development, a crackdown on informal economic activities, and the emergence of early indicators of gentrification such as art projects and coffee shops. Tracing the development of such urban policies and interventions for nearly a decade following the state of emergency, I end with an analysis of Jamaica's urban security governance as characterized by a nonlinear, prototyping logic.

Dons

For decades, Kingston's low-income areas have been governed by dons, local community leaders who are generally involved in criminal activities such as extortion or drug trafficking. Historically, these dons have been local political brokers, tied to either the Jamaica Labour Party (JLP) or the People's National Party (PNP). Following Jamaica's independence from Britain in 1962, these two main political parties both channeled weapons and money to dons, relying on them to secure electoral turf by any means necessary. Within the neighborhoods they controlled in downtown Kingston, dons ensured that loyal party supporters received state housing or jobs, while intimidating or forcing out supporters of the "wrong" party. In so doing, dons were central to the emergence of a violent system of political clientelism known as "garrison politics," which transformed downtown Kingston's low-income neighborhoods into "garrison communities," fiercely defended party-political enclaves (see Stone 1980; Sives 2010).

From the 1980s, dons' connections to the transnational drug trade allowed them to gain financial independence from politicians. The most influential and wealthiest dons have been central to a system of local governance, providing neighborhood residents with access to social welfare and to employment, either within their own organizations or through their political and business connections. They have also played an important role in extralegal security provision, resolving local disputes and punishing crimes ranging from theft to rape. In various instances, the Jamaica Constabulary Force condoned or even supported this self-help form of law and order, often based on violent retribution. As their governance practices grew increasingly entangled with politicians, bureaucrats, and the police, the most powerful dons became corulers, whose interests influenced political decision making as much as vice versa (see Harriott 2008; Lewis 2012; Jaffe 2013).

This long-standing entanglement explains the initial reluctance of then Prime Minister Bruce Golding to extradite Dudus. Golding's party, the JLP, had historically close ties to Dudus and his neighborhood of Tivoli Gardens, known as "the mother of all garrisons." The "Tivoli incursion" took place in May 2010, after nearly nine months of increasing pressure from the United States and from local media, civil society, and the opposition PNP. While the security operation and the state violence it involved shocked the Jamaican public, many citizens, politicians, and businesspeople also saw the crisis as an opportunity to "dismantle the garrisons" and to fashion a new urban future without dons.

Formal and Informal Crime Prevention

Realizing this future Kingston involved, first of all, implementing new types of security strategies. Some of the interventions that took shape during and after the state of emergency were formal policing policy; others appeared to be unofficial but coordinated actions. Here I focus on two related sets of future-oriented policing measures: the compilation of rudimentary databases through place-based curfews and "processing," and the production and dissemination of security lists of "persons of interest," several of whom were killed by the police.

Curfews and "Processing"

Amidst widespread calls to bring an end to the rule of dons, the Jamaican security forces—the Jamaica Constabulary Force (JCF) together with the Jamaica Defense Force (JDF)—implemented a series of military curfews directly after the May 2010 security operation, primarily in West and Central Kingston. These interventions involved cordoning off spaces categorized as risky and preventing residents from leaving for the duration of the curfew. As in Tivoli Gardens, entrances to each neighborhood would be sealed off and converted into military checkpoints (see fig. 1), while soldiers conducted searches of residents and properties throughout the curfew area, with "getting the guns" as one stated goal. In addition to temporarily controlling the mobility of residents and searching for illegal weapons, however, the curfews were central in compiling a database of suspected criminals and can be understood as a first step in making legible, governable spaces out of former "no-go areas."

Closely related to the general curfew was a procedure euphemistically called "processing," which functioned as a crucial part of the production of legibility. During the 2010 curfews, under the legal exceptionalism of the state of emergency, the security forces summarily rounded up thousands of men and teenaged boys from Tivoli Gardens and other inner-city neighborhoods. While these men were never charged with any crime, they were detained and "processed," arrested without charges and held overnight in the National Arena, the city's main indoor sports stadium. This processing involved photographing and fingerprinting the men, a strategy designed to create a biometric database for future reference.

In Brick Town, the inner-city neighborhood in West Kingston where I worked most closely, this processing took place in early June 2010. During a two-day military curfew, the soldiers went from building to building searching for contraband. Their total catch consisted of four guns (an Uzi submachine gun and three pistols) and 140 rounds of ammunition—not a very large number of illegal weapons for a neighborhood considered to be a hotbed of organized crime. In addition, the military presence enabled the public-private utility companies to come into the neighborhood and disconnect the ubiquitous illegal electricity and water connections. While this measure did not appear to have an immediate connection to combatting organized crime, it was promoted as part of a so-called regularization

453

Figure 1 Military curfew in downtown Kingston, 2010. Photo by author.

strategy that sought to regularize (rather, recommodify) the "irregular" or free use of electricity, water, and housing in neighborhoods run by dons.

The Brick Town raids did not appear to be very effective. Many people who would otherwise have been detained had removed themselves from the neighborhood well before the security forces came in, either because they had inside sources notifying them of a pending curfew, or because they could guess that the neighborhood was a high-priority area that would be targeted early on. Other residents told me that they had escaped being detained and processed because they were recognized by individual police officers involved in the raids who vouched for them. Some of my main contacts fled to the countryside to stay with family there, and some of them had still not come back years later. (This permanent displacement may in fact have been an anticipated effect, as I discuss in further detail below.) Many of the water and electricity taps were quickly reconnected as soon as the military left—during follow-up visits in the months and years that followed, I found many people had managed to circumvent the various antitheft technologies the electricity company had tried to implement, and they were back to the old system of "bridging light." Three of the four weapons seized during the curfew had been found hidden away in one business establishment, but over the years that followed, it became clear that the proprietor could not be prosecuted for illegal possession of weapons, as it could not be proven beyond a doubt that he knew they were on his property.

What, then, was the function of such curfews and processing, beyond a performative show of force? I suggest that we can see them as playing a central role within the development of future-oriented policing in Kingston. The identification, measurement, and management of risk necessitates an ongoing process of data collection, organization, and analysis. In other contexts, the "actuarial archive" that enables governance actors to know and manage insecurity may involve large quantitative datasets and complex proprietary algorithms (e.g., Amoore and Raley 2017). In low-income, high-crime urban areas, the possibilities of compiling statistical databases for purposes of preventive repression are often limited. In Kingston's inner-city neighborhoods, the security forces work with blunter tools, both in compiling rudimentary databases of risky persons and in repressively preventing future crime. Biometric data is collected through force, risk calculations are made based on simple correlations of bodily identity markers and place of residence, and preventive policing often involves the violent curtailing of the lives of those expected to commit future crimes.

In an interview,[2] a retired senior JCF officer, whom I call Edmund, explained to me that the processing of inner-city men was an intentional police strategy, necessary for the compilation of a database of real and potential criminals. Under normal circumstances, the police have very limited means of identifying suspects. There is a widespread reluctance for witnesses to testify against suspects, making material evidence such as fingerprints and eventually DNA all the more important. But even when certain individuals have been identified as suspects, the police are often at a loss regarding how to find them, as there is no national registry of names and addresses. In addition, some inner-city residents, including criminals, simply do not exist within the state's bureaucracy. Their existence has never been registered through birth certificates, educational degrees, or tax regis-

---

2. Interview, November 2014.

tration numbers, and they remain true unknowns to the formal system: unidentified, unregistered, nonexistent.

Edmund explained: "You have a suspect by an alias, you don't even have a true name . . . just, known as 'Jughead' or 'Skatalite.' It's very, very complex." There had been attempts to pass legislation making it mandatory for all Jamaicans to carry identification cards. Similar schemes in Brazil have been used mainly as a means of surveillance intended to make low-income populations more legible (see Koster 2014). In Jamaica, politicians have been highly reluctant to pass a national ID law because, as Edmund put it delicately, their constituencies do not always stand to benefit—the collusion between politicians and dons is a major impediment. Given this lack of political support, the police looked for other ways to compile a database, not so much even for crime prevention but for the future apprehension of suspects. They had had no legal basis on which to photograph or fingerprint suspected criminals, but the state of emergency provided the chance they had been waiting for, to collect biodata for future use, for solving future crimes that they would most likely not be able to prevent.[3]

The curfews and processing, then, can be understood as an anticipatory form of policing that frames citizens as potential criminals based on their area of residence. The construction of a crude database of names, photographs, and biometric data was explicitly place based, relying on a conception of criminogenic spaces, where future crime risk is calculated through a combination of residential location and "suspicious" markers such gender, skin color, and styles of clothing.

"Persons of Interest"

An additional form of future-oriented policing was also initiated during the 2010 state of emergency, when the police began to publicize lists of "persons of interest" who were summoned to police stations. These persons were alleged dons, who were sometimes listed by their real names and sometimes only by their aliases. The newspapers and television news shows put out calls for people known as "Not Nice" and "Government," naming their general address. As a researcher

---

3. Human rights organizations came to similar conclusions, noting: "It appeared that the security forces believed the State of Emergency gave them carte blanche to detain young men for the purpose of developing an unlawful database of young men who can then be tracked as being 'known to police.' The State of Emergency was operated in a discriminatory fashion as security forces focussed their operations in inner-city (socioeconomically depressed) neighbourhoods, rounding up only and almost all young men in these areas for the purpose of 'processing'" (Byers et al. 2011: 24).

working on donmanship, I used this publication to gain a more comprehensive understanding—an informal database of my own—of who was in power where. However, the legality of this practice of public naming and criminalizing was highly questionable.[4]

Those who showed up at the police stations were held for a little while, processed, and generally released, as the police had no evidence on which to detain them beyond what the state of emergency allowed; they were not suspects, just persons of interest. In Brick Town, I soon heard rumors of what residents called an "embargo": if the police see persons of interest with other people or hear that they are getting in trouble, they will "crack down on you," that is, kill you. The Brick Town don, who had succeeded his more popular father, left the place following the "person of interest" listing and never returned to a leadership position, taking seriously the warnings he had apparently received.

In mid-2012, Keith, one of my main interlocutors in Brick Town, explained to me that this "persons of interest" strategy, which had continued after the state of emergency ended, seemed to have had some effect on local gunmen: "If you notice, as they are named you see them run go give up themselves. One time you wouldn't find them do those things, but now them just run go in to the police. 'Cause them know if them don't come in when the police say to come in by certain time, when time police see them, them liable to die."[5] The fear of being killed by police resonated more broadly throughout downtown Kingston. In the Central Kingston neighborhood of Tel Aviv, the man commonly held to be the local don, Donovan "Pepsi" Ainsworth, had announcements posted through the area stating, "I Donovan Ainsworth, otherwise known as 'Pepsi' or 'Calla Danks,' write this notice to officially inform all politicians and members of the security forces who have classified me as a gang leader or a don that I am neither" (see fig. 2).

The consequences of being listed as a person of interest cannot be seen separately from a more long-standing practice of police killings (see Amnesty International 2016). For several years, the JCF killed around 200 citizens annually, peaking to

4. In addition, the differentiated nature of the practice was glaringly evident in the case of the so-called X6 killer, a wealthy, politically connected businessman who shot at a taxi that had run into his BMW X6 vehicle, killing a teenage passenger. Initially, none of the main newspapers published the alleged killer's name, arguing that it was very important that the privacy and anonymity of suspects of serious crimes be protected. The blatant "outing" of alleged dons emphasized the extent to which this concern for privacy is applied according to class position and political protection.

5. Interview, August 2012.

382 persons in 2010.[6] In a context in which a majority of Jamaicans sees the justice system as largely incapable of successfully prosecuting crimes, extrajudicial killings are often understood popularly as a more effective way of bringing criminals to justice. However, these killings are not necessarily punitive or framed as criminal justice per se. Rather, police understand them as having a clear preventive character. In a media interview, Reneto Adams—a former senior superintendent of police who retired from the JCF following a brutality scandal—explained the preventive logic of police killings: "I use a 'crocodile and alligator' analogy—you don't kill the ferocious alligator and the ferocious crocodile; you have them killed or terminated in the eggs before they are hatched. It is simple logic" (Green 2011). As such, the lists of suspected criminals, followed by the permanent displacement or death of those listed, can be understood as a strategy intended to mitigate urban uncertainty by preventing future crime in specific sections of urban Jamaica. As a technique of government and a sometimes lethal form of normative

Figure 2 Poster disavowing the status of don, 2011. Photo by author.

ordering, Jamaica's list of persons of interest is not entirely dissimilar from the "kill lists" and "no fly lists" developed by the US government in the context of preventing terrorist attacks (see, e.g., de Goede and Sullivan 2016).

Inner-City Regeneration and Real-Estate Speculation

I consider these future-oriented crime prevention strategies—which were largely focused on the neighborhoods bordering the historical commercial district in West and Central Kingston—in relation to activities associated with increasing the real-estate potential of the same area: a crackdown on informal economic activities, a major commercial construction project, and a number of indicators of nascent gentrification.

6. A total of 3,514 persons were killed by police in the period 1991–2010 (Byers et al. 2011: 12). The number of police killings dropped sharply in 2014 following the establishment of the Independent Commission of Investigations (INDECOM), which initiated the first meaningful prosecution of such killings.

Many Jamaicans hoped that the "clean-up" of downtown Kingston that the state of emergency set in motion would herald a new era of commercial redevelopment. A letter writer to the *Jamaica Observer* who described himself as a "20-year-old hopeful citizen" expressed these sentiments rather poetically (Edwards 2014):

> Travelling through the infamous Tivoli Gardens for the past couple of years has been rather exhilarating. Beyond the barricades, stripping paint, empty buildings, and criminal associations, Tivoli is perfect. . . . With less juice boxes strewn across the area, space is available to build businesses. If you observe, there are mechanic shops, restaurants, boutiques, furniture stores, funeral parlours, bars. . . . The community also has multiple recreational spaces, churches, schools, a theatre, a cemetery, a police station, a health centre, a home for the aged, and a stadium. . . . No gilded residential area, with all their pompous occupants, cultured lawns, endearing security systems, and magic dust can trump such sustainable genius. I'm jealous. Minus the criminality, splash a new coat of paint, get the schools up to par and watch and see this bewildered titan resurge beyond the stigma and heal its vilest lacerations. Then I tell you, it will be the platinum real estate no one will refuse."

While perhaps a little overoptimistic regarding the potential of Tivoli's 1960s public housing development, these hopes seemed slightly more realizable a few blocks down, where the city's past and perhaps future glory was evident in the crumbling but still impressive facades of its colonial Georgian architecture. Realizing the platinum potential of this real estate, however, required concerted effort on the part of both public and private actors.

Speculative policing involved not only the preventive repression of organized crime but also the more general removal of economic activities considered both criminogenic and aesthetically incompatible with urban modernity. In addition to their antigang measures, in the months and years following the 2010 security operation in Tivoli Gardens, JCF activities in downtown Kingston also concentrated on removing informal activities, with frequent sweeps intended to permanently remove informal vendors, cook shops, and other small-scale enterprises. In a similar move to the "aesthetic criminalization" Asher Ghertner (2015: 99–124) identifies in his work on slum removal in Delhi, the Jamaican authorities classified informality as a visual and legal nuisance incompatible with post-Dudus urban renewal. The importance of optics was evident in the practice of removing vendors and their goods from only the main commercial thoroughfares, while allowing them to continue in the less visible lanes and back alleys.

Another letter writer commended this crackdown, which appeared more sustained than previous half-hearted attempts to remove informal vending, and connected it to a major construction project by telecommunications giant Digicel: "The heart of our city must be free from the chaos that was once downtown Kingston. The police force must be unreservedly congratulated for its action, no matter how belated; I truly hope this is not just another nine-day wonder. In the same breath, the move by Digicel to headquarter their operations downtown must be congratulated and exemplified by other private and public entities" (Chambers 2010).

Construction for Digicel's regional headquarters, an eleven-story office tower featuring wind turbines, solar paneling, and a geothermal cooling system, started in 2010, and the building was officially opened in 2013. Located on the border of Tivoli Gardens, the structure was among the largest developments to have been completed in downtown Kingston in years, and it was difficult not to interpret this investment as a major indication of urban regeneration. In welcoming Digicel to downtown Kingston, then Prime Minister Bruce Golding said, "We are delighted with Digicel's commitment to spearheading the rejuvenation of downtown Kingston and will continue to partner with the company not only to ensure a smooth transition to its new home, but to drive the redevelopment of downtown Kingston" (Digicel Jamaica 2010). While the construction work provided an important employment opportunity for local residents, observers hoped that more long-term economic effects would emerge as hundreds of middle-class employees moved from Digicel's former offices in uptown Kingston to the new downtown headquarters.[7]

In addition to the authorities, middle-class Jamaicans were enthused about the new presence of such a modern, environmentally friendly space in downtown. Karin, a middle-class blogger and yoga teacher, joined the politicians in praising the corporation, asking:

> Will the relocation of the Digicel headquarters downtown . . . be a catalyst for further development downtown? I'm hoping that the hundreds of people that will undoubtedly work and visit the building will be eating, shopping and generally spending money with the surrounding downtown businesses, large and small, and not simply staying indoors in the "food court" to be included in the building. Downtown Kingston has amazing potential. The waterfront views are beautiful, the neighbourhoods historic, the shopping great, and the people warm and welcoming. . . . Big up to Digicel for having the vision. (Edmonds 2012)

7. For more on Kingston's uptown-downtown divisions, see Carnegie (2014, 2017).

Few commentators dwelled on the question whether the warm and welcoming low-income population would benefit from this economic development, or whether these commercial activities might eventually result in their displacement. The Brick Town residents I spoke to were equally hopeful that Digicel would mean an improvement to their lives.

Nevertheless, I began to wonder if gentrification could be imminent, especially as I began to notice a number of standard early indicators. The food court in the Digicel building sold lattes and smoothies—one online review noted that "it's super clean and doesn't even feel like downtown which is important if I'm actually gonna stomach eating here" (Yanique 2013).[8] A local chain of coffee shops that had previously only had branches in the fanciest commercial areas of uptown Kingston opened a space in Central Kingston. A well-connected Australian artist opened an art gallery and vegetarian café in a former beer brewery on the border of Tivoli Gardens. While art enthusiasts would on occasion visit the National Gallery of Jamaica, one of the few elite institutions in downtown Kingston, this new project persuaded wealthy Jamaicans to venture into backstreets they would have avoided at all costs just a few years before. Could this mean domestication by cappuccino, and a slow encroachment of the creative class and their edgy art projects (Atkinson 2003; Ley 2003)?

Prototyping Urban Regeneration

Following the various policies and interventions affecting Kingston over time, I became increasingly aware of the provisional, experimental nature of Jamaica's security governance. The "success" of police actions and urban regeneration— whether assessed in terms of homicide rates or sustained changes in investment patterns—rarely appears to be more than partial or tentative, but this does not seem to perturb politicians and policy makers. Decreases in the homicide rate prove only temporary, real-estate investments wax and wane, and legal challenges force certain policies to be deemphasized. Yet to focus on such measurable outcomes may be to miss one of the main points of speculative policing. Concrete, quantifiable results, I suggest, are less important than facilitating and normalizing new ways of administering urban life.

In November 2013, I sat on the steps of a small business in Brick Town, talking to the owner, Lion, about the attempts to regenerate downtown Kingston, includ-

8. Another reviewer, however, commented, "The security guards are awful . . . maybe it's because my complexion isn't as light as they'd like it to be. I am constantly harassed whenever I dine there" (Junior Byrd 2014).

ing the construction of the nearby Digicel building and the ongoing attempts to remove informal vendors from the streets. I asked him whether he thought the changes would affect Brick Town positively or negatively. I tried to explain the concept of gentrification to Lion, but he interrupted me: "Yeah man, I seen it happen in New York." The same thing had happened to Jamaicans he knew in Brixton: "Them cyaan [cannot] pay the rent." He knew exactly what gentrification was, but he still thought it would be a good thing for downtown Kingston, even if it involved the displacement of poorer residents. When I asked him whether he thought urban renewal could ever affect him negatively, he shook his head adamantly and told me he was not at risk, as he was renting his shop from a "brethren" who lived in the United States, and "him no go sell me out."

Gesturing across the road from his shop toward the wholesale grocery stores run by Chinese immigrants, I asked Lion if he could imagine them being replaced by little boutiques. He surprised me by informing me that the buildings now housing the wholesales had previously been tenement yards occupied by families: "In the 1980s, all of the wholesale used to be yards. People used to live there, but the man who used to run the place run them out." The General, the neighborhood's former don, had forced the families to leave to make place for the Chinese wholesalers. Perhaps the post-Dudus form of speculative policing had incorporated the dons' informal policing tactics (see Meikle and Jaffe 2015), effecting a strong-arm displacement of low-income residents while advancing commercial interests, and evidencing an analogous assessment of the respective value of real estate and of certain groups of citizens.

When I visited Brick Town a few years later, Lion had moved his business to a shabbier building in a quieter part of the neighborhood. His US-based brethren had asked him to move out of the other place so that a family member could set up a business there. While a financial disagreement with Lion had played a part in this decision, it appeared possible that the new commercial opportunities in the downtown area had also been a factor. Yet it remained unclear whether any of the changes would endure. Elsewhere in West and Central Kingston, the fancy coffee shop had closed, and the art space folded after the Australian artist moved back home. The Digicel building remained a busy hub, but its office workers rarely ventured outside, and security guards still cast suspicious glances at neighborhood residents. Still, a new cluster of commercial properties on the downtown waterfront—a coffee shop, a branch of a well-known ice-cream parlor, a swanky bar, and an outpost of a seafood restaurant popular with tourists (fig. 3)—seemed to signal further attempts to introduce uptown consumer spaces in former no-go

Figure 3 New commercial complex in downtown Kingston, 2019. Photo by author.

areas. The construction of Chinese-funded government offices suggested that state actors were also continuing to invest in downtown Kingston's new future.

If real-estate investment and other signals of economic regeneration developed in an uneven, tentative fashion, the provisional character of the post-Dudus security policies and practices seemed even clearer. Human rights activists and news media challenged the ethical and legal permissibility of publicly naming "persons of interest" and noted the discriminatory, class-based character of its implementation (Byers et al. 2011: 14; *Jamaica Gleaner* 2011). In response, the JCF (2011: 3–6) issued procedural guidelines for the "naming, publication and general handling" of persons of interest, but it is unclear whether this affected the extralegal practices associated with this form of listing.

Other formal and informal security policies appeared to be more of a "success," in that they were subject to less legal and public scrutiny and in fact were formalized, expanded, and/or institutionalized. This "prototyping" of policies appeared to be at work in relation to both the formation of databases and the spatial logic of the curfew. More broadly, it is conceivable that the policing strategies first trialed under the state of emergency paved the way for normalizing a previously unacceptable degree of militarization of urban policing.

The rudimentary database that the security forces began to construct in 2010 certainly seems to have worked as something of a prototype. In 2017 the Jamaican government passed the National Identification and Registration Act, which will establish the National Identification System, a database assembling biographic, demographic, and biometric information. This mandatory system of registration will record each person's name, address, sex, citizenship, marital status, facial image, fingerprints, signature, and eye color. This database, set to be rolled out in 2019, is promoted explicitly as an important tool in the fight against crime (NIDS Project 2019).

Meanwhile, murder rates went back up, and in 2017–18 the government passed the Zones of Special Operation Act and established a new state of emergency in sections of the island, which lasted until January 2019. These acts involved a new series of spatially circumscribed curfews in areas declared "zones of special operation" or ZOSOs, including Denham Town in the West Kingston area and neighborhoods in the tourism hub Montego Bay, where the security forces were granted legal powers to stop, search, and arrest persons without a warrant. By mandating a military-police joint command to administer these special operations, the ZOSOs furthered the militarization of policing, a tendency compounded by the appointment of a JDF major-general as commissioner of the JCF. In addition to extending policing powers to the military within the ZOSOs, the government pledged to quadruple the JDF's annual recruits and to invest US$66 million to enhance JDF capabilities, suggesting a more general shift toward military predominance in security.

Was the 2010 state of emergency a failure, in that it was followed so quickly by another one? Or might we read it as a successful prototype, in that it paved the way for another to follow so quickly, without major political or popular pushback? I suggest that the policing interventions developed from 2010 onward can be understood as beta versions of a form of "agile" future governance, testing and prefiguring the concept of accumulation by militarized dispossession.

Conclusion

Speculative policing emerges at the intersection of multiple engagements with risk, combining a preventive approach to future crime with an interest in enhancing risky investments and an experimental logic of governance in the making.

In Kingston, citizens are framed as potential criminals based on their area of residence, but major interventions tend to materialize primarily when these areas have significant commercial potential. Such framings approach some urban spaces and populations as threatening yet amenable to techniques for managing them with greater certainty, so that businesspeople feel safe to make investments. Speculative policing involves a combination of future-oriented urban interventions, in which different governance actors align to recalibrate the existing sociopolitical order. This form of urban policing need not involve a mastermind or even a master plan; rather, it stems from a shifting alliance of the security forces with political and business elites. Senior police officers seek to follow international trends in compiling anticipatory databases, while politicians and investors see opportunities to shift power relations and enhance profits. While relations between and among these different interest groups are often marked by conflict and competition, when crisis erupts, a shared project may emerge around urban change. By making unruly areas and their residents more legible, they act to render uncertainty more knowable and risk more calculable.

However, as recent developments in Kingston show, these combined urban interventions are themselves a gamble. This form of urbanism rarely follows a linear process, and its modes of engaging risk are provisional and tentative. Where politicians, business leaders, and senior police officers saw the state of emergency as a chance to make don-controlled urban spaces safe for investment, the "success" of this new form of policing is by no means guaranteed. In some cities, the political-economic-security coalitions that seize on such moments of rupture or disaster see their efforts pay off (Gotham and Greenberg 2014), but the possibility of failure is real. This may be a disappointment for some investors and policy makers, while leaving others indifferent. Such failure may in fact come as a relief to some residents of areas targeted for regeneration. The uncertainty of success and the uneven distribution of gains are part of the speculative nature of these interventions.

References

Amnesty International. 2016. *Waiting in Vain: Jamaica: Unlawful Police Killings and Relatives' Long Struggle for Justice.* London: Amnesty International.

Amoore, Louise. 2014. "Security and the Incalculable." *Security Dialogue* 45, no. 5: 423–39.

Amoore, Louise, and Rita Raley. 2017. "Securing with Algorithms: Knowledge, Decision, Sovereignty." *Security Dialogue* 48, no. 1: 1–8.

Atkinson, Rowland. 2003. "Domestication by Cappuccino or a Revenge on Urban Space? Control and Empowerment in the Management of Public Spaces." *Urban Studies* 40, no. 9: 1829–43.

Browne, Simone. 2015. *Dark Matters: On the Surveillance of Blackness.* Durham, NC: Duke University Press.

Byers, K., C. Gomes, C. Lee, T. Muhammad, and P. Mutzenberg. 2011. *Jamaica: Civil Society Report on the Implementation of the ICCPR (Replies to the List of Issues CCPR/C/JAM/Q/3).* tbinternet.ohchr.org/Treaties/CCPR/Shared%20 Documents/JAM/INT_CCPR_NGO_JAM_103_9243_E.pdf.

Campbell, Yonique. 2015. "Doing 'What Wisdom Dictates': Localized Forms of Citizenship, 'Livity', and the Use of Violence in the 'Commons.'" *Caribbean Journal of Criminology* 1, no. 2: 53–75.

Carnegie, Charles. 2014. "The Loss of the Verandah: Kingston's Constricted Postcolonial Geographies." *Social and Economic Studies* 63, no. 2: 59–85.

Carnegie, Charles. 2017. "How Did There Come to Be a 'New Kingston'?" *Small Axe* 21, no. 3: 138–51.

Chambers, Phillip. 2010. "Stop the Lip Service and Restore Downtown Kingston." *Jamaica Observer*, October 31.

Corsín Jiménez, Alberto. 2014. "Introduction: The Prototype: More than Many and Less than One." *Journal of Cultural Economy* 7, no. 4: 381–98.

Davis, Diane E. 2013. "Zero-Tolerance Policing, Stealth Real Estate Development, and the Transformation of Public Space: Evidence from Mexico City." *Latin American Perspectives* 40, no. 2: 53–76.

De Goede, Marieke. 2012. *Speculative Security: The Politics of Pursuing Terrorist Monies.* Minneapolis: University of Minnesota Press.

De Goede, Marieke, and Gavin Sullivan. 2016. "The Politics of Security Lists." *Environment and Planning D* 34, no. 1: 67–88.

De Koning, Anouk. 2015. "'This Neighborhood Deserves an Espresso Bar Too': Neoliberalism, Racialization, and Urban Policy." *Antipode* 47, no. 5: 1203–23.

Digicel Jamaica. 2010. "Digicel Breaks Ground on Downtown Kingston Global Headquarters", November 30. www.digicelgroup.com/jm/en/mobile/explore /other-stuff/news---community/2012/11/30/digicel-breaks-ground-on-downtown -kingston-global-headquarters.html.

Dodman, David. 2007. "Post-independence Optimism and the Legacy of Waterfront Redevelopment in Kingston, Jamaica." *Cities* 24, no. 4: 273–84.

Dodsworth, Francis. 2016. "Risk, Prevention, and Policing, c. 1750–1850." In *Governing Risks in Modern Britain*, edited by Tom Crook and Mike Esbester, 29–53. London: Palgrave Macmillan.

Edmonds, Karin Wilson. 2012. "New Digicel Building Downtown Kingston—A Catalyst for Development?" YardEdge, March 10. www.yardedge.net/yard-life /new-digicel-building-downtown-kingston-a-catalyst-for-development.

Edwards, Dave. 2014. "The Republic of Tivoli." *Jamaica Observer*, January 8. www.jamaicaobserver.com/None/The-Republic-of-Tivoli_15748885.

Freeman, James. 2012. "Neoliberal Accumulation Strategies and the Visible Hand of Police Pacification in Rio de Janeiro." *Revista de estudos universitários* 38, no. 1: 95–126.

Ghertner, Asher. 2015. *Rule by Aesthetics: World-Class City Making in Delhi.* New York: Oxford University Press.

Gotham, Kevin Fox, and Miriam Greenberg. 2014. *Crisis Cities: Disaster and Redevelopment in New York and New Orleans.* New York: Oxford University Press.

Green, Jonathan. 2011. "Life and Death in the Police State of Jamaica: The Scandal of the Officers Who Double as State Executioners." *Daily Mail Online*, February 5. www.dailymail.co.uk/home/moslive/article-1352885/Jamaica-Life -death-police-state-officers-double-executioners.html.

Halpert, Oren, Jesse LeCavalier, Nerea Calvillo, and Wolfgang Pietsch. 2013. "Test-Bed Urbanism." *Public Culture* 25, no. 2: 272–306.

Harriott, Anthony. 2000. *Police and Crime Control in Jamaica: Problems of Reforming Ex-Colonial Constabularies.* Kingston: University of West Indies Press.

Harriott, Anthony. 2008. *Organized Crime and Politics in Jamaica: Breaking the Nexus.* Kingston: University of West Indies Press.

Jaffe, Rivke. 2013. "The Hybrid State: Crime and Citizenship in Urban Jamaica." *American Ethnologist* 40, no. 4: 734–48.

Jamaica Gleaner. 2011. "Double Standard Rule on Persons of Interest." *Jamaica Gleaner*, July 11. jamaica-gleaner.com/power/30034.

JCF (Jamaica Constabulary Force). 2011. *Jamaica Constabulary Force Orders, Part 1: Administration and Notifications*, August 25, Serial No. 3351. library.jcsc .edu.jm/xmlui/bitstream/handle/1/116/Force%252520Orders%2525203351A %252520dated%2525202011-08-25.pdf?sequence=1.

Junior Byrd. 2014. "Digicel Food Court." Foursquare, November 21. foursquare .com/v/digicel-food-court/51782738e4b0b71b11341b37.

Kimbell, Lucy, and Jocelyn Bailey. 2017. "Prototyping and the New Spirit of Policy-Making." *CoDesign* 13, no. 3: 214–26.

Knight, Frank. (1921) 2006. *Risk, Uncertainty, and Profit.* Mineola, NY: Dover.

Koster, Martijn. 2014. "Fear and Intimacy: Citizenship in a Recife Slum, Brazil." *Ethnos* 79, no. 2: 215–37.

Lewis, Rupert. 2012. "Party Politics in Jamaica and the Extradition of Christopher 'Dudus' Coke." *Global South* 6, no. 1: 38–54.

Ley, David. 2003. "Artists, Aestheticisation, and the Field of Gentrification." *Urban Studies* 40, no. 12: 2527–44.

Meikle, Tracian, and Rivke Jaffe. 2015. "'Police as the New Don'? An Assessment of Post-Dudus Policing Strategies in Jamaica." *Caribbean Journal of Criminology* 1, no. 2: 75–100.

NIDS (National Identification System) Project. 2019. *National Identification System*. Kingston: NIDS Project. The Office of the Prime Minister. opm.gov.jm /wp-content/uploads/2017/02/NIDS-brochure.pdf (accessed February 26, 2019).

Pilo', Francesca. 2017. "A Socio-technical Perspective to the Right to the City: Regularizing Electricity Access in Rio de Janeiro's Favelas." *International Journal of Urban and Regional Research* 41, no. 3: 396–413.

Sives, Amanda. 2010. *Elections, Violence, and the Democratic Process in Jamaica, 1944–2007*. Kingston: Ian Randle Publishers.

Smith, Neil. 1996. *The New Urban Frontier: Gentrification and the Revanchist city*. London: Routledge.

Stone, Carl. 1980. *Democracy and Clientelism in Jamaica*. New Brunswick, NJ: Transaction.

Wright, Melissa W. 2013. "Feminicidio, Narcoviolence, and Gentrification in Ciudad Juárez: The Feminist Fight." *Environment and Planning D: Society and Space* 31, no. 5: 830–45.

Yanique. 2013. "Digicel Food Court." Foursquare, April 24. foursquare.com/v /digicel-food-court/51782738e4b0b71b11341b37.

Zaloom, Caitlin. 2004. "The Productive Life of Risk." *Cultural Anthropology* 19, no. 3: 365–91.

Zedner, Lucia. 2007. "Pre-crime and Post-criminology?" *Theoretical Criminology* 11, no. 2: 261–81.

Zeiderman, Austin, Sobia Ahmad Kaker, Jonathan Silver, and Astrid Wood. 2015. "Uncertainty and Urban life." *Public Culture* 27, no. 2: 281–304.

....

Rivke Jaffe is professor of urban geography at the University of Amsterdam. Connecting geography, anthropology, and cultural studies, her research focuses primarily on intersections of the urban and the political. Her current work studies security dogs in Jamaica. Her publications include *Concrete Jungles: Urban Pollution and the Politics of Difference in the Caribbean* (2016) and *Introducing Urban Anthropology* (with Anouk de Koning, 2016).

Policing Intensity

Andrew M. Carruthers

Policing and Passing in East Malaysia

*Qualifications admit of a more and a less; for one thing is
called more pale or less pale than another, and more just than
another. Moreover, it itself sustains increase (for what is pale
can still become paler)—not in all cases though, but in most.*
—Aristotle, *Categories*

*Every voyage is intensive, and occurs in relation to thresholds
of intensity between which it evolves or that it crosses. One
travels by intensity.*
—Gilles Deleuze and Félix Guattari, *A Thousand Plateaus*

In Tawau—a town in the East Malaysian state of Sabah situated only a hop, skip, and a jump from the Indonesian border—two plainclothes policemen sit drinking coffee at a busy intersection. They're not on traffic duty, but their eyes are nevertheless cast upon the traffic of bodies across the street. Both watch the hustle and bustle of comings and goings unfolding at a nondescript harbor, where men, women, and children from nearby Indonesia disembark from schooners, luggage in tow, sidestepping official immigration channels in the process.

"They're the same, but different" (*Mereka sama, tapi berbeza*), the first man says in Malay, referring to the disembarking passengers. "We're the same, but different" (*Kita sama, tapi berbeza*), the second corrects him. "We're more-or-

Thank you to Madiha Tahir, Shamus Khan, and the participants at the October 2018 "Violence and Policing" conference at Columbia University for their generous and incisive feedback. Any lingering "lessnesses" in the essay's final form remain my sole responsibility.

Public Culture 31:3   DOI 10.1215/08992363-7532715
Copyright 2019 by Duke University Press

less the same" (*Kita lebih kurang sama*), the first one replies. "The same, but not the same" (*Sama tapi tidak sama*), the second one laughs, as if delivering the punchline to a shared joke. "We're virtually the same" (*Kita hampir sama*), the first man adds.

The two men watching the passengers unload their cargo are self-identified Malaysians of Bugis descent, and the disembarking passengers are undocumented Bugis migrants from Indonesia. Far from "street-level bureaucrats" (Lipsky [1969] 2010) or "petty sovereigns" (Butler 2004: 56) seeking to police an area in which so-called illegal immigrants do not belong, our two plainclothes policemen look upon these disembarking passengers with a curious sense of hospitality, despite state-level efforts to "cleanse" (*membersihkan*) Sabah of their kind. They are "fellow Malays" (*sesama Melayu*), one notes. They are "family."

The Bugis are renowned as a mobile, seafaring people who consider the contemporary Indonesian province of South Sulawesi to be their *tanah air*, or "homeland," but have migrated throughout archipelagic Southeast Asia and beyond over the course of several centuries.[1] More than a century ago, Bugis migrants from Sulawesi began traveling to Tawau, where, under the auspices of British colonial rule, they became "the most energetic and successful cultivators" of coconuts and came to "own nearly all of the large and valuable land . . . East and West of Tawau town" (*British North Borneo Herald* 1912, cited in Sintang 2007: 31). In 1963, British North Borneo was incorporated into the independent postcolonial state of Malaysia as "Sabah," and the Bugis—a bilingual Muslim people who speak Malay in addition to their Bugis ethnic language—came to be assimilated as "Malay" members of the newly formed Malaysian nation, a place where "Malay" people are constitutionally defined as Muslim speakers of Malay and practitioners of "Malay custom."[2] In the decades following Malaysian and Indonesian independence, Bugis migrants from Indonesia continued traveling to Tawau and greater Sabah, availing themselves of a "diasporic infrastructure" (Carruthers 2017b: 128) linking their homeland in the Indonesian island of Sulawesi to the East Malaysian state of Sabah. And for almost forty years following Sabah's incorporation into Malaysia, undocumented Bugis migrants from Indonesia were welcomed as migrant laborers, readily assimilating among their coethnic Bugis-Malaysian counterparts as Malay-speaking Muslim members of the "Malay race."

Recent state-level sociopolitical and economic developments, however, have

---

1. For foundational overviews of the Bugis, see Mattulada 1985 and Pelras 1996.
2. See "Malaysian Federal Constitution, As at 1 November 2010," article 160, clause 2.

cast these undocumented immigrants as an unwelcome, elusive, and parasitic force in need of expulsion. Sabah's indigenous stakeholders—non-Malay Christian groups like the Kadazandusun or Murut peoples—have dwindled demographically in the decades following Malaysian independence. This erstwhile majority of indigenous Christian people has been displaced by a growing Malay population, and they're crying foul. The East Malaysian state's indigenous people allege that undocumented Bugis immigrants have been mobilized by Malaysia's founding race-based Malay party, the United Malays National Organization (UMNO), to reengineer Sabah's ethnic and political demography and are the beneficiaries of Malaysian national identity cards that enable them to illegally vote for UMNO at the political polls. Sabah's indigenous peoples allege that undocumented Indonesians, by virtue of their ascribed status in Malaysia as Malay-speaking Muslim members of the greater "Malay race," have been mobilized as "phantom voters" (*penghundi hantu*) by UMNO, turning out to the polls in droves in support of a party that "genuine Sabahans" (*Sabahan tulen*) would otherwise never vote for.

These concerns culminated in a 2012 Royal Commission of Enquiry on Illegal Immigrants (Shim et al. 2014: 3) in Sabah:

> Sabah is often referred to as the "Land below the Wind," a kind of paradise on earth. It is endowed with great beauty, both in terms of land and people. It is rich in natural resources. Tourists flock to see its natural wonders and heritage. They are in awe of its multi-racial, multi-cultural, and multi-religious settings. . . . Sabahans should have good reason to feel contented. And yet . . . there is, at least from one perspective, a sense of gloom. For decades, Sabahans have been plagued and haunted by an insidious problem which has turned out to be an all-consuming nightmare. It is endemic. It has grown into a crisis of humongous proportions. . . . It is, of course, the lingering problem of illegal immigrants in Sabah.

Despite the Commission's efforts to assuage indigenous Sabahans' concerns, many feel like they face an insurmountable challenge: how might they police undocumented immigrants who look and talk like local Malays and who carry identity cards marking them as Malaysian citizens? "It's hard to know the *border* [*sempadan*] between them," one told me.

With an eye to these ongoing developments in East Malaysia, this article asks the following: How might a focus on intensities—provisionally understood as those perceptible yet seemingly prequantitative variations in the more-or-lessness of things—help us better understand the borders (qua thresholds) between nation-states, people, languages, and much else besides?[3] How might intensity as an orienting object for ethnographic inquiry revise or reshape our understandings of policing across thresholds of belonging? I explore these questions with tacit reference to Jacques Rancière's (2004: 12) conception of policing as that which regiments "system[s] of self-evident facts of sense perception," and I address these issues in two expository steps that trope on the idea of the threshold.

First, and in a longer sketch stretching across interactional and infrastructural time scales, I examine how intensive processes (Deleuze [1968] 1994; Delanda 2002, 2005)—those "anexact yet rigorous" flows, crossings, and coalescences (Deleuze and Guattari: 367; see Delanda 2002)—have come to shape the extensive, "virtual idea" of a contested border or threshold in continuous flux between nation-states: Malaysia and Indonesia. Here I attend to the curious case of Sebatik, an island situated off the eastern coast of Borneo cleanly bisected by the Indonesia-Malaysia international border.

Second, and in an abbreviated ethnography of sensible intensities, I shift focus to certain constellations of signs that distinguish Malaysian citizens from noncitizens, examining how Malay(sians) and Indonesian(s) are contrastively evaluated in Sabah's shifting sociopolitical scene. I do so by channeling linguistic anthropological approaches to intensity gradients. Qualities (e.g., hotness, coldness, hardness, softness) vary in their intensity or "more-or-lessness" across spatiotemporal contexts and are in turn subject to grading—a process prior to measurement or counting whereby we discern, evaluate, and regulate such intensities (Sapir 1944; Carruthers 2017b; Kockelman 2016). Grading processes effectively demarcate intensive deviations from semiotically salient and experientially grounded thresholds, which serve as "point[s] of departure," in Edward Sapir's (1944: 94) parlance, for determining what "counts" (so to speak) as "more" or "less." Put differently, these presupposed thresholds or points of departure reflect and shape the ways we—like Goldilocks or Alice in Wonderland—differentially weigh and react to the "mores" or "lesses" of sensuous experience, from the relative hotness or coldness of porridge, to the largeness or smallness of chairs, to the hardness or softness of beds. In Sabah, a place where citizens and noncitizens are widely cast as "more-or-less the same" with respect to the bodily and behavioral signs they are assumed to evince, everyday grading practices are, I argue, central not only

3. The "thing" in "the more-or-lessness of things" is a hypernym or superordinate, enveloping or extending to any entity or event whose contents admit of a "more" or a "less" in some context. For genealogical approaches to the issue of intensity or intensive magnitudes see Mader (2014) and Solère (2001). For a foundational critique of the notion of intensive magnitudes see Bergson ([1889] 1910).

for policing but also for "passing" (see Garfinkel [1967] 2006; Goffman [1963] 1986).

I conclude with a discussion of what I mean by "policing intensity," while bringing the foregoing issues to bear on Rancière's problematic yet curiously enduring distinction between "politics" and "the police."

Policing Virtual Thresholds I: Space

*A "surface" is not simply a geometric composition of lines. It is
a certain distribution of the sensible.*
—Jacques Rancière, *The Politics of Aesthetics*

In the Indonesian village of Aji Kuning, Hasidah—a middle-aged Bugis seamstress—rises from a chair in her living room and glides toward the kitchen to prepare coffee for her guests visiting from Malaysia. "Lots of folks have already visited here," one guest asserts in Malay. Hasidah replies, explaining in her Bugis-inflected Malay that "lots of reporters, lots of all kinds of people [have come here]," owing in no small part to her home's putatively "unique" location. As she approaches the threshold dividing her living room from her kitchen, one of her visitors alerts her to the danger of border crossing "without documents" (*tanpa surat*). This tongue-in-cheek warning elicits a chuckle and a knowing smile from Hasidah as she moves toward her kitchen. Only briefly pausing before the strip of wood dividing her living room and kitchen, she makes a dramatic show of stretching out her foot and confidently planting it on the kitchen floor. Having crossed the threshold, Hasidah looks back at her guests assembled in the living room, declaring that she has safely reached Malaysian soil. She later explains that although she "uses a passport" (*pakai paspor*) to visit Tawau proper, she can safely "cross" (*limpas*) between Indonesia and Malaysia in the comfort of her own home.

Hasidah's house has become something of an international spectacle, straddling as it does the Indonesia-Malaysia border on Sebatik Island. As is so often pointed out by the Indonesian and Malaysian journalists or curious dignitaries who flock to her home, Hasidah's "kitchen is in Malaysia," while her "living room is in Indonesia" (*Dapur di Malaysia dan ruang tamu di Indonesia*) (*Utusan Melayu* 2014). Standing over the threshold dividing her kitchen and living room, Hasidah drives this point home, remarking that she has "one foot in Indonesia" and the "other in Malaysia" (see fig. 1). One of the guests begins what for Hasidah is a by-now predictable line of inquiry, asking, "What does it feel like cooking in Malaysia and . . . ," only to be cut off by their Bugis host, who, anticipating where

Figure 1 Threshold crossing(s).

the question was going, laughingly explains that she feels "just the same" (*sama sahaja*) whether she's cooking in her "Malaysian" kitchen or sitting down in her "Indonesian" living room.

Sebatik Island is a study in thresholds. Located only one kilometer from the eastern coast of Indonesian Borneo, Sebatik is cleanly bisected by the international Indonesia-Malaysia border. The island's northern half lies within the East Malaysian state of Sabah, with its southern half falling within the Indonesian province of North Kalimantan. Aside from a sequence of inconspicuous stone border markers that dot the island's diameter, and notwithstanding the presence of a small Indonesian army border station adjacent to Hasidah's house, the thirty-nine-kilometer border is unfenced, unmarked, and relatively unpatrolled. And yet, this unenforced, putative threshold between nations has a kind of "world-configuring function" (Balibar 2002: 79) for Sebatik's residents, especially those like Hasidah, who imagine themselves to be dwelling on both sides of an invisible fence.[4]

4. For definitive accounts of life on Sebatik, see the important work of Ramlah Daud (2010).

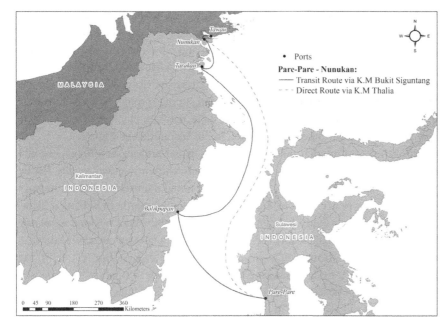

Figure 2 Channels of movement. Map provided by ISEAS-Yusof Ishak Institute.

On the one hand, the everyday salience of this invisible, virtual threshold stems from Sebatik's positioning as a kind of "zone of intensity" (Delanda 2005: 80), one in which ongoing flows and crossings between the places we today call "Indonesia" and "Malaysia" came to shape the extensive boundaries of an island-based community over the course of a century. Since the late nineteenth century, Sebatik has served as one of many penultimate way stations on Bugis migration trails leading from Sulawesi to Sabah. Indeed, and beginning in the late nineteenth century, intensive flows between these places gave rise to an extensive, self-regulating Bugis diasporic infrastructure linking Tawau to the Bugis homeland of Sulawesi. Today, Bugis migrants in search of new lives in Malaysia continue along these well-trodden paths or channels (Carruthers 2017b, 2017c) (see fig. 2).

On the other hand, this ostensibly arbitrary border that shapes and constrains contemporary movement across national thresholds is a curious artifact of colonial-era cartographic imaginaries. The 1824 Treaty of London between the British and Dutch empires divided the geographical expanse of an imagined "Malay world" between the two colonial powers. The treaty carved a line across the Johor-Pahang-Riau-Lingga Malay Sultanate, and, while distant territories like Borneo went unmentioned in the treaty, it nevertheless "signaled to other European powers the possibility of future British and Dutch accommodation in this area as well" (Andaya and Andaya 2016: 124). The virtual idea of a transcendental, transregional border meandering eastward across Borneo—carving out the borders of Sarawak, Brunei, and Sabah—and slicing through Sebatik at exactly 4°10' N was established in 1912 as a threshold between empires (Trocki 2000). This border was later inherited by postcolonial Indonesia and Malaysia.

After the constitutional incorporation of Sabah, Sarawak, and Singapore into Malaysia in 1963, the salience of this arbitrarily chosen line was keenly felt by Bugis communities on Sebatik, who suddenly found themselves divided in ways they hadn't experienced before. Immediately following northern Sebatik's incorporation into Sabah (and by extension, Malaysia), the island became a volatile crucible of violent engagements and interactions during the Indonesian-Malaysian *konfrontasi* or "confrontation"—an undeclared war in East Borneo stemming from Indonesian President Sukarno's opposition to the formation of Malaysia. "Konfrontasi was because Sabah wanted to be part of Malaysia," recounts one sixty-five-year-old inhabitant of the Malaysian side of Sebatik. "Konfrontasi was scary. We were afraid to go to the jungle to tap our rubber trees or to the sea to catch fish because Indonesian soldiers would disguise [themselves] as farmers or fishermen and they would catch us" (*Star Online* 2012). He recalled how Malaysian troops (accompanied by British forces) appeared in his village not far from the newly demarcated border. "The troop[s] set up a camp about two hundred meters from the village's perimeter. They told us to dig a 2.4 by 1.2 meter hole under our stilt houses. They told us to jump into the hole if there was shooting," he remembers. One skirmish came too close for comfort, with Indonesian and Malaysian troops shooting across Sebatik's invisible border that had by that time reached a kind of "critical point" (Delanda 2005: 80) of intensive tension. "We were scared as bullets were flying. You could not see the enemy. They were at the other side of the border," he noted, explaining that villagers had to withdraw from their homes and move to jungle areas more far afield until the neck and neck conflict's formal resolution in August 1966 (*Star Online* 2012).

The *konfrontasi* dispute testifies to the tempestuous, topological nature of borders and boundaries that meaningfully materialize across zones of intensity. So, too, and nearly half a century later in 2005, bilateral disputes between Indonesia and Malaysia regarding their respective borders once again focused both countries' joint attention on Sebatik's islandwide invisible fence. Both countries were contesting an international maritime border in the Ambalat sea block directly east of Sebatik in the Celebes Sea. Perhaps tacitly reopening older, *konfrontasi*-era wounds, the Indonesian army began actively policing the Indonesian side of the border, establishing a barracks adjacent to Hasidah's house and the invisible fence that cuts across it.

The fence (qua threshold) dividing Hasidah's living room and kitchen is invisible—but clearly not qualitatively insensible—and virtual—but definitely not un-"real" (see Balibar 2002; Delanda 2002; Deleuze [1968] 1994; Kockelman 2017; Massumi 2002). On the one hand, the virtual idea of the border (or Hasidah's invisible fence) is real insofar as it acts as a "structure of a space of possibilities" (Delanda 2005: 83) for certain trajectories, mobilities, and becomings. So, too, it is "fully real" (Deleuze [1968] 1994: 208) insofar as it materializes or "actualizes into extended spatiality" (Clisby 2015: 139) in the form of the wooden threshold that divides her kitchen from her living room, or the *batu* or "rock" border markers that dot the diameter of the island. As Kockelman (2017: 131) puts it, "the best way to 'intuit' the virtual is to inhabit it," and our everyday, tacit intuitions are closely linked to habitus and "sense" (2017: 177).

Hasidah and other inhabitants of Aji Kuning Village have common-*sense* intuitions as to where the virtual border lies: it is congruent and coextensive with a variety of materially sensible thresholds, from strips of wood dividing kitchens from living rooms, to sequences of stone markers. That they jointly orient toward the same markers suggests how Hasidah and her neighbors share the same "map" as they navigate this virtual border. Here a "map" might be thought of as a set of assumptions about the places that populate a given terrain, and a "terrain" might be considered not only a physical space but also a meaningful ensemble of enactable mediations between selves and others (e.g., Indonesian versus Malaysian) and "here's" and "there's" (e.g., Indonesia and Malaysia) across imagined thresholds (e.g., the Indonesia-Malaysia border) (see Kockelman 2012: 183).

Sebatik's fence is not a strict, impenetrable border but a prototypical "threshold" in one of the word's classic senses: it is a point of departure. Consider Hasidah's home: as she gestured toward the wooden threshold dividing two rooms of her house, she characterized it as a kind of *pintu masuk* or "entry door" or "point of entry" linking not only her kitchen to the living room but also Indonesia to Malaysia. In this sense, (in)visible or indexically sensible thresholds are affordances (Gibson 1977). Just as George Herbert Mead's chair "invites us to sit down" (1962: 280; see Keane 2016), thresholds invite certain actors to transgress or cross them. Thresholds do not simply "block or obstruct" intensive flows (Mezzadra and Neilson 2012: 64) but instead serve as "essential devices for their articulation" (64).

For those Indonesian Bugis migrants seeking new lives in Malaysia, Sebatik's imaginary fence is considered one such threshold qua clandestine point of departure. Some Bugis migrants travel by way of "official channels," taking ferries from Nunukan Port in Indonesia to the immigration department in Tawau, Malaysia, at a cost of IDR200,000 ($14.05 at the time of this writing), accompanied by an additional IDR15,000 ($1.05). However, many Bugis migrants avoid officially sanctioned channels of movement to Malaysia, considering them to be costly with respect to time and money, and potentially disastrous given mandatory document checks and frequent boardings by Malaysia's maritime police. Instead, they cross a different, so-called clandestine threshold widely known to migrants and Malaysian police alike. These migrants take a speedboat from Nunukan to Sebatik Island's Aji Kuning Village. Once there, and only a few meters from Hasidah's house, they walk confidently past a more-or-less indifferent Indonesian border barracks, crossing the island's invisible fence, and descend into a winding, narrow river populated by Bugis speedboats, and characterized by migrants as a "mouse path" (*jalan tikus*). Speedboat captains navigating the snakelike river will "smuggle" (*somokol*) and deposit these migrants at "safe zones" along Tawau's coastline (see fig. 3).

For undocumented Bugis migrants, Sebatik's porous borders enable emancipatory lines of flight. This is not to imply that smooth sailing awaits those undocumented migrants who cross this threshold. Migrants are aware of Malaysia's "necropolitics" (Mbembe 2003) of detection, detention, deportation, and sometimes death—a necropolitics that has itself become the focus of popular songs written by well-known Bugis singers and frequently sung by itinerant migrants en route to Malaysia.[5] What concerns undocumented Bugis migrants today is the felt intensity of these policing practices, practices that many Bugis migrants characterize as having increased in their scope and scale of brutality. One former Bugis migrant I met in one of Nunukan's karaoke bars told me that cross-border surveillance has intensified to such a degree that many Bugis migrants no longer consider traveling to Sabah. "It's not like it was before," he told me, explaining Sabah's agenda to "cleanse" (*membersihkan*) itself of "illegal immigrants" has become "too cruel" (*terlampau kejam*).

On the other hand, and for Sabah's state officials, the intensity of these policing practices is causally and necessarily linked with the imagined intensity of cross-border clandestine flows. Sabah state officials have sought to police this intensity by homing in on particular thresholds.

---

5. See the songs of Ansar S., "TKI Ilegal" ("Illegal Indonesian Migrant Worker") in particular.

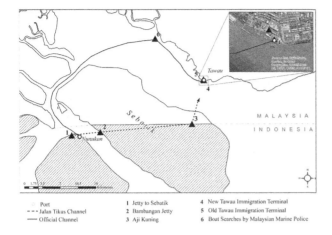

Figure 3 Official and clandestine threshold crossing(s). Map provided by ISEAS-Yusof Ishak Institute.

In 2016, as a temporary salvo, Sabah imposed a two-week interregnum on cross-border barter and movement between Nunukan (especially Sebatik) and Tawau, which had entailing effects on the socioeconomic well-being of inhabitants living on both Indonesian and Malaysian sides of Sebatik Island. The attempt was widely considered a failure. As one Malaysian of Bugis extraction told me, these effects indicate how cross-border clandestine barter and movement are inextricably linked to the well-being of the island's whole, and suggest how the inhabitants of both sides of Sebatik "mutually shape" (*saling membentukkan*) and depend on one another.

Sabah state forces have intensified crackdowns on *jalan tikus* or "mouse paths" and those thresholds that Hasidah characterized as *pintu masuk* or points of entry. This has been no easy feat for Malaysian forces fatigued by the prospect of policing Sabah's notoriously porous borders, where clandestine "mouse paths" and points of entry weave and wander along narrow waterways and circuitous jungle paths. The chief representative of the Indonesian Consulate in Tawau once described the sheer impossibility of policing these clandestine channels, estimating cross-border clandestine paths to be around one thousand in number, and saying, "There aren't just a thousand roads to Rome, but there are also a thousand roads to Tawau" (*Pro Kaltara* 2015).

Malaysian security forces have attempted to redress this seemingly insurmountable problem by targeting widely known clandestine paths and points of entry. These activities (and the responses to them) reaffirm the ontological status of borders as "necropolitical sites par excellence" (Mezzandra and Neilson 2012: 64). These activities have shaped the trajectories of those migrants who—having found their go-to channels and threshold crossings figuratively plugged by Sabah security forces—must reorient themselves toward tempestuous terrains with which they are unfamiliar, with potentially devastating results. In January 2017, for instance, a boat ferrying forty undocumented Bugis Indonesian migrants departed for Sebatik Island. Rather than traversing closely monitored Tawau-Nunukan channels, the ferry departed from an undisclosed location in Tawau under the cover of darkness. Due to overcrowding, stormy conditions, and an alleged lack of familiarity with points of entry outside the gaze of the Sabah surveillance state, the ferry capsized, and all but one passenger drowned. Uncensored images of dead women and children floating in the sea off Sebatik Island circulated on messenger applications and social media, provoking an uproar among Indonesians who interpreted the event as diagnostic of the lengths that undocumented migrants will go to avoid intensifying state surveillance.[6]

Amidst ongoing crackdowns on cross-border clandestine channels of movement and illicit points of departure and entry, the ideological and geopolitical salience of one particular threshold—the one that served as the topical point of entry for this expository section—has intensified. Sebatik's invisible fence has become an object of joint attention among Malaysians and Indonesians alike. An article published in a major East Malaysian newspaper highlighted the invisible fence's renewed ideological salience for Sabah state forces and noted various remedies currently under consideration by the Malaysian state:

> Over the years, Sebatik has gained notoriety as the entry and distribution point for goods smuggled from Malaysia. . . . Untold billions of Ringgit are believed to have flowed out of Malaysia through this illegal channel. . . . A recent two-pronged government strategy in the form of removal of some subsidies and tighter enforcement by Marine Police and Customs have helped minimize the problem somewhat. [But] then there is the problem of immigrant arrivals as well as human and drug trafficking. Just like United States President-elect Donald Trump who envisions building a wall among

6. For a review of these recent events, see Carruthers 2017a.

the Mexican border to keep illegals and would-be criminals out, [Malaysian] Sebatik Assemblyman Datuk Abdul Muis Picho thinks only something similar would tackle the problems once and for all. (*Daily Express* 2016)

Assemblyman Muis has allegedly long dreamed of building such a wall, one that would dramatically actualize "into extended spatiality" (Clisby 2015: 139) the virtual idea of the geopolitical border that bisects Sebatik cleanly in two. Here his efforts to construct a wall to police an extensively demarcated border must be read as an effort to define "an organizational system of coordinates that establishes a distribution of the sensible or a law that divides the community into groups, social positions, and functions," one that "separates those who take part from those who are excluded, and . . . therefore presupposes a prior aesthetic division between the visible and the invisible" (Rancière 2004: 3).

The assemblyman, however, has hit a wall of his own. Malaysian and Indonesian inhabitants of Sebatik use competing and conflicting "system[s] of self-evident facts of sense perception" (12), "common imagined perceptual ground[s]" (Bebout 2016: 204), ontologies, or maps for determining the "actual," extensive spatiality of a "virtual" border. For Indonesians like Hasidah and the barracks officers stationed adjacent to her home, the border's location is commonsense—it materializes in the form of wooden thresholds, planted flags, or rock markers. These landmarks constitute a coordinating infrastructure or common perceptual ground for reckoning thresholds between nations.

In contrast, Muis's perceptual grounds, ontologies, and maps conflict with those of his Indonesian counterparts to such a degree that he and his Malaysian colleagues allege that houses like Hasidah's are fully within Malaysian soil. The assemblyman alleges that the stone markers that serve as key landmarks for Sebatik's Indonesian residents "were being removed and thrown away by folks on the Indonesian side so that they can open up farms, plantations, and settlements" (*Daily Express* 2016), and that "records from the Surveying and Mapping Department confirm these areas that are being encroached [upon] are [Malaysian]" (*Daily Express* 2016). Colleagues of Assemblyman Muis suggested using GPS technologies to determine whether his claims are "out of bounds," so to speak (see fig. 4). For the assemblyman, wall building is a method to forestall a loss of sovereignty, in which the idea of "loss" itself presupposes certain assumptions about intensity gradients: "We need integrated enforcement badly in these villages and I suggest the area be occupied, especially by military and assisted by police. . . . [We] must coordinate to look after our border and minimize the illegal activities."

The curious case of Sebatik Island—a zone of intensity and site of policing

Figure 4 Policing virtual thresholds. Map provided by ISEAS-Yusof Ishak Institute.

at the Indonesia-Malaysia border—throws into stark relief the various ways in which perceptual grounds, ontologies, or maps configure the ways thresholds are detected and policed. It also shows how indexical signs that point such and such about certain states of affairs are "simultaneously important and elusive" (Kockelman 2017: 136), their detection or discernment contingent on the maps and media (e.g., stone markers or GPS) available to particular semiotic agents.

In the following section, I continue examining how agents' indexical sensitivities to particular intensities inflect the policing of bodies in motion.

Policing Virtual Thresholds II: Signs of "Moreness"

"We're the same, but not the same, that's our philosophy," my older acquaintance tells me as we drive through Tawau Town, passing by *batu* or "stone," the name for the once conspicuous jetty for undocumented migrants from adjacent Indonesia, now ostensibly closed and closely monitored by *imigresen*. My friend, whom I refer to as Abang (a fictive or tropic use of the Malay kin term for "older brother"), works in intelligence, though he never goes into detail as to what that entails. His by now familiar philosophy of "same, but not the same" refers once again to that contrastive commonality obtaining between coethnic Bugis citizens and noncitizens in contemporary Sabah. He offers a preliminary example: the "tightness" or relative "sexiness" of jeans. Undocumented Indonesian migrant women, he explains, are distinguishable on the basis of their form-fitting clothing, vis-à-vis more modest, flowing gowns favored by Tawau's Bugis women. Thinking me suitably convinced, he offers a second example: the "thickness" of migrant talk. Though some undocumented Indonesians may, with varying degrees of success, sartorially assimilate into the fabric of everyday life in Sabah, their talk in Malay is thicker (*lebih pekat*) relative to that of local Malays (*Melayu tempatan*).

Abang's observations reflect certain ontological assumptions—widely shared in Tawau and greater Sabah—about index-kind or index-identity relations: undocumented Indonesian women have a projected propensity to wear tighter (*lebih ketat*) jeans or sexier (*lebih sexy*) clothing, and undocumented Indonesians in general have thicker speech. This projected propensity toward cross-modal "moreness"— note the presence of the Malay degree adverb *lebih* corresponding to the English degree morpheme *-er* in *sexier, tighter,* or *thicker*—has been the object of mediatized representation in national news portals. Consider, for example, a profile of Muliyati, a Bugis woman living on Sebatik, in Malaysia's *Star Online* (2012) news portal.

Muliyati was born in Aji Kuning on the Indonesian side of Sebatik but raised on the Malaysian side of the island. "I was living in Indonesia because in the 1970s we did not know whether this house was in Malaysia or Indonesia," she says. "We are all the same. We are Bugis, we speak Bugis language. We are all the same because in this village, the Malaysians have mixed with the Indonesians and the Indonesians have mixed with the Malaysians." Her half-sister, born in Boné Regency in the Bugis homeland of Indonesia's South Sulawesi Province, was also raised in Aji Kuning, but she currently lives on the Indonesian side of the island. "Take my sister Asirah. She's an Indonesian. But I don't see any difference between her and me. Maybe the way we dress and speak," she says. Muliyati's reported speech is interlineated with commentary by the *Star*: "Indonesian women, Muliyati observes, tend to wear sexier clothes while Malaysian women are more conservative. For instance, an Indonesian might wear leggings and a blouse, whereas a Malaysian wearing leggings would conceal it in a *baju kurung* [enclosed dress]." Muliyati continues, highlighting that second point of contrast regarding habits of talk. "We also speak differently," she notes. "When Indonesians speak Bahasa Malaysia, it is thick [*pekat*] with Bahasa Makassar. They also pronounce the words differently." Here she effectively refers to Makassar Malay, a regional Malay variety spoken throughout the Bugis homeland of South

Sulawesi resulting from the assimilation of the phonology and morphosyntax of two of the region's "local languages" (*Bahasa daerah*) with Malay or Indonesian lexical material (Carruthers 2017b, 2017c). And she marks a certain thickness that distinguishes the Malay spoken by Bugis Indonesians from that spoken by Bugis Malaysians.

Sexiness, tightness, and thickness are abstract qualities stipulated by a predicate that relate to a subject or materialize in a substance: clothes, jeans, and talk.[7] Much linguistic anthropological ink has been spilled regarding the issue of qualia, or sensuous instances of abstract qualities that "materialize" cross-modally.[8] Comparatively little work, however, has examined how human beings (as semiotic agents) grade or weigh the relative intensities (or prequantitative "mores" or "lesses") of qualities, and the causal effects that such weighings entail.[9] Framed with an eye to Sapir (while telescoping back to Aristotle) by way of Muliyati and Abang, abstract qualities like sexiness, tightness, or thickness "admit of a more and a less" (Aristotle 1963). Statements as to the relative sexiness of one's clothes, tightness of one's jeans, or thickness of one's talk make propositionally explicit the assumptions that undergird one's semiotic ontology (Kockelman 2012: 65).[10] They reveal something about the contextually salient and experientially grounded thresholds that, returning to Sapir (1944), double as one's points of departure for determining the relative moreness or lessness of entities and events.

The idea of moreness matters, not only because it helps mediate our understanding of intensity and grading, but primarily because it is regularly invoked and predicated about by Bugis migrants, relating not only to their aspirational orientations but also to processes of policing and passing. A certain item in Malay—*kelebihan*—recurs as an articulated object of desire in the narratives of Bugis migrants in Malaysia or return migrants in Indonesia. Frequently glossed

7. Framed in another way, the predicates that refer to or stand for the embodied qualities in things—*tight, sexy, thick*—can become subjects of thought in and of themselves (tightness, sexiness, thickness). C. S. Peirce (1906) called this process hypostatic abstraction, a process that "turn[s] predicates [e.g., *tight, sexy, thick*] from being signs that we think or think through, into being subjects thought of [e.g., tightness, sexiness, thickness]" (Peirce 1906: 522). Recall Peirce's (1867: 288) example of a black stove: "If we say 'The stove is black,' the stove is the *substance*, from which its blackness has not been differentiated, and the *is*, while it leaves the substance just as it was seen, explains its confusedness, by the application to it of *blackness* as a predicate."

8. For an important overview and synthesis of the qualia literature, see Harkness 2015.

9. For exceptions, see Carruthers 2017a, 2017b, and Kockelman 2016, inter alia.

10. In this sense, they are examples of Peircean representational interpretants (in contrast to affective and energetic interpretants) (Peirce 1955: 276–77, 1998 [1907]: 398–433; see Kockelman 2012: 64–67).

in the literature as "surplus," "excess," or "advantage," *kelebihan* is defined in one Malay dictionary as "the quality of being more than usual" (Dewan Bahasa dan Pustaka 2005: 906). Attending to the word's morphology, however, provides us with a more precise understanding of its meaning: it is a nominalized form of the degree adverbial *lebih* or "more." In this formal sense, *kelebihan* (ke-lebih-an or NOM-more-NOM) is best understood as moreness: a kind of meta-quality that migrants stipulate about some (unstated) but semiotically salient quality whose intensity exceeds normative thresholds.[11] Bugis migrants often characterize their movement to and from Malaysia as a "search for moreness," either in their regional variety of Malay (*mencari kelebihan*), or in Bugis (*kelebihangngé isappa*). Moreness is also used by migrants, however, to indicate certain recognizable intensities that they evince in their everyday speech.

In what remains, I examine two named excesses of migrant speech that are jointly recognizable by migrants and Malaysians alike: *kelebihan G* or a moreness or excess in the letter *G*, and *kelebihan lagu* or a moreness or excess in intonation. Both of these excesses emerge, as Muliyati alluded to earlier, from the assimilation or "mixing" of Bugis phonology with Malay lexicon. The first—an excess in the letter *G*—stems from a phonotactic constraint in the Bugis language that stipulates the glottal stop and velar nasal (ng) as the only consonants appearing in word-final position. This stipulation or constraint is "carried over" by Bugis migrants from Bugis to Malay, shaping the ways they pronounce common Malay words like *fish* (migrants pronounce *ikan* as *ikang*) or *eat* (*makan* is pronounced *makang*), the names of cities in Sabah (Sandakan becomes Sandakang), or even *kelebihan* itself (*kelebihan* becomes *kelebihang*). For speakers, this excess in the letter *G*—sometimes jokingly referred to as an "excess in vitamin *G*" or *kelebihang vitaming G*, in which *kelebihan* and *vitamin* evince the excess *G* in question—reflects an orthographic orientation, in which the excess is visualized through writing, not phonetics. The second named excess—*kelebihan lagu* or intonational excess—stems, like *G*, from mixing, in which prototypically Bugis intonation contours featuring high and low pitch targets are carried over by migrants from Bugis to Malay. Like *G*, a Bugis Indonesian propensity to *malagu-lagu* or evince a moreness or excess in melodic or singsong pitch movement is one that distinguishes Bugis migrants from Bugis Malaysians.

---

11. See Carruthers (forthcoming) for a closer examination of *kelebihan* qua moreness.

Sketch 1

An indigenous Sabahan sits at a table at a nonhalal restaurant in Tawau. "They're taking our jobs," he notes between sips of his beer. "And they're everywhere," referring to Bugis Indonesians who irregularly enter Sabah. "Everywhere?" I ask. "Yes," he says, noting that they look "just the same" (*sama sahaja*) as Bugis Malaysian locals. But, by attending to their habits of talk, he explains, they are distinguishable:

Text 1

F: Pertama, dia punya loghat. Sebutan	1	**F**: First, they've got an accent. Their pronunciation
kadang-kadang sama, sama! Cuman	2	is sometimes the same, the same! It's just
ada punya sleng, ada punya timing,	3	that they've got some slang, they've got timing,
macam dia punya, apa itu,	4	like they have, what is it,
lagu-lagu itu.	5	a melody.
AC: Lagu-lagu==	6	**AC:** A melody==
F: ==Lagu. Lagunya,	7	**F:** ==Melody. Their melody,
punya soun-soun itu tidak sama.	8	their sounds aren't the same.
Kalo orang di sini, kan, macam	9	If people here, right, like
orang lokal, lokal di sini ada juga	10	local people, locals here we've also got
Bajau, ada lah Tidung, kan? Murut.	11	Bajau, there's Tidung, right? There's Murut.
Dusun, Murut, dan Tidung itu saya	12	The speech of Dusun, Murut, and Tidung I
tidak bezakan, sama dengan	13	can't differentiate, it's just the same with
loghat saya. Nah, tapi kalo tempatan	14	my accent. Now, if we're talking about locals
yang di sini, Bugis, saya tahu.	15	here who are Bugis, I can tell.
AC: Kenapa dengan Bugis itu?	16	**AC:** What is it about those Bugis?
F: Sebab dia ada ikut-ikut dengan dia	17	**F:** Because they follow their
punya Ibunda punya . . . ini, sleng,	18	native . . . uh, slang,
lagu-lagunya lah. Lebih kurang	19	it's their melody. It's more or less
begitulah.	20	like that.

"Their melody, their sounds aren't the same," he says, tracing the ups and downs of a virtual mountain range in the air with his left hand. This up-and-down topsy-turvy tracing emulates the Bugis tendency to *malagu-lagu*, a habit of speaking that instantly distinguishes them from Bugis *tempatan* or locals whose habits of talk are "more flat" (*lebih rata*). By characterizing the sensual singsong of "illegal" immigrants' habits of talk with respect to the "flatter" intonation contours of their coethnic, "legal" counterparts, this petty sovereign has not only engaged in acts of grading. He has also identified a certain intensive excess that might be seized on to identify "illegal" interlopers in contemporary Sabah—one that hinges on the highs and lows or the mores and lesses of pitch movement. He continues in a similar vein, identifying "illegal" Bugis from their coethnic Malaysian counterparts by way of a graded excess in another feature of speech:

Text 2

F: Nah, ini Bugis, kita tahu sahaja	1	F: Now, these Bugis, of course we know
kerana selalu "G" dia orang tidak boleh	2	it's them because it's always "G" they can't
pakai.	3	use.
AC: Selalu "G"?	4	AC: Always "G"?
F: Ah, "N," "N!" "N" kah,	5	F: Ah, "N," "N!" Is it "N,"
"**pulang**," "**pulan**."	6	"**return**" (pulang), "**return**" (pulan).
"G" kah dia tak boleh pakai? "N" kah?	7	Is it "G" that they can't use? Is it "N"?
"**Ikang**" ah "N" tak boleh	8	"**Fish**" (ikang) ah it's "N" that they can't
sebut! Kalo, kan "**ikan**,"	9	pronounce! If, right, they say "**fish**" (ikan),
"**ikang**."	10	they say "**fish**" (ikang).
AC: "**Ikang**."	11	AC: "**Fish**" (ikang).
F: Kalau "**Sandakan**," "**Sandakang**,"	12	F: If "**Sandakan**," it's "**Sandakang**," if
asal "N" hujung . . . "N" dia tak boleh	13	"N" is at the end . . . "N" they cannot
sebut.Tapi oleh kerana dia orang-orang	14	pronounce. But because they're people
di sini, kan, dia harus learn itu supaya	15	who live here, right, they should learn it so
boleh sebut "NG" sama "N." Tapi	16	they can pronounce "NG" as "N." But
macam mana, sudah lancar sudah	17	how can they, if they're already fluent
bercakap keluar juga itu.	18	when they speak, it still comes out.
AC: Dan masih ada [anunya.	19	AC: And there's still the [um.
F: [ah, masih ada	20	F: [ah, still is.
AC: Masih ada [lagunya itu.	21	AC: Still have that [melody.
F: [tak boleh hilang.	22	F: [cannot disappear.
Masih ada.	23	Still there.

In homing in on a certain sound, this Sabahan identified a certain intensity or excess that obtains in the speech of undocumented Bugis migrants from Indonesia. Just like those singsong pitch contours that migrants "bring" to Malay from their Bugis language, one of those features is the velar nasal in the word-final position. Much like those prototypically Bugis singsong pitch contours, an intensive or graded excess in this sound is one that indigenous Sabahans have indexically homed in on as an aural sign of outsidership (Carruthers 2017b, 2017c). And it's one that undocumented immigrants' coethnic, Malaysia-born counterparts have homed in on as well.

Sketch 2

"What's more important, Bugis language or Malay language?" a Malaysian Bugis woman asks her Indonesian Bugis interlocutor on a palm oil plantation. The Malaysian woman, herself a descendent of Bugis extraction, is accompanied by two Bugis Malaysian friends, one of whom is an active member of UMNO. "Bugis is important!" she exclaims. "I don't know half of Malay!" (*Nda' tahu separuh itu Melayu*), she continues, evincing that prototypically Bugis singsong in the process (see fig. 5).

Rather than focusing on the denotational content of her interlocutor's response, the UMNO member homes in on the singsong pitch contours of her utterance, interrupting and characterizing it as "very Bugis" (*Bugis sangat*). "Too Bugis" (*terlampau Bugis*), she tells me later.

The Indonesian Bugis woman's dramatic phrase-final fall on *Melayu* (see fig. 5) is what triggered her Malaysian interlocutor, leading her to characterize the woman's utterance as "very Bugis" (*Bugis sangat*) and "too Bugis" (*terlampau Bugis*). Again, note the presence of intensifiers *sangat* and *terlampau*, corresponding to English intensifiers *very* and *too*. Both utterances are implicit comparative constructions which imply that the woman's speech is in excess of itself, in a manner of speaking. Indeed, to say that the woman's speech is too Bugis is to imply it transgresses locally salient thresholds or points of departure. It is to say that her *lagu* or intonation is, as our UMNO member would inform me later, "very Bugis compared to the speech patterns of local Bugis people."

This Malaysian woman would later explain to me that people such as this woman—card-carrying "Malaysians" actually from Indonesia—must "reduce" certain features of their speech such that it aligns with locally salient norms and forms, and such that the speakers might effectively pass as Malaysian citizens. "It's best if they [Bugis immigrants from Indonesia] correct their pronunciation as best they can, because from their pronunciation one can tell if they've lived a long time in Sabah or just a few years, even though they're identity card holders," she

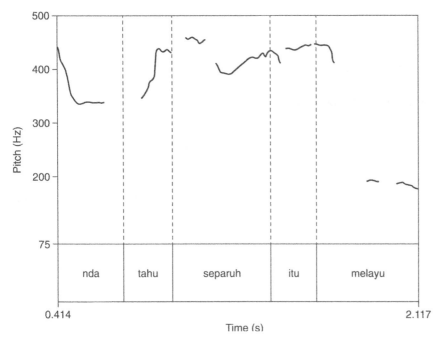

Figure 5 Intonational "excess."

told me. To pass as local Malays (and avoid potential arrest), such migrants must modulate, minimize, or "hide their Bugisness" (*tapok kebugisannya*) by masking certain sonic excesses that distinguish them from their coethnic Malaysian counterparts. In contemporary Sabah, an excess in singsong pitch or velar nasals in the word-final position is "enregistered" (Agha 2007: 144) or conventionally understood to index or point toward "illegal" presences, and speakers who exhibit such excesses may be subject to capture by police (Carruthers 2017b, 2017c). To effectively pass as local card-carrying Malays, then, such migrants must modulate their habits of talk, lest the sounds they evince deviate from a normatively regimented distribution of the sensible.

In this crucial sense, then, processes of policing—of detecting a putative excess or moreness in certain features of migrant speech—serve as the very points of departure for processes of passing. By mapping regimes of sensible intensities, and by coming to understand where the thresholds between such regimes lie, migrants might minimize embodied excesses, enabling them to effectively travel under thresholds of detection. Like agentive, "thermodynamic gods" (Schneider and Sagan 2005: 326), they might pass by using their "consciousness to direct energy, to tap into local muscle gradients in [the] body," modulating certain intensities by policing laryngeal and articulatory settings.

Conclusion: Policing Intensity

In *The Policing Web*, Jean-Paul Brodeur (2010: 41) argues that "a theory of policing aiming to be (relatively) complete should provide an account of what is being referred to when we use the word 'police' as a common noun (the police), as a verb (policing), and as an adjective (as in police apparatus)." With an eye to Brodeur's parts of speech, *policing* in *policing intensity* may be alternatively read as a noun or verb, meaning the phrase may refer to the relative intensity or magnitude of policing practices on the one hand, and to the practice of policing or monitoring intensity (qua direct object) on the other.

First, and in the absence of readily available or regularized data of arrest of deportation, *policing intensity*, or the relative magnitude or intensity of policing practices in Sabah, is a notion that migrants speak of with respect to a more or a less. Recall here the comment by our Nunukan karaoke patron who, drawing on the Malay intensifier *terlampau* or *too*, noted that the policing of undocumented migrants in the East Malaysian state has now become "too cruel," in which a present magnitude of cruelty is weighed or graded with respect to past magnitudes. This current intensity is one that forecloses (at least for now) the possibility of this patron's return, and it is one that, following a political sea change in the 2018 Malaysian general election, has a nebulous future. In May 2018, the Alliance of Hope–led opposition won a simple majority over and against the UMNO-led National Front coalition. This has led to a degree of uncertainty regarding the future of undocumented immigrants in Sabah, a place once considered a "fixed deposit" for the National Front and UMNO, the Malay race-based party alleged to have illegally disseminated national identity cards to Bugis immigrants in exchange for votes. Leading up to the election, Sabah's "illegal immigrant problem" was characterized as "the mother of all problems of Sabah," with calls for "the government to resolve the issue of illegals getting their hands on genuine Malaysian identity documents through the back door" (*Borneo Post* 2018). Subsequent to the opposition's win, calls reemerged for what we might call the re-"fabrication of social order" (Neocleous 2000) in Sabah, where all extant Sabah identity cards would be made null and void, with new ones issued only to "genuine Sabahans" holding birth certificates. The policing apparatus presupposed and potentially entailed by this policy proposal, would, as I've written elsewhere, have devastating entailments in the lives of those Bugis Indonesians who have come to pass as card-carrying Sabahans (Carruthers 2016).

Second, and returning to the issue at the heart of this essay, *policing intensity* refers to the monitoring of intensity as a discernable dimension of everyday experience. I have addressed how policing practices take aim at the "more-or-lessness" of flows and forms that transgress institutionally and normatively regimented thresholds—be they putatively "intransitive" borders between nations or borders between speaking subjects. Put differently, in the Indonesia-Malaysia borderlands, encounters with and evaluations of moreness—or what William James (1890: 151–52) called "the immediate feeling of an outstanding plus"—reflect and shape certain distributions of the sensible.[12]

Rancière (2004: 12) defines his "distribution of the sensible" or *partage du sensible*—where *partage*, an item that "combines the sense of both division and connection" (Mezzadra and Neilson 2012: 66)—as a *langue*-like "system of self-evident facts of sense perception that simultaneously discloses the existence of something in common and the delimitations that define the respective parts and positions within it." There is a rather ubiquitous term floating about today that resonates with Rancière, if defined accordingly: *ontology*—that set of assumptions that semiotic agents have about the signs and kinds that constitute a world (see Kockelman 2012, 2017). If we approach *le partage du sensible* in this way, then we might also personify or recharacterize Rancière's abstract notion of the police as those keepers of kinds—that is to say, as agents who have militantly common-*sense* intuitions about where the thresholds or borders between different kinds of entities lie, on the basis of the signs they evince.

Let's recall Rancière's (2004: 39) assertion that the political "defines models of speech and action but also regimes of sensible intensity," maps "the visible" and "trajectories between the visible and the sayable," and defines "variations of sensible intensities, perceptions, and the abilities of bodies." If this is the political, then how do those keepers of kinds—that is to say, the police—not engage in political acts in their everyday lives?

To bring this observation to bear on this essay's foregoing ethnographic particulars, how is Assemblyman Muis's agenda not explicitly political, insofar as it seeks to regulate or redefine certain "variations of sensible intensities, percep-

---

12. Note here the rhetorical resonances between James's sense of moreness as "an outstanding plus" and Mimi Thi Nguyen's (2015: 793) notion of the hoodie as "an example of Hortense Spillers's signifying property plus."

tions, and the abilities of bodies" in the act of building his wall along a virtual border that conflicts with Hasidah's notion of the invisible fence that cuts through her home? And, with an eye to Sapir's (1944) work on grading, how are undocumented migrants' efforts to pass as locals—efforts that entail the minimizing or masking of certain qualities—not contingent on their contrastive evaluation of sensible intensities, an act that Rancière resolutely defines as political but one that, in this case, might best be defined as a mode of self-policing?

The police is political and the political polices, and this is more than evident in the Indonesia-Malaysia borderlands, a setting where people and places are characterized as more-or-less the same on the basis of certain sensible intensities. With respect to high-stakes situations or settings where one's failure to pass "lexical [or phono-lexico-grammatical] border guards" (Suleiman 2013: 21) may mean life or death, the stakes discussed here may seem decidedly lower.[13] Recalling the plainclothes policemen depicted in my introduction, this fact could perhaps reflect a historically cultivated sense of kinship or cross-border commonality that obtains between Bugis Indonesians and Malaysians. Nonetheless, the setting described here—one where border crossing is decidedly not a movement between radical worlds or incommensurate domains, as is so often alleged in the literature—allows us to consider policing from a different angle of vision. It encourages us to consider how the police act within a slippery continuum that they themselves orchestrate or seek to do so.[14] And, with an eye to the mediating role played by intensity or more-or-lessness within such a setting, it indicates something about the foundationally fuzzy logic that undergirds certain processes of policing.

References

Agha, Asif. 2007. *Language and Social Relations*. Cambridge: Cambridge University Press.

Andaya, Barbara Watson, and Leonard Y. Andaya. 2016. *A History of Malaysia*. London: Palgrave MacMillan.

Aristotle. 1963. *Categories and De Interpretatione*, translated by J. L. Ackrill. Oxford: Oxford University Press.

Balibar, Étienne. 2002. *Politics and the Other Scene*. London: Verso.

13. See the shibboleths associated with the "Parsley" massacre of the Dominican Republic, Palestinian versus Lebanese pronunciations of *tomato* in the Lebanese civil war, or Mojaddedi's work (this issue) on language, translation, and wartime exchange. See *Boys Don't Cry* (dir. Kimberly Peirce; 1999) for another high-stakes depiction of the perils of passing.

14. I thank Stuart Schrader for suggesting this point.

Bebout, Lee. 2016. *Whiteness on the Border: Mapping the US Racial Imagination in Brown and White*. New York: New York University Press.

Bergson, Henrie. (1889) 2010. *Time and Free Will: An Essay on the Immediate Data of Consciousness*, translated by F. L. Pogson. London: Swan Sonnenschein & Co.

The Borneo Post. 2018. "Upko Asks How DAP Can Easily Forgive Dr M on Projek IC." March 1.

Brodeur, Jean-Paul. 2010. *The Policing Web*. Oxford: Oxford University Press.

Butler, Judith. 2004. *Precarious Life: The Powers of Mourning and Violence*. London: Verso.

Carruthers, Andrew M. 2016. "Sabah ICs for Sabahans." *ISEAS Perspective*, no. 11.

Carruthers, Andrew M. 2017a. "Clandestine Movement in the Indonesia-Malaysia Migration Corridor: Roots, Routes, and Realities." *ISEAS Perspective*, no. 58.

Carruthers, Andrew M. 2017b. "Grading Qualities and (Un)Settling Equivalences: Undocumented Migration, Commensuration, and Intrusive Phonosonics in the Indonesia-Malaysia Borderlands." *Journal of Linguistic Anthropology* 27, no. 2: 124–50.

Carruthers, Andrew M. 2017c. "'Their Accent Would Betray Them': Clandestine Movement and the Sound of 'Illegality' in Malaysia's Borderlands." *SOJOURN: Journal of Social Issues in Southeast Asia* 32, no. 2: 221–59.

Carruthers, Andrew M. Forthcoming. "The Meaning of 'Moreness': An Essay for James T. Collins." In *Bukit sama Didaki: A Festschrift for Professor Emeritus Dr. James T. Collins*, edited by Chong Shin, Andrew M. Carruthers, and Dedy Ari Asfar. Bangi, Malaysia: Institut Kajian Etnik.

Clisby, Dale. 2015. "Deleuze's Secret Dualism? Competing Accounts of the Relationship between the Virtual and the Actual." *Parrhesia* 24: 127–49.

Daily Express. 2016. "How M'sia is slowly 'losing' Sebatik." December 26.

Daud, Ramlah. 2010. "Identiti dan penghidupan komuniti sempadan etnik Bugis: Satu kajian kes di Pulau Sebatik" ("The Identity and Livelihood of the Ethnic Bugis Borderland Community: A Case Study on Sebatik Island"). MA thesis, Universiti Malaysia Sabah.

Delanda, Manuel. 2002. *Intensive Science and Virtual Philosophy*. London: Continuum.

Delanda, Manuel. 2005. "Space: Extensive and Intensive, Actual and Virtual." In *Deleuze and Space*, edited by Ian Buchanan and Gregg Lambert, 80–88. Toronto: University of Toronto Press.

Deleuze, Gilles. (1968) 1994. *Difference and Repetition*. London: Athlone.

Deleuze, Gilles, and Félix Guattari. 1986. *A Thousand Plateaus*, translated by Brian Massumi. Minneapolis: University of Minnesota Press.

Dewan Bahasa dan Pustaka. 2005. *Kamus dewan edisi keempat (The Institute Dictionary, Fourth Edition)*. Kuala Lumpur, Malaysia: Dewan Bahasa dan Pustaka.

Garfinkel, Harold. (1967) 2006. "Passing and the Managed Achievement of Sex Status." In *The Transgender Studies Reader*, edited by Susan Stryker and Stephen Whittle, 58–93. New York: Routledge.

Gibson, James. 1977. "The Theory of Affordances." In *Perceiving, Acting, and Knowing*, edited by Robert Shaw and John Bansford, 67–82. Hillsdale, NJ: Lawrence Erlbaum.

Goffman, Erving. (1963) 1986. *Stigma: Notes on the Management of Spoiled Identity*. New York: Simon & Schuster.

Harkness, Nicholas. 2015. "The Pragmatics of Qualia in Practice." *Annual Review of Anthropology* 44: 573-589.

James, William. 1890. *The Principles of Psychology*. Vol. 2. New York: Henry Holt.

Keane, Webb. 2016. *Ethical Life: Its Natural and Social Histories*. Princeton, NJ: Princeton University Press.

Kockelman, Paul. 2012. *Agent, Person, Subject, Self: A Theory of Ontology, Interaction, and Infrastructure*. Oxford: Oxford University Press.

Kockelman, Paul. 2016. *The Chicken and the Quetzal: Incommensurate Ontologies and Portable Values in Guatemala's Cloud Forest*. Durham, NC: Duke University Press.

Kockelman, Paul. 2017. *The Art of Interpretation in the Age of Computation*. Oxford: Oxford University Press.

Lipsky, Michael. (1969) 2010. *Street-Level Bureaucracy: Dilemmas of the Individual in Public Service*. New York: Russell Sage Foundation.

Mader, Mary Beth. 2014. "Whence Intensity?: Deleuze and the Revival of a Concept." In *Gilles Deleuze and Metaphysics*, edited by Alain Beaulieu, Edward Kazarian, and Julia Sushytska, 225-248. Lanham, MD: Rowman & Littlefield.

Massumi, Brian. 2002. *Parables for the Virtual: Movement, Affect, Sensation*. Durham: Duke University Press.

Mattulada. 1985. *Latoa: Satu lukisan analitis terhadap antropologi politik orang Bugis (Latoa: An Analytical Sketch of the Political Anthropology of the Bugis)*. Yogyakarta, Indonesia: Gadja Mada University Press.

Mbembe, Achille. 2003. "Necropolitics." *Public Culture* 15, no. 1: 11–40.

Mead, George Herbert. 1962. *Mind, Self, and Society*. Chicago: University of Chicago Press.

Mezzadra, Sandro, and Brett Neilson. 2012. "Between Inclusion and Exclusion: On the Topology of Global Space and Borders." *Theory, Culture & Society* 29, nos. 4–5: 58–75.

Mojaddedi, Fatima. 2019. "The Closing: Heart, Mouth, Word." *Public Culture* 31, no. 3.

Neocleous, Mark. 2000. *The Fabrication of Social Order: A Critical Theory of Police Power.* London: Pluto.

Nguyen, Mimi Thi. 2015. "The Hoodie as Sign, Screen, Expectation, and Force." *Signs* 40, no. 4: 791–816.

Peirce, C. S. 1867. "On a New List of Categories." *Proceedings of the American Academy of Arts and Sciences* 7: 287–98.

Peirce, C. S. 1906. "Prolegomena to an Apology for Pragmaticism." *The Monist* 16, no. 4: 492–546.

Peirce, C. S. (1907) 1998. "Pragmatism." In *The Essential Peirce, Vol. 2, 1883–1913*, edited by Nathan Houser and Christian Kloesel, 398–433. Bloomington: Indiana Univeristy Press.

Pelras, Christian. 1996. *The Bugis.* Oxford: Blackwell.

Pro Kaltara. 2015. "Tak Tahu Kapan Selesainya, TKI yang Dideportasi Selalu Kembali" ("Not Knowing When It Ends, Indonesian Migrant Workers Who Are Deported Always Return"). December 17.

Rancière, Jacques. 2004. *The Politics of Aesthetics*, translated by Gabriel Rockhill. New York: Continuum.

Sapir, Edward. 1944. "Grading, A Study in Semantics." *Philosophy of Science* 11, no. 2: 93–116.

Schneider, Eric D., and Dorion Sagan. 2005. *Into the Cool: Energy Flow, Thermodynamics, and Life.* Chicago: The University of Chicago Press.

Shim, Steve Lip Kiong, Herman J. Luping, K. Y. Mustafa, Kamaruzaman Hj. Ampon, and Henry Chin Poy Wu. 2014. *Report of the Commission of Enquiry into Illegal Immigrants in Sabah. Presented to Seri Paduka Baginda Yang Di-Pertuan Agong.* Kota Kinabalu, Malaysia: The Royal Commission of Enquiry.

Sintang, Suraya. 2007. *Sejarah dan Budaya Bugis di Tawau, Sabah (The History and Culture of the Bugis of Tawau, Sabah).* Kota Kinabalu, Malaysia: Penerbit USM Dengan Kerjasama Persatuan Kebajikan Bugis Sabah.

Solère, Jean-Luc. 2001. "The Question of Intensive Magnitudes According to Some Jesuits in the Sixteenth and Seventeenth Centuries." *The Monist* 84, no. 4: 582–616.

Suleiman, Yasir. 2013. *Arabic in the Fray: Language Ideologies and Cultural Politics.* Edinburgh: Edinburgh University Press.

The Star Online. 2012. "Proud to Be Malaysian." September 16. www.thestar.com
.my/lifestyle/features/2012/09/16/proud-to-be-malaysian/.

Trocki, Carl. 2000. "Borders and the Mapping of the Malay World." Paper presented at the Association of Asian Studies Annual Meeting, San Diego, CA, March 9–12.

Utusan Melayu. 2014. "Dapur di Malaysia, ruang tamu di Indonesia" ("Kitchen in Malaysia, Living Room in Indonesia"). April 1.

Wong, Jane. 2000. *The Sabah Malay Dialect: Phonological Structure and Social Functions.* Kota Kinabalu, Malaysia: Universiti Malaysia Sabah Press.

Andrew M. Carruthers is an assistant professor of anthropology at the University of Pennsylvania.

The Closing: Heart, Mouth, Word

Fatima Mojaddedi

First of all, for a moment at least, empty space—the place
where the thing stood or the victim lived. Someone is sure to be
found who needs this space without occupying it.
—Walter Benjamin, "The Destructive Character"

By 2013 the sense of distress and anarchic upheaval was palpable in Kabul, rising like a cacophony of voices and memories of past deeds. It meant accusation and swift vengeance, for some a knife to the neck, and made both country and language feel smaller and more volatile. The protean atmosphere was one of strangeness, and of the quality of feeling Georg Simmel describes as the sense that "he, who is close by, is far, and strangeness means that he, who also is far, is actually near" ([1950] 1964: 402). But this ambivalent unity of remoteness and proximity is also a matter of the heart, of the relation between languages in moments of violent confusion that exposes speakers to the demand for perspective and coherence, while also to space, memory and the approach of the stranger. One wet, biting cold afternoon my friend Mahmud told me he is *dil tang*. This means he feels like his heart is tight and closed. Like innumerable

This essay is an expansion of a talk delivered in the Departments of Anthropology at the University of California, Davis, and University of California, Berkeley. I am especially indebted to Rosalind C. Morris and Stefania Pandolfo for their guidance, and to Marilyn Ivy and Nadia Abu El-Haj, who read an earlier version. I would also like to thank Cristiana Giordano, Alan Klima, Victoria Gross, Natacha Nsabimana, Michael D'Arcy, and Milad Odabaei. This essay would not have been possible without the generous invitation to participate in this special issue. For that, and for their suggestions as part of a larger collective review, I thank Madiha Tahir, Shamus Khan, Jesse Goldberg, Caren Kaplan, and Andrea Miller.

Public Culture 31:3   DOI 10.1215/08992363-7532703
Copyright 2019 by Duke University Press

people Mahmud believes speaking and listening to another person, offering a glimpse into one's life and thoughts, can enable a chest-opening experience. He doesn't seek a witness. But he does want the particular, intimate kind of relief found in dialogic moments of baring oneself. He speaks to lessen his pain, which is both a physical feeling, one we all know, and something much more. Mahmud knows that there is strangeness found in speech and that speech is itself a strange and never self-same thing, and that it is inseparable from the lessening and intensifying of the tightness in his heart.

More generally, Mahmud understands that in Afghanistan speech is part of a much larger, more international endeavor, and that in the midst of the irresolution of war and the world's largest display of industrial and modern firepower, speech contributes to this by providing an additional medium of access to subjects of violence and wartime propaganda. In this milieu, often described as a destructive, even barbaric country threatening to destabilize the greater region, it becomes difficult to discern when someone intends to cause you harm in lieu of desiring a relation. The problem is not just group and wartime formations but also the inescapable sense of fear and distrust that subtend both war and the upheaval of social, even neighborly, and linguistic life. He—in war the stranger is typically male—is crucial to the idea that it is a place without peace, at once deeply isolated from the world, and full of difficult people to understand. But from within the world of everyday relationality, urban-rural exchange, and translation, the experience of strangeness is also accompanied by the inexorable force of words and voicing. It is part of the power of verbal command and interpellation, the scenes of interrogation, peals of laughter, slips of the tongue, and moments of translational authority when the proximity between languages becomes the occasion for the violence of language as wartime exchange.[1]

Mahmud works in the Afghan National Archives. It is in a converted summer palace, close to the Kabul River and the city's old and storied bazaars. The river has dried, and the peripheral neighborhood evokes a sense of nostalgia for what has since been feverishly passed over in the name of the *nau* (the new). Its oldness lingers in the makeshift shops and farm carts that line its dirt roads and in the animal power and child labor that animates it with the sounds and chatter of petty commerce. I spent time with him in the archives and even came to assume he lived a good life. He labors indefatigably, and although his task is underfunded by the Afghan government's Ministry of Information and Culture, and seemingly endless, he finds joy in categorizing and reading the trove of materials hidden

1. On hearing from different languages and the notion of "sound blindness" see Boas 1889.

underground until recently during decades of armed conflict. The fear was they would be set on fire. Mahmud now seeks to preserve them. He gave me files to read and showed me the former Afghan royal family's photo albums hidden in the basement. They had never been seen before: "You are the first person I am showing. They were so beautiful. Look at their stylish clothes and class and now they have vanished," he said.

Hundreds of thousands of Afghans died in the large-scale conflicts (the Soviet War of 1979–1989, the Afghan Civil War of 1992–1996, the Taliban Regime of 1996–2001 and the Afghan-American War (2001–) that came to define modern Afghanistan and entwined its political trajectory with those of global and regional powers. Like many, Mahmud lived through these conflicts and rebuilt his house after it was destroyed. He lives in one of Kabul's poorer neighborhoods where unpaved side streets intersect, and the acrid smell of urine is unavoidable. The alleyways evoke a sense of mystery and haunting absence: of domestic and familiar scenes that are not without tragedy and violence. He didn't invite me to his home but describes it and asks me to imagine: "The curtains in my home are always shut," he said. "Why do you feel *dil tang*?" I asked. "It is hard to explain how life makes your heart close," he replied. He admits he has put up secondhand curtains and that they are tasteless but are always drawn shut even if the neighbors see their inferior quality and red color. He no longer cares what his neighbors think. The house is darker still because he insists on the unforgiving aura that makes his heart feel so small. "I accept this feeling," he also said. I learned that Mahmud did not live a good life. His twenty-one-year-old son Taha was brutally murdered one afternoon when Mahmud was sitting with him in their kitchen. There was a repeated knock on the back door: "Tak. Tak. Tak," Mahmud recalled. The door led to one of the alleyways and outside a group of young men, boys almost, stood in an odd state of solemnity. "I opened the door and Taha recognized them as our neighbors. They said they wanted to talk and Taha went outside to talk."

To speak is to be exposed to memory and the other. The boys looked hardened to Mahmud but not like they were secreting a horror. At the end of the alley behind another house the young men quickly overpowered and stabbed Taha with a long blade in the abdomen and vitals. Mahmud heard his screams and ran out to find him on the ground in a pool of blood. He died within minutes in his father's arms. Mahmud showed me an old passport-size photo of his son that he keeps in his wallet and cried openly. I didn't ask the most obvious question, but he quickly intuited my curiosity: "Oh, we know why! He was killed for having worked as a translator [*tarjomon*] for the US military. There is no doubt about that. People say it. Everyone knows it." Mahmud speaks in a pained and haunted voice of certitude, but like in a spectral encounter, he gains this certainty only when everything else he thought he knew, about life and speaking with others, and sharing the only city he has ever known was tragically undone. "Now you know," he said, "this is what the situation is for us."

By 2013 the situation Mahmud warns of became harder to control. Its fault line reshaped the social as the phantomlike and deadly division between the living and those suddenly closer to being marked for death. Guilt was in the air, and revenge seeking became common in Kabul and rural towns. Ordinary people were suspected of harboring dangerous affiliations, of having secret sources of money or ties with the insurgents. Liquid cash (mainly dollars) flooded the national economy and informal money market. The ingress of foreign capital and the destruction of traditional agriculture, large-scale bombing campaigns in the countryside, and the violence of the black market abetted the cultivation of opium crops and the deadly exchange of ransom, drugs, precious and semiprecious gems, timber, weapons, and suicide bombers sourced from the growing pool of unemployed young men.

This experience and sense of danger was especially invoked by *Kabulis* as the fantasia of a rural insurgency closing in on their city. People feared for their lives and the dissolution of social bonds, and the inescapable, arbitrary distrust of the other proliferated alongside insurgent and counterinsurgent groups, and also new reconnaissance and biometric technologies and older networks of political and military-urban violence. In some places, men were sloppily decapitated and became random lessons for each other, some were poisoned or tortured, others ambushed, and one woman, Farkhunda, was killed and her body set on fire in broad daylight in central Kabul and then tossed in the barren Kabul River. Fear became the object of social discourse to such an extent that it was a metonym for the general experience of social disintegration and wartime catastrophe. People found it nearly impossible to evade the kind of random and horrifying violence that is a common feature of war and siege, its key signifier even, but nonetheless leaves people with the singular feeling of being persecuted: "There is no place left to live. We'll all die. Tell us, where should we go?" an acquaintance and a day laborer, now imprisoned on false charges, asked me.

The Translator

In "The Task of the Translator" Walter Benjamin ([1955] 1968) imagines translation as the provisional encounter with difference in the mode of supplemental and poetic license. Translation, he proposes, reveals the kinship of languages not through likeness but in the mode of intention that exists in every language and allows it to become other and greater than itself. It is a greatness realized only in relation to difference. Benjamin describes it as an enlightening through which translation "catches fire on the eternal life of the works and the perpetual renewal of language" (74). Translation creates strangeness and the possibility of rupture, and death, but also of a rising into a "higher and purer linguistic air . . . the predestined, hitherto inaccessible realm of reconciliation and fulfillment of languages" (75).[2]

Understanding this requires that we reckon with how translation introduces the possibility of rupture and absence, and therefore to think about translation as a "theoretical metaphor through which to think about difference" (Giordano 2014: 15; see also De La Cadena 2015 and Pandolfo 2018). It is in the latter mode, particularly in moments when speech is central to this logic, that translation subverts what Ibn Khaldûn refers to as "group feeling," and makes it possible to wage war on those who were previously kindred.[3] In these moments, the translator must also reckon with the specter of incommunicability and the rare "total linguistic barrier" that Primo Levi (1988: 88) evokes as the difference between life, the domain of war, and human finitude.

I met Matin in 2012 when he had just quit his job as a translator for the United States and the International Security and Assistance Force (ISAF) and lived with his parents in a poor neighborhood next to the Kabul International Airport. His neighborhood was heavily bombed by the American military in 2001 and is still under threat from surrounding construction projects. Matin remembers using a small propane lantern to help locate the bodies of his dead neighbors. On the day of our meeting he was lost trying to find the Flower Street Café in the neighborhood of Taimani. He didn't call me for directions because he thought his willingness to initiate a phone call, and unexpectedly inject his voice without his physical presence, would cause me to think he intends harm. In conversation, he also

2. In the introduction to *Illuminations* Hannah Arendt (1968: 49–50) explains that this purer language is about the place of history in language, and that for Benjamin language is not "the gift of speech which distinguishes man from other living beings, but, on the contrary, 'the world essence . . . from which speech arises.'" Arendt explains that this is the language "whose existence we assume unthinkingly as soon as we translate from one language into another."

3. Ibn Khaldûn (1989: 223–24) describes the wartime notion of "group feeling" as the site of loss and intensification. It enables war to erupt not only between enemies but former neighbors once close to each other, and hence those privy to social envy. His discourse is distinct from Sigmund Freud's ([1915] 2005) understanding of ambivalence and guilt in relation to the dead, but it shares the assumption that warfare possesses a psychic force and requires the bond of sentiment to also transcend it.

seemed fearful that he might betray himself, and he would emphatically add to his stories, "I say all of this only because I trust you like a sister."

In Afghanistan, the social body is marked by the coexistence of the demand for speech and its lack, and in some moments, speech becomes the site of a dangerous double bind: the medium of persuasion and, as I understand its power, an uncontrollable instrument of war that proceeds alongside the translator.[4] The voice is violent, but it is interpretation, and the possibility of listening at any moment or in any place, that makes that violence brutal.[5] Matin does not articulate this from within his speech, but I believe he intuits the possibility and wants to protect himself from its force by listening to different voices differently. Thus, even though he fears his own disembodied voice, and the displacement of being a subject in dialogue by the power of misunderstanding, he still speaks to me and he speaks to me differently than he does with those he meets on his military missions.

On his way to meet those people, in the vast landscape outside Kabul he refers to as "the countryside," Matin had access to military radio transmissions through wired headphones. He would listen to them inside large armored tanks to better acquaint himself with different languages and military vocabulary. He did this not to understand the meaning and content of the transmission but to learn how to speak and thereby to lessen his chances of making mistakes in speech or when listening to different accents: for example, when he tries to understand British, American, and Scottish soldiers. He is especially terrified of mistakes like a mispronounced or misplaced word, which interpreted in a certain way, can result in the accusation that he is giving false information or even part of a covert "green on blue" plot against his unit.[6] Unlike other instruments of war, speech is mysterious

4. When I describe the transmission of words as uncontrollable, I am also thinking with Jeanne Favret-Saada (1976: 9–10) and the nature of words in witchcraft, when "deadly words" become the source of a power that precludes the impartial participant and "tie or untie a fate." I also draw on James Siegel (2005: 50), who illustrates that the phenomenon of witchcraft is also about speaking and immediate access to unconscious power, a power such that words and signifiers can suddenly "link anything with anything even if the result is catastrophe." Translation and witchcraft are not the same thing, but they do share the proclivity for excess that begins with the word and is realized in the uncontrollable linkages that emerge from the act of saying. For an evocative account of another way of thinking the power of words in relation to the emergence of excess(es), and therefore understanding the translation between languages and worlds to simultaneously be about the partial connection of differences and similarities (which are never simply just one or the other), see Marisol De La Cadena's *Earth Beings: Ecologies of Practice across Andean Worlds* (2015).

5. It is important to note here that all voice is also interpretation, and that even the presymbolic voice, for example a child's scream, is about desire and anticipating the other. See Dolar 2006: 29.

6. "Green on blue" attacks refer to incidences of violence when embedded Afghans turn on their foreign military units, usually in the form of a shooting.

to itself in this way, and it thickens the space of encounter with the expectation of an excess that cannot be contained in a relation of exchange, a transcendental power Matin is painfully conscious of.

With me he seemed relieved of the weight of foreign language, and our shared mother tongue became an opening to the possibility of trust between us. Matin admits, like Mahmud, that speaking makes his heart feel better: "Sometimes I feel myself *dil tang*, you know, like my chest is closed, but I feel better when I talk to you," he said. But elsewhere Matin speaks and seeks to hear something other than this kind of change in heart. When his voice is dislodged from Persian, and therefore from what I imagine he understands as the possibility of control, there is less of an opening, and it becomes more possible (even likely) that the people he encounters are also not quite themselves either, that their tongues are overtaken and that their hearts have also closed.[7] He navigates this kind of strangeness and what he perceives as the difference between reality and the appearance of things. For him it is particularly dangerous when the disjuncture emerges in the City of Kabul, where, ideally, he envisions a city of articulateness and order. He tells me this hope is diminishing and that his close friend was murdered midday in his own taxi when a man, disguised as a woman in a classic blue burqa, stole his cash, shot him, and drove away in the car. "What will become of us?" Matin asks me. "We are not safe in Kabul," he insists.

For Matin, to live in Kabul is to know something about life and the way the world works, and therefore to have a voice capable of openings that lead to more life and which is both a voice and a sign of the fullness of life and intellect.[8] Thus, as he speaks in his *Kabuli* dialect, and professes he is media savvy, he undoubtedly feels closer to a "language-of-power" (Anderson 1991) that is not only a sense of national duty but a duty to life and being. Outside Kabul he has to speak

7. The voice (and song) is also the rendering of testimony to the event, and the voice that is both a "present corporeality" and "an impersonal agent of strangeness, inscription of alterity" (Pandolfo 2008: 109).

8. I would contrast this sense of voice, which indicates for Matin the powers of intellection and also lawfulness, with what Roland Barthes (1977: 181) describes as the "grain of the voice." For Barthes the grain is the dimension and materiality of voice inseparable from body, and it illustrates the "encounter between a language and a voice" while remaining irreducible to personality (or civil identity). It is the singularity of voice (something more than its timbre) that is like a separate body and "bears along *directly* the symbolic" (i.e., renders the symbolic) and speaks from within body and within language the significance of language as opposed to communication or the mere expression of feeling (1977: 182). This twin sense of voice, at once bodily and structural, is what Stefania Pandolfo describes as the possibility of a voice and counterpart that is (in the experience of Amina in the setting of a psychiatric hospital) "corporeal expression, material and 'insubordinate' . . . yet which is rooted in a field of power of which her voice is the trace and 'condensation'" (2018: 67).

in a different voice, one that sets him on the path of discerning the failure of this potential in rural places, where words and propaganda are readily exchanged in the effort to bring those populations under government control, but where the speech of the local remains without sense and life.[9] "They are all illiterate," he remarks, and "they don't know how to speak," and because they only possess unintelligible speech and cannot write, Matin believes they misunderstand both image and word; he tells me they are immune to accountability: they compulsively lie, deceive, and live like violent "brutes," he says.[10]

The rest of the country, and its unpredictable populations, weigh down on him like rocks on his chest. It changes the way he speaks to me. Matin reckons with the partial and "simple truths" of these stories; he tells me these are things I must "already know," and he confesses them again as the truths of the countryside that are predictable like the rhythm of its seasonal economy. He wants me to envision a volatile and vast backwater where people shepherd animals and tend to crop in lonely fields, and because of this extreme isolation, "they talk nonsense and are all nomadic." "There is no life there," he adds. He resents that country folk desperately try to "pour into" Kabul from the other side of its mountains to feel safe, and although he acknowledges, having barely survived the early years of war himself, that "to feel safe is a very precious feeling," he doesn't think it justifies their arrival. The difference between Kabul and the provinces is like the infinite one "between ground and the sky," he triumphantly describes. The chasm is wide enough to contain not only the variations of geography and dialect but also the preponderance of life and death drives, of true intellect and its woeful, destructive mimesis.[11]

9. On the relationship between voice and capital for Karl Marx, and of voicing to representation and dialectical thought, see Morris 2016. Rosalind Morris (2016: 235) illustrates that in the context of the working day "voice names the quality of a saying that cannot be reduced to the said but also of a real that contradicts (speaks against) the concept."

10. On the disavowal of language in lieu of image fetish see Morris 2004.

11. Historically, the project of linguistic assimilation is part of "print-as-commodity" and the rise of national consciousness alongside the age of mechanical reproduction and generalized experience of reading print language (Anderson 1991). Anderson ([1983] 1991: 44) argues, "Nothing served to 'assemble' related vernaculars more than capitalism, which, within limits imposed by grammars and syntaxes, created mechanically reproduced print-languages capable of dissemination through the market." This not only enables national consciousness but also creates "languages-of-power" and dialects that are closer to print-language. Vicente Rafael (1993) offers a different account of how native vernacular circumscribed the universalizing impulses of Christian colonial rule in the Philippines and the ways conversion and translation between Spanish and Tagalog "produce the vernacular as that which simultaneously institutes and subverts colonial rule" (1993: xv). For a beautiful account of the "grain of voice" and its reemergence at the margin of national culture and its desire(s) in Japan, see Ivy 1995.

Matin carries with him the conviction that there is a latent danger inside rural peoples that translation can help reveal. It kindles the fire of perspective. "Have you been to Helmand?" he asked me. "Not yet," I replied. "You should never go even if someone promises your safety. You may not make it back alive and, speaking as someone who has transported bodies back to Kabul, it's a horrible sight. Bodies bloat, and bruise. It's horrible, just horrible." He also imagines himself being seen and recognized by "one of them." He says: "I look different now, from when I was on missions. But can you imagine if one of them recognizes my face? They'll know. They'll kill me right away." "But what about all of the time you have spent in Kabul, without harm, and all the relationships and friends you have?" I ask. "That doesn't matter," he replies, and he continues:

> Listen. In Mazaar-e Sharif [a city in the north of the country close to the border of Tajikistan] "they" [the Taliban] caught a guy I knew on the side of the road. You'll never guess what happened. They took his cell phone from him. Poor guy must have been terrified and he handed it over, of course. They called someone from his recent call list and pretended they were merely helping him out after an accident. An ordinary act of goodwill! They asked about his identity.

Matin quickly reenacted the hypothetical conversation on the other line: "'Oh! Dear God! He's my good friend! He's a commander in the Afghan National Army. One of our own. Please take good care of him brother!' Well, they hung up and slit his throat right then and there. They are primitive people, they care nothing for humanity."

He voices the imagined voice of the other to indicate there is no place left to go, and that even from within the symbolic order of narrative, there is a closing. Even his face, which looks different in Kabul because it is clean shaven, bared of disguise, no longer assures he can traverse between place and mode of appearance. For Matin, the closing is not only of dialogue but of city and countryside, two atmospheres that have become spaces of reciprocal strangeness and dangerous crossings, offering no respite from the possibility of violent retribution. The figure of the stranger that determines the ordinary spatial and psychic boundaries of the group and city has now transformed into the much more dangerous corollary of the "inner enemy" who moves between spaces and retains, as Simmel (1950: 404) also describes, an objective air composed of "distance and nearness, indifference and involvement." And owing to this, for Matin, both country and language are smaller.

Helmand is an ancient agricultural province in the south of the country where

British forces launched an enormous operation called "Operation Panther's Claw" in 2009 in an attempt to wrest control from the Taliban and establish an ISAF military presence. It is now the world's largest opium-producing region, and a place of dialect that Matin encounters not through headphones but with his naked ears.[12] One afternoon while he was out on patrol by a large cornfield he thought he saw someone. Suddenly a shot was fired at him and his commander. He recounts how bewildered he felt, and that he was taken aback both by the loud burst of gunfire but especially the green color of the field. The dusty haze and thick air came together like two additional elements of an effortless camouflage that nearly killed him. Out of nowhere, a *mard-e-ajeeb* (strange man) appeared. He was out in the open holding a large cob of corn in front of his face and trying to hide a sardonic look. Matin didn't actually see his face, but this is the look he suspects was on it as the inimitable trace of a sinister truth-being. Things were as clear as day:

> I knew it was him. I know he shot at us. It was as obvious as day. But he pretended like he had gone into the field to get some corn to eat, he tried to cover his face with a shawl and then he started pretending to be insane, so we just let him go, but I knew it was him. I remembered his face. You won't believe what happened next! A few days later that same man, now clean shaven, was introduced to us as the local police chief who we were supposed to support and train. He had trimmed his beard and cut his hair. That's how it is. You don't know who anybody truly is. I confronted him, and he denied the whole thing. He was very articulate, he started to laugh, and he said, "OK. OK. It was me. Let it go." One day they are with the local police force and the next they hide in cornfields and shoot you. They mock and fool you.

Matin encounters disguise as a natural feature of the landscape, first on the man's face, which is clean shaven like Matin's will be later, and then the ultimate disguise: the false bearer and representative of the Afghan state. The space of translation, and therefore of his paid expertise and the easy exchange he has come to take for granted between language and money, is the uncontrollable scene of shifting representations where no expert intervention or condition of knowledge can prevail. In its stead, Matin encounters radical alterity as the other side of translation: a side impossible to surveil and control, irreducible to madness, but

---

12. For a mapping of this operation see *BBC News* 2019. For an account of the relationship between policing and the calibration of intensity (the "more-or-less-ness" of things and ethnic identities) in crossings between Indonesia and East Malaysia, see Andrew Carruthers's "Policing Intensity," in this issue.

nonetheless a space where the reality principle is entirely overtaken by the dangerous play of representations. This duality, between his desire to know the truth of the place and the proliferation of false signs, renders interpretation impossible for him. He encounters a redoubled world of strangeness where an already ambivalent relationship intensifies into a nonrelation.

Matin implores me to understand and fear this as much as he does. When he senses my reluctance, he offers another story. He urges more caution. He changes his tone. He wants me to perceive, like he has seen and heard, the truth of rural society as the impossible task of translation. This is the aporia he repeatedly encounters, and there is only an uncontrollable opening, toward uncertainty, rupture, and maybe toward death. Matin repeats his warning to me: "You should never go to Helmand." He recounts his initial bewilderment, a moment even more disorientating than the man from the cornfield:

> I had never been to Helmand before. They are so different! I'd never seen or heard anything like that before, it was my first time, but the difference between those people and *Kabulis* is like the difference between the ground and sky. They don't know how to speak! I couldn't bear it. They are completely illiterate. There are basic things they don't understand, that they don't know how to say or express. But that's not all. We would give them gifts and in return they would plant IEDs [improvised explosive devices] and land mines by the roads. All they cared about was their crops. Mainly corn and wheat. We would have to use their lands because all the major roads had roadside bombs and mines. Our convoys would pass through their agricultural fields, and of course, the chained tires would destroy the crops and land, and they would come to us for compensation. We always gave them more than the price of their harvest, and sometimes they invited me over for dinner and sometimes they tried to kill us.

To go to Helmand and speak with the locals is to open himself up to the possibility of a total failure of the gift, which he gives in the form of monetary compensation for the destruction of agricultural land, and thus the collapse of the reciprocity of exchange he understands as the logic of relation between war and the compensation of its brutal violence. Instead he encounters the dangerous mimesis of exchange: the planting of bombs and roadside mines in a place where the planting of crops had become impossible. He faces strangeness again, and in the midst of this confusion, he also cannot escape the voice of the stranger. He hears it as the truth of what he already knows, of something familiar, for example, a dinner invitation, but also the voice of remoteness that disrupts his sense of space and narrative: "They don't know how to speak! I couldn't bear it," he says.

Matin experiences the dissonance with a sense of transporting anguish. He feels he has entered a different time and ascribes precisely the kind of remoteness that is a hallmark of modern warfare and the will to kill (Freud [1915] 2005) to those on whose behalf he is tasked to speak and bring peace. There is what Carlo Ginzburg (1994: 50) describes as an "inward shift" in his perception "projected into a geographical scene." The scene is the space of nonrelation. It is a kind of social world that raises enormous problems for him, especially as he struggles to convey meaning between English and local dialects, mostly in Pashto. He describes this struggle as "the only way." For Matin the shift is also the terror of an encounter indifferent to shared meaning, and therefore alien to the promise of translation from the very outset. For him, Helmand is strange and foreign because it is also foreign to signification as he understands it.[13] I believe this is the difference he perceives between "ground and sky" and between social life and violence, and also between the generality of law and sense making and the chthonic lure of drives that find expression in the heightened experience of a mobile power that later "finds" him in Kabul city. "How much money is worth the risk to your life?" I asked him. Matin replies:

> Well, $715 a month is a pittance for this kind of work. My God, we are in an active war zone! At my old job the American soldiers would give us some charity sometimes, hand-outs and such, but it wasn't enough. Now, from here [Kabul], when I think about the risks I took I am horrified. You know, I used to not even tell my own parents where I was. I'd lie and say I was in Mazaar-e-Sharif, and that my cell phone reception wasn't working and that's why I hadn't called. They had no idea I was in the middle of a battle.

Matin lies. The more he calls home and speaks to his family in Persian, the more he conveys in his mother tongue, and the higher the chances he is suspected of harboring the same proclivity for violence as those he encounters on the missions. He understands this:

> You see, they [the Americans] were very scared. Even though I wasn't allowed to use my phone. They didn't trust us entirely and thought we might be cooperating with the insurgents.

---

13. To think signification and meaning in relation to the foreign, I turn to Jacques Derrida's (1997: 262–63) reading of Georges Bataille on the question of sovereignty, specifically, on how sovereign silence and a continuum that is the experience of a "sovereign operation" is also, as Derrida contends, the "experience of absolute difference."

"How so?" I asked.

Well after a long time, they would learn to trust us. Initially they suspected us of helping the insurgents plant the roadside mines and explosives. But we deserve that kind of surveillance because Afghans behave in suspicious ways. Some of them fight with the foreigners or steal from them. Even the Afghan police officers behave like that. This has an impact on how we are perceived and treated. When they [foreign militaries] transition their teams every six months the new commander has to be informed about the local area, its topography, the strength of insurgency, and the quality of the Afghan translators. As a result, there were many problems between Afghan and foreign security services. There was always a lot of theft. The Americans were afraid of the Afghans. Afghans, well you know this, we are a very stubborn and proud people. The Americans hate that more than anything.

I can give examples. The Americans would send an Afghan to clear the road mines, and he would refuse to do the job. He'd say, "Why should I care about a mine here or there? Why should I be the one who clears them? I've traveled all these mountains and roads, and I've never been hit by a mine so let these guys take their chances too. They are not better than us." That kind of talk. I'd try to explain that this was an area prone to mines. I'd explain this is war and he just wouldn't care. They would do other things too. They would steal from the fridge that was only for the Americans. Things like milk and juice. Just lift something if they wanted it.

"Why do you think they steal?" I asked.

Listen. I've been on the frontlines. I've seen how it is. The American soldiers they get their goods, supplies, and food from helicopters, but not the Afghan soldiers. They only have rice and beans. Sometimes they don't even have bread. I understand why they steal milk, juice, and food. You have to understand these are areas with very heavy fighting, with ambushes on all the roads that connect to surrounding towns and villages. This means the roads are effectively closed off and you cannot do anything via land. Only via air. Translators were moved around in heavy-lift helicopters—we call them "chinooks"—and so were the soldiers, but the problem for our Afghan soldiers is they don't have anything of the sort, nothing like the Americans. As a result, they do what they have to do. It's natural.

Matin's voice cannot be contested, and yet he returns to the problem of speech. He doesn't see the predicament of the Afghan soldiers and translators to be only the lack of resources, nor the apparatus of surveillance they were themselves under, even as they were imposing it on the native population. The problem is that native speech necessarily leads to confusion and therefore to the subversion of strategic interests (which abound on all sides), and this opens up its political force, a force he would like to silence even while he cautions that it cannot be taken too seriously. It is like a bad dream. He explains the predicament to the American soldiers:

> I'd say: "Look these people are different from you. They are uneducated. They don't know how to use language. They don't know how to talk. They talk for an hour and the translation takes five minutes because these people are undereducated. They'll repeat themselves ten times. They never get to the point. They add so much flourish to their words. They absolutely hate responding in a straightforward manner. They will make you dizzy! Running around this way and that way with their words and after an hour they get to the damn point you wanted from the beginning. They'll repeat it in ten different ways. They don't want to shed light on your questions or give you answers. You have to force them. They daydream while talking."

Their language is a version of collective dreamwork verging on lunacy, and they do not offer straightforward answers to his questions. We have reached a moment in Matin's experiences that is also a turn in the nature of his bewilderment. For him the figure of the Afghan "brute" now speaks an unreal truth while directly standing in for the chasm between the desired effect of speech as a medium of wartime suasion (i.e., ideological conversion and military pacification) and the failure of translation to secure a space of meaningful exchange. The brute has become the forbidding difference between the content and capacity for speech. But at the same time, and I presume this is equally bewildering for him, the power of speech is revealed to the degree that it is also about its absence: about speech as the site of lack, and most certainly about what has not been said.

And then there is the surrounding land. One afternoon he was out on patrol in a village when someone shot at him and his accompanying soldiers with a pistol from inside a lone house. There was no doubt it was from the house. It was the only one in the area and "surrounded by all land," he describes. The pop was unmistakably that of a pistol. Usually, the soldiers would carry a ladder to get into houses, which they asked Matin to carry on his back this time. Matin refused. "We pay you to do this!" a solider yelled at him. "I am here to give you my tongue. You pay me for language. Nothing more," Matin replied. He recalls that he pulled out his contract, which he kept in his back pocket: "Show me right now where it says I am to carry a ladder on my back. I am not here to lift ladders!" He mobilizes the language of contract and value, the relationship between language and exchange that he now connects to the violence of inclusion in war, and to the problem of supplement he has come to embody in this most literal of ways.

We are a long way from Benjamin's understanding of a supplemental relation between languages. For Matin, the experience of proximity in alienation, of closeness to the scene, to uncertainty in power, to the ideology of war and resources of battle: tanks, headphones, field manuals, but also local crops, dialect, and foreign languages make Matin feel stranger still. He cannot be both translator and supplement. His refusal offers itself as a complex moment of reckoning, but unlike Taha, who paid with his life, tragedy is avoided here in part because Matin does not yet live in the aftermath of translation. He still wields a powerful foreign code: English, and he retains the power, however shifting, to bring war to the inside of peoples' homes, where English demands its own translation, and where Persian and Pashto signify what Afghans either do not know or cannot communicate through speech alone.

Matin's body, as an instrument and precaution, is unambiguous. It is an enhancement to ground warfare and access, an addition that intensifies the reach of his military unit, adding itself to an already rich arsenal of weapons. But on the other hand, his body is also a representation, a sign that sovereignty does not proceed unaided, that it incorporates the danger it seeks to neutralize, and therefore that the fiction of wartime translation as a medium of exchange is as much about the hierarchizing of difference as it is the structuring of local life around the twin imperative of question and answer: around interrogation and senseless reply. They had no ladder that afternoon and so they banged on the door instead. "Put your women in another room!" they yelled. They barged in, and several men were sitting in the main room. No women in sight. The American soldier ordered Matin to ask the obvious question: who shot the gun? "Shots? What shots? We didn't hear anything. What a shame. Someone shot at you? We're sorry to hear that," one man, speaking on behalf of the others, clumsily responds.

The incredulous soldiers searched the isolated house and also tested the men's fingertips for gun powder residue. They eventually found the gun. The man who was speaking pleaded with the soldiers, and they spared him. But he never admitted to actually shooting anyone. Instead, he implored and wanted them to try to understand the radical contingency of the situation. He wanted them to understand the shift in reality when strangers approach your house and tell you to hide your women: "Wouldn't you be afraid if you lived in a place like this? One lone house in the middle of nothing. And, out of nowhere, all of a sudden, a bunch of men show up! You'd shoot too! Just to show, for the sake of showing, that you are ready to defend yourselves."

I imagine the men were in a double bind they understood as a part of their rural life. In many areas, like in other guerrilla wars that bear heavily on the role of rumor and gossip in the countryside (Taussig 1987), and where personal disputes are readily solved by going to foreign military personnel and framing other locals, they were perhaps suspects before the shot was even fired. And yet, despite living with the possibility of interminable accusation, they do not remark on it. But they do perceive that there is no room for their language, for the possibility of speech in the moment of wartime encounter, and by extension a meaningful place in the symbolic domain that can also secure, through the abstract order of political right, what Hannah Arendt (1968: 296) calls "the existence of a right to have rights." At the same time, they had to demonstrate that they understood this. They shot the pistol to say they live in the house surrounded by all land, and also with the competing forces of language and war. This is in part also revealed by the fact of a single shot, which is not nearly enough to counter the firepower of a military unit typically armed with rifles, machine guns, long- and short-range sniper rifles, grenade launchers, and more. There is an unexpected truth in the men's feigned incredulity when they ask, "What shots?" The men express how invasion changes the nature of relations between persons on either side of the conflict as mediated by the translator: in the context of total war, where civilians and combatants are presumed indistinguishable, the locals understand that to speak (instead of shooting first) is to risk their life. It is precisely their readiness to shoot at the translator and the soldiers first—because they need to demonstrate they are willing to engage in self-defense and do not believe speaking will defuse the situation—that Matin cannot fully understand, translate, or escape, because as part mediator, and part instrument of war, he is caught in it.

The Closing

In Kandahar, a province in the southern part of the country, surrounded again by what he understands as a "brutish" atmosphere of deceit, these tensions become impossible for Matin to balance as part of translation's promise. There is no longer any language for the madness, and along with the Afghan soldiers, he discovers he must resort to excess, the kind of reckless mimesis he ascribes to the locals but that now becomes his own prerogative. The Afghan soldiers typically make do with much less food and supplies than the Americans, and this was as true in Kandahar as it was in Helmand. As a result, they sought access to roads and towns, but in Kandahar, again like in Helmand, the roads were effectively closed off by roadside mines. Aside from the dramatic possibility of airlift and support, Matin and his Afghan National Army counterparts (who he was conveying information to over the radio) felt blindsided in yet another place they simultaneously desire to transform into the purview of government control. Things became so difficult that Matin had to go into the mountains:

> I went on a lot of missions in the mountains when I was with the special forces. Their missions were almost always in the mountains. We were close to a village, and our mission was to support the local Afghan police. There were a lot of ambushes. That was their tactic, and of course they laid roadside mines and bombs on the major roads. So we would go out primarily at night, at two or three a.m., and wait for them in the mountains so they would not attack the Afghan police. They would try to attack every single night. Every single night members of the Afghan police were killed, at least two or three dead and I'd see their bodies. There were too many dead bodies, sometimes even six or seven of them. Or they would be badly hurt.

"What did you do?" I asked.

> What did we do? We tried to ambush first. We would try to ambush them beforehand, while they were traveling to the villages, sometimes we got caught by an ambush instead. I got hurt when a mine went off and hit the person in front of me.

Matin casts the situation for us as one in which anticipatory attacks are merely the expression of state interest. There is in fact no distinction here between the state and terror, a real and planned ambush attack, between the event and its ideation or even the taking of native life and "access" to his environment, in this case the roads, the escape path "they" had also presumably booby-trapped. It is the scene of a total collapse. From the mountain, the difference between ground and sky Matin understands as the domain of enclosure and local life becomes the space of the abandonment of translation, and instead, the taking on of the deadly play of destruction: the reply not in dialogue but in the form of a *kameen* (ambush). Matin finds himself engulfed in the same attitude of readiness he misunderstood as the singular expression of local life and language. The situation deteriorates rapidly. Nobody knows who was responsible for the ambushes or laying of the mines. The locals were terrified, accusations proliferated on all sides; the play of ambush-before-ambush and of shadows and planting in the middle of the night created an atmosphere so terribly pervasive that Matin recalls even his own nearly deadly injury during an explosion with chilling nonchalance. He even jokes, "I'd show you my scars, but it is a shame they are on my legs."

What is the role of the translator during an actual ambush? In the scene of fighting? I ask.

> There isn't a lot of communication during those moments, but state [Afghan] security forces are in touch with us. They communicate the attacks that *will be* [emphasis mine] made on them. They perceive dangers, and we have to relay that, their perceptions, to the Americans who are in turn supporting the Afghan forces. The Americans tell them what to do, how to respond to situations, and of course the local villagers play a role too.

The atmosphere is devoid of speech in the present tense, but also of the attempt to speak on behalf of others. Matin describes his role during this encounter as communicating between two parties, on the same side of war (American and Afghan soldiers) but separated by the foreignness of tongues. By contrast, this is precisely what fails when it is demanded of the locals themselves, who suffer for speaking in a representative capacity, despite what Matin says is everyone's shared interest in resolving the problem of the land mines. By the time Matin comes down from the mountains, speech had become impossible. The locals would not communicate what was "in their hearts."

> We would sit with them and hold councils [*jirgas*]. The local villagers were hard to understand. They wouldn't open up to us. They wouldn't communicate to us what was in their hearts, if they helped us the Taliban would punish them later. We couldn't be there to protect them, and the Taliban kill, literally cut the necks off of anyone who talks with foreigners or helps them. They have no tolerance or mercy. At one village meeting, a man got up, like a representative, and spoke and encouraged the other villagers to help us, to not let the Taliban use their village to plant mines. That very night they found him. They cut his head off. He wasn't young, maybe thirty years old.

The disembodied voice Matin thought I would fear over the telephone is here the voice of address, the attempt to speak to and on behalf of others, and then, by that same evening, a headless body incapable of future speech. Perhaps there is nothing more vivid than a beheading to illustrate the rupture of the real, and while it recounts for us one of the key presuppositions of counterinsurgency, that Afghans live in an intractable, acephalous society, the scene of the *jirga* realizes that representation in literal form; it transforms the idiom of territorial and organizational difference, and of asymmetric warfare, into the redoubling of revenge and lack. We know from Matin that by this point it was impossible to tell who was planting which mine, and that the nature of one anticipatory ambush attack for another resulted in an atmosphere of chaotic confusion and limited access to the closest town, and therefore a sense that nobody could quite escape the village where they were all in deadly proximity. I imagine they felt strange and yet intimate with one another.

The young man was in fact very young, and he was beheaded because he spoke on behalf of another double bind. In this context, to allow a convoy to officially stay the night was to not only appear to collaborate with the foreigners but, more crucially, to accede to the force of ambush-style attacks as the condition for entry into rural villages and therefore as the basis for holding that ground (as opposed to being entrapped in it). In a sense, the young man was beheaded to communicate that nobody else should dare communicate on behalf of such a state of affairs. He was beheaded for bringing into language the reality of a situation in which nobody could protect or trust one another, and a state of affairs that the locals and foreigners shared with no end in sight, and thus a state too early to put into language or a fixed representation. There was only a general sense of what was transpiring, and to speak on its behalf was to make it more real than anyone could bear.

On another afternoon, in a remote village, there was another *jirga*. Again, representatives of both sides came to speak to each other. Matin describes it as a particularly dangerous place, where combat was fierce, and that the locals had gathered in an open field to be addressed by Matin and his unit. Taliban fighters had cordoned off the village. The level of tension was high, and nobody was quite in control of the exchange of words or the situation. Matin addressed the Afghans and asked for a night of safe rest in the village for the entire convoy, and as a gesture of goodwill offered to play a game of soccer. Some of the village men asked Matin, "What is a soccer ball?" Matin was stunned. He demonstrated by putting together a bunch of scrunched up plastic bags. They tried to play that way, and the local men fumbled and fell; Matin recalls the comical scene: grown men tripping like children.

The soldiers pulled out their smartphones and began to take pictures and video. They laughed at the scene unfolding before them and archived it for future amusement. Matin felt very uncomfortable, and the horror he intuited was realized the next day when his unit rode over a massive roadside bomb on the side of the same field they used for the game. They hadn't checked for mines because they assumed that even through the laughter, or perhaps owing to it, even though it was never

515

shared, that a bond was forged nonetheless. They were confused, in a way they could not permit Afghans to be, and they were also dead wrong.

> They were crying, the ones who survived, one man was crying a lot, and would ask "how could they do this? We just played a game of soccer with them yesterday and today they tried to kill us all." I said to him, "take out your phone." I showed him the pictures and videos he had taken. He was completely unaware of how offensive that had been, how murderous offending someone can be around here. He still didn't understand. "Why would they kill us for taking pictures?" I had to explain: "You played music, you made fun, you turned them into entertainment and they did that in response. You have to respect them." They listened to me after that, I told them not to walk around without their shirts off or go swimming in their underwear, which they used to do regularly. They only learned to listen to me after something this violent occurred. Otherwise they were deaf.

The nature of playing a game in this place was misunderstood in the same way that the nature of speaking out was misunderstood in the first *jirga*. The defeat that photography and laughter was to preserve, a form of capture James Siegel (2009: 60) describes in colonial Indonesia not as "a tool for the preservation of a culture, but a technological device devoted to its defeat and to the recording of the remnants of that defeat," becomes the scene of another game. This game is one of refusal and destruction. It is a game in which there could be no recording and no shared laugh but only the violence intensified by proximity to the *jouissance* of laughter. But unlike the outcome of the first *jirga*, this was a severance in keeping with the photographic form, the kind of severance Marilyn Ivy (2009: 828) tells us "severs the moment as event"; by severing the real and continuity of signs, it "incites desire to bring something unapproachable closer . . . the photograph 'transcends' time and space as it feverishly circulates, without origin and without final destination." So too, we might say, does the laugh of the invader. Refusing its own origin, the laughter instead becomes about exchange and death. Matin is the only person in his unit who now seems to understand this. He understands that the atmosphere has become impossible to mitigate, that no translation will suffice to make it clearer, to make the foreigners less "deaf" to the reality of the lifeworld they have structured along the fatal divide between play and annihilation.

By way of concluding I'd like to consider a final story about exchange. Matin was hiding in what he describes as the thick of the jungle, close to the agricultural town of Marjah, in Helmand Province. A group of Taliban fighters were hiding there too, and their bodies and weapons were in deadly proximity. The Taliban fighters would come out at night. Matin says they were "stealthy and sneaky," and they came out to plant roadside mines. They didn't realize Matin and his unit put surveillance cameras in the trees, and so they walked through some ponds, Matin describes, some marshland, and on land. There were only two homes in the vicinity, and Matin, who wore real camouflage during these missions, befriended one of the owners. The owner was an elderly man. In return for his friendship and goodwill Matin promised to protect him from any retaliatory violence. He couldn't bear another fatal outcome like the young man who spoke in the *jirga* and was beheaded. One night, Taliban fighters snuck into the old man's backyard and planted an explosive mine inside an old can of cooking oil. They fled afterward. Unbeknownst to them, the man would typically stay up all night long and guard his own home. He saw everything that transpired, and the next day he went to see Matin, or as he calls him, "Mr. Translator."

"Hi, Mr. Translator. I brought you something." Matin immediately took the oil can in his hands, mistaking it for cooking oil, or the gift of homemade food.

"What is it?" Matin asked.

"Oh. It's a mine."

Matin said he almost collapsed on the spot, but the old man spoke some more: "Don't worry. I removed the battery, don't worry," he said.

Matin alerted the military personnel and they immediately came out to examine it. The old man kept repeating: "Relax I removed the battery. It doesn't work. Relax. I removed the battery it will not go off."

By this point, the man's fingerprints were all over the device, and Matin, knowing how readily accusations were made against locals on the basis of biometric evidence, didn't want him questioned or biometrically enrolled. The biometric system used in Afghanistan is called the Handheld Interagency Identity Detection System, and many men in rural areas are routinely "enrolled" (as they are in Kabul when they seek employment on military bases). Enrollment means having your fingerprints and iris scan entered in the system. It produces the potential for complicated scenarios; for example, if someone handles a piece of scrap metal before it is used by someone else to construct an improvised explosive, their fingerprints might still be on it, and if after testing the explosive the fingerprint matches someone in the system, who may have been entered after obtaining a job on a military base, they can easily be accused of both constructing the device and gaining entry into the base to plan an insider attack. Matin understands all of these possibilities. Thus, fearing that the enrollment would likely result in the man's interrogation, possible torture, or even deportation to Guantanamo Bay, Matin struck a deal with all sides instead. They would go back to the man's backyard and bury the mine again. They would replant it and watch the house until the original perpetrators returned to take back what was left of it in the event of explosion (and thereby remove their own fingerprints from the scraps and scene of the crime). Matin planted the mine, and after a day, when the perpetrator-strangers did not arrive, went back and unearthed it himself. He spared his friend any further involvement. In the south of the country, he said, "people do support the Taliban, and I was very afraid. They demand your respect, and if you show it to them, they are kind."

To end here is not to say the final word is "kind." It is ironic that the planting is a substitute for the structures of recognition and speaking on behalf of others that have come undone in this agricultural place, and that amidst the proliferation of false representations, it is the human capacity and gaze (certainly not the camera's) that discerns this falsity for what it is: an opportunity to rescue others from the violence of literalism. But to accede to the possibility of exchange in the aftermath of translation's failure, and the violence of total war, is to still reckon with the empty places where victims stood to speak, where the improvised mine, first mistaken as a gift, did not detonate. It is to traverse, as I've attempted, across transcripts and places of ambush and disguise, the cornfield and the destruction of agricultural land, the fields where men were beheaded, inside the tenuous link between the translated phrase and maddening dreamwork of local dialect, and finally in the closing of the heart (the *tangi*, or tightness) that becomes the predicament between languages. But alongside these spaces there is perhaps one more, one that requires the opening Matin and Mahmud desire as the compensation for their survival, not to attest to the force of translation but to witness the catching on fire of dialogue in the place otherwise left unoccupied.

References

Anderson, Benedict. (1983) 1991. *Imagined Communities*. London: Verso Books.
Arendt, Hannah. 1968. *The Origins of Totalitarianism*. New York: Harcourt.
Barthes, Roland. 1977. *Image-Music-Text*. New York: Hill and Wang.
BBC News. 2019. "Mapping Operation Panther's Claw." news.bbc.co.uk/2/hi/uk
   _news/8172556.stm (accessed February 18, 2019).

Benjamin, Walter. (1955) 1968. "The Task of the Translator." In *Illuminations*, edited by Hannah Arendt and translated by Harry Zohn, 69–82. New York: Schocken Books.

Boas, Franz. 1889. "On Alternating Sounds." *American Anthropologist* A2, no. 1 (January): 47–54.

Carruthers, Andrew M. 2019. "Policing Intensity." *Public Culture* 31, no. 3: 469–496.

De La Cadena, Marisol. 2015. *Earth Beings: Ecologies of Practice across Andean Worlds*. Durham, NC: Duke University Press.

Derrida, Jacques. 1997. *Writing and Difference*, edited and translated by Alan Bass. Chicago: University of Chicago Press.

Dolar, Mladen. 2006. *A Voice and Nothing More*. Cambridge, MA: The MIT Press.

Favret-Saada, Jeanne. (1980) 2010. *Deadly Words: Witchcraft in the Bocage*. Cambridge: Cambridge University Press.

Freud, Sigmund. (1915) 2005. "Timely Reflections on War and Death." In *On Murder, Mourning and Melancholia*, edited by Adam Philips and translated by Shaun Whiteside, 167–194. London: Penguin Books.

Ginzburg, Carlo. 1994. "Killing a Chinese Mandarin: The Moral Implications of Distance." *Critical Inquiry* 21, no. 1: 44–60.

Giordano, Cristiana. 2014. *Migrants in Translation: Caring and the Logics of Difference in Contemporary Italy*. Oakland: University of California Press.

Ibn Khaldûn. (1967) 1970. *The Muqaddimah: An Introduction to History*, translated by Franz Rosenthal, edited by N. J. Dawood. Princeton, NJ: Princeton University Press.

Ivy, Marilyn. 1995. *Discourses of the Vanishing*. Chicago: University of Chicago Press.

Ivy, Marilyn. 2009. "Dark Enlightenment: Naitō Masatoshi's Flash." In *Photographies East: The Camera and Its Histories in East and South-East Asia*, edited by Rosalind C. Morris, 229–57. Durham, NC: Duke University Press.

Levi, Primo. 1988. *The Drowned and the Saved*, translated by Raymond Rosenthal. New York: Summit Books.

Morris, Rosalind C. 2004. "Images of Untranslatability in the US War on Terror." *Interventions: International Journal of Postcolonial Studies* 6, no. 3: 401–23.

Morris, Rosalind C. 2016. "Dialect and Dialectic in 'The Working Day' of Marx's *Capital*." *boundary 2* 43, no. 1: 219–48.

Pandolfo, Stefania. 2018. *Knot of the Soul: Madness, Psychoanalysis, Islam*. Chicago: University of Chicago Press.

Pandolfo, Stefania. 2008. "Testimony in Counterpoint: Psychiatric Fragments in the Aftermath of Culture." *Qui Parle* 17, no. 1: 63–123.

Rafael, Vicente. 1993. *Contracting Colonialism: Translation and Christian Conversion in Tagalog Society under Early Spanish Rule*. Durham, NC: Duke University Press.

Siegel, James T. 2006. *Naming the Witch*. Stanford, CA: Stanford University Press.

Siegel, James T. 2009. "The Curse of the Photograph: Atjeh 1901." In *Photographies East: The Camera and Its Histories in East and South-East Asia*, edited by Rosalind C. Morris, 57–78. Durham, NC: Duke University Press.

Simmel, Georg. (1950) 1964. *The Sociology of Georg Simmel*, translated and edited by Kurt H. Wolff. Glencoe, IL: The Free Press.

Taussig, Michael. 1987. *Shamanism, Colonialism, and the Wild Man: A Study in Terror and Healing*. Chicago: University of Chicago Press.

Fatima Mojaddedi is an assistant professor of anthropology at the University of California, Davis, and obtained her PhD from Columbia University. Her research is based in Afghanistan where she considers questions of modernity and language; theories of subjectivity, memory, and the cultural unconscious; as well as archival histories of empire and economy.

James Baldwin and the Anti-Black Force of Law: On Excessive Violence and Exceeding Violence

Jesse A. Goldberg

*I think that one thing that remains constant for me is that the
system—the prison industrial complex—isn't broken. The
system of mass criminalization we have isn't the result of
failure. Thinking in this way allows me to look at what's going
on right now in a clear-eyed way. I understand that white
supremacy is maintained and reproduced through the criminal
punishment apparatus.*
—Mariame Kaba, "Towards the Horizon of Abolition:
A Conversation with Mariame Kaba," interview

*I do not claim that everyone in prison here is innocent, but
I do claim that the law, as it operates, is guilty, and that the
prisoners, therefore, are all unjustly imprisoned. . . . Does
the law exist for the purpose of furthering the ambitions of
those who have sworn to uphold the law, or is it seriously
to be considered as a moral, unifying force, the health and
strength of a nation? . . . Well, if one really wishes to know how
justice is administered in a country, one does not question the
policemen, the lawyers, the judges, or the protected members*

This essay was catalyzed by the teaching of Grant Farred and Dagmawi Woubshet and the organizing of Decarcerate Tompkins County. I also thank my fellow contributors to this special issue—
especially Michelle Velasquez-Potts and Graham Denyer Willis—as well as Madiha Tahir, for their
invaluable comments on this article.

Copyright 2019 by Duke University Press

of the middle class. One goes to the unprotected—those, precisely, who need the law's protection most!—and listens to their testimony. Ask any Mexican, any Puerto Rican, any black man, any poor person—ask the wretched how they fare in the halls of justice, and then you will know, not whether or not the country is just, but whether or not it has any love for justice, or any concept of it.

—James Baldwin, "No Name in the Street"

It has become a refrain in abolitionist activism that, as Mariame Kaba (2017) argues, events marked by apparently excessive violence (such as the killing of an unarmed person by police or the abuse of incarcerated people by correctional officers) or seemingly obvious miscarriages of "justice" (such as the nonindictment of a police officer caught on camera choking an unarmed and nonresistant man to death) are not aberrations of the so-called criminal justice system but in fact register the system working as it is constructed to work. For some thinkers and organizers, such a diagnosis is too pessimistic insofar as it forecloses the possibility that the problems of racism, classism, ableism, queer antagonism, and sexism that abound in carceral institutions and practices can be solved by reforming those institutions and improving those practices.

In this essay, I lean into rather than away from this pessimism to think alongside James Baldwin. There has been recent resurgent attention to Baldwin as academics, public intellectuals, filmmakers, and curators engage with his work through the lens of the Movement for Black Lives. Continuing this turn, I read Baldwin as a theorist of the law and, ultimately, an abolitionist. By reading "The Fire Next Time" (1963) and "No Name in the Street" (1972) through a theoretical framework (primarily) formed by Saidiya Hartman, Jacques Derrida, Alexander Weheliye, and Christina Sharpe, I argue that policing in the United States is inherently organized by a(n) (il)logic of anti-Blackness that necessitates racist violence as a structural component of its practice. This pessimistic diagnosis is then extended through Baldwin's own theorizing on the Black Panthers' conception of "self-defense" to illustrate that while policing in the United States can never not be excessive in its racist violence, the Black subjectivity that would seemingly be obliterated by this excessive force of law ultimately exceeds the reach of the policeman's club or bullet, without losing sight of the bodies left in those weapons' wake.

Black Studies as Critical Legal Studies

The work this essay seeks to do in mining Baldwin's interrogations of law, police, and prisons is and has been the work of the field of Black studies at large for decades. This brief initial section will thus outline work by a small number of theorists key to my particular argument and how it will frame my reading of Baldwin. There are two currents of this framework. On one side, Hartman and Baldwin supplement the caesura in Derrida's articulation of "the force of law" by outlining how Black subjectivity within the law is formed through excessive violence. On the other side, Weheliye and Sharpe highlight that though Black subjectivity is formed by and through violence, Blackness simultaneously exceeds violence. These two strands of thought converge in the abolitionist impulse of Baldwin's work.

In *Scenes of Subjection: Terror, Slavery, and Self-Making in Nineteenth-Century America* (1997), Hartman argues that the Black subject comes into existence as the object of the law's violence without ever being subject to the law's protection. For her, "attempts to assert absolutist distinctions between slavery and freedom are untenable," both in terms of conceptual coherence and historical event (13). That is, the "freedom" granted by law to its subjects is inseparable from the violence of slavery, and so maintaining law's order conceptually entails the maintenance of the violence structuring the Black subject as non-Human. As a matter of historical fact, Hartman's work thus focuses on how the institution of policing emerges out of the institution of slavery, which she traces as "the shift from the 'power of police' all whites exercised over slaves to the supreme police power exercised by the state, and what occurred in its wake was the banishing of Blacks from public society" (170).

This insight supplements Derrida's argument in "Force of Law: The Mystical Foundations of Authority" (1990). Here Derrida thinks with Walter Benjamin's "Critique of Violence" (1921) in distinguishing between justice and law, characterizing the former as "undeconstructable" and the latter as inseparable from violence or "force." For Derrida, there is no law without enforceability, and enforceability denotes the use of violence. He thus spends much of his energy in "Force of Law" considering the im/possibility of a distinction between the violence that inaugurates the law and the violence that maintains the law while asking if it is possible to separate "just" or "legitimate" force from "unjust" force. While Derrida briefly mentions the police as the physical instantiation of the force of law, Hartman—and ultimately even more clearly, I argue, Baldwin—flesh out what is only thinly theorized by Derrida's otherwise generative abstraction. Namely,

Hartman and Baldwin name the object of the law's violence that goes unnamed in Derrida's essay: the Black subject.

In *Habeas Viscus: Racializing Assemblages, Biopolitics, and Black Feminist Theories of the Human* (2014), Weheliye draws on the work of Hortense Spillers and Sylvia Wynter to critique Michel Foucault and Giorgio Agamben's theorizations of bare life, social death, and biopolitics. In doing so, Weheliye recognizes that "the legal conception of personhood comes with a steep price" (78) but moves from habeas corpus to *habeas viscus* to underscore that "the flesh is nothing less than the ethereal social (afterlife) of bare existence" (72). In short, the law's violence both marks the bare life of racialized assemblages such as the Black subject *and* is exceeded by a "fleshy surplus" through which alternative genres of the Human are practiced beyond the law's force. Similarly, in *In the Wake: On Blackness and Being* (2016), Sharpe invokes the term *wake* through multiple registers, implying genres of mourning the dead as much as the after flows of a ship through water and the process of awakening to consciousness. She writes, "To be in the wake is to live in those no's, to live in the no-space that the law is not bound to respect, to live in no citizenship, to live in the long time of Dred and Harriet Scott; and it is more than that. . . . To be in the wake is also to recognize the ways that we [Black people] are constituted through and by continued vulnerability to overwhelming force though not *only* known to ourselves and each other *by* that force" (16). That is, Blackness is undoubtedly characterized through a precarious proximity to death, but Black subjects are not reducible to that vulnerability.

So the framework is as follows: law's violence exceeds the capacity for justice insofar as anti-Blackness is its condition of possibility (Derrida and Hartman). Black being, even as the object of law's excessive violence, proceeds to exceed that violence (Weheliye and Sharpe). This doubleness is at the heart of Baldwin's theorizations of the law.

(Anti-)Blackness as the Law's Condition of Possibility

In "The Fire Next Time," Baldwin meditates on the position of Black Americans, whom he calls American Negroes, in contrast to Black Africans. Baldwin ([1963] 1998: 335) insists that the American Negro is a particular construct existing only in the United States: "I am, then, both visibly and legally the descendant of slaves in a white Protestant country, and this is what it means to be an American Negro, this is who he is—a kidnapped pagan, who was sold like an animal and treated like one, who was once defined by the American Constitution as 'three-fifths' of a man, and who, according to the Dred Scott decision, had no rights that a white man was bound to respect."

The historical content in this sentence is probably familiar to most critical students of American history: Africans were brought to America mostly as enslaved chattel; colonial law evolved from the early 1600s to further solidify the construct of race throughout the seventeenth century, eventually basing the condition of enslavability on the criterion of legible Blackness in the eighteenth century; then US law was inaugurated to continue the propagation of slavery as an institution that reduced enslaved people to the status of property, a paradox of which gets articulated in the often celebrated "three-fifths compromise." And eventually, the law sutured Blackness so tightly to enslavement through a legal framework that privileged property rights over civil rights that even African Americans who found themselves on land where slavery was illegal could still be claimed as property because whites were not bound to respect the rights of Black people. The law of slavery is what gives the Negro his existence as a recognizable piece of the US political structure, and so in the case of Blackness, race is produced by law.[1]

If we take seriously the intermingling of Baldwin's recollection of his "prolonged religious crisis" with his recollection of interactions with police officers describable only in terms of verbal and physical violence, Blackness emerges as an identifying marker of the American Negro produced not only by the law as a set of rules but also by the law as violence. This is because Baldwin does not write about the law in the abstract or even as a matter of textuality; he writes about being cursed at, frisked, thrown to the ground, whipped, and secreted into precinct basements by police officers. Baldwin knows the law through bodily contact.

Throughout "The Fire Next Time," Baldwin assumes the role of a witness giving testimony before the law. He recalls having "seen men dragged from this very corner" by police, who dispersed crowds "with clubs or on horseback" (314); he writes of having "been carried into precinct basements often enough" (317); he

1. This paragraph is attempting to do the work that entire other books do. One such book would be *Scenes of Subjection*, which I would argue deserves to be read as a legal history as much as a piece of critical theory or literary and cultural analysis. A small sample of other relevant works include Edward Baptist's *The Half Has Never Been Told* (2014), Sarah Haley's *No Mercy Here: Gender, Punishment, and the Making of Jim Crow Modernity* (2016), Douglas A. Blackmon's *Slavery by Another Name: The Re-enslavement of Black Americans from the Civil War to World War II* (2009), Ibram X. Kendi's *Stamped from the Beginning: The Definitive History of Racist Ideas in America* (2016), Stephanie Smallwood's *Saltwater Slavery: A Middle Passage from Africa to American Diaspora* (2008), Khalil G. Muhammad's *Condemnation of Blackness: Race, Crime, and the Making of Modern Urban America* (2011), and Edmund S. Morgan's *American Slavery, American Freedom* (2003).

remembers being thirteen years old and hearing a police officer, on passing him in the street, complain about "niggers" not staying uptown, as well as "two police-men amus[ing] themselves with me by frisking me, making comic (and terrifying) speculations concerning my ancestry and probable sexual prowess, and for good measure, leaving me flat on my back in one of Harlem's empty lots" when he was just ten years old (298). And so when he reflects that "it was absolutely clear that the police would whip you and take you in as long as they could get away with it" (299), such a conclusion about the function of the law as a race-producing force is reached by claiming the veracity of embodied experience.

Generalization from embodied experience is an interpretive tool for under-standing the functions of law, as the broad field of legal scholarship known as criti-cal race theory has established. In her article, "Looking to the Bottom: Critical Legal Studies and Reparations," Mari Matsuda ([1987] 1995: 63) writes, "What is suggested here is not abstract consideration of the position of the least advan-taged. . . . Instead we must look to what Gramsci called 'organic intellectuals,' grassroots philosophers who are uniquely able to relate theory to the concrete experiences of oppression." Matsuda's point is that we can learn as much about the phenomenology of law from reading Frederick Douglass as we can from Oliver Wendell Holmes. And while her initial statements suggest that organic intellectu-als like Douglass merely relate theory to experience, as her argument develops she points to one way in which this testimony from the bottom opens new conceptual ground by theorizing in the seemingly uncrossable lacuna of critical legal studies. Matsuda asks, "How could anyone believe both of the following statements? (1) I have a right to participate equally in society with any other person; (2) Rights are whatever those in power say they are. One of the primary lessons [critical legal studies] can learn from the experience of the bottom is that one can believe both of those statements simultaneously, and that it may well be necessary to do so" (65). Looking to the bottom opens the theorization of the "both/and" demanded by the politics of deconstruction: the insistence on deconstructing law while believing that "justice in itself, if such a thing exists, outside or beyond law, is not decon-structable" (Derrida 1990: 945).

In every stroke of his pen, Baldwin is theorizing in this difficult both/and. We see this in "The Fire Next Time" as he holds on to both the assertion that "there is absolutely no reason to suppose that white people are better equipped to frame the laws by which I am to be governed than I am" (342) and the diagnosis that "there is simply no possibility of a real change in the Negro's situation without the most radical and far-reaching changes in the American political and social structure" (335). The first assertion is a demand to be included in the representative mechanism of the United States' democratic republic, while the second is a demand to rethink the very foundation of that republic. Baldwin is not contradicting himself. He does not believe that America as it was at the time was capable of making Black freedom truly possible, since America's condition of possibility was and is Black unfreedom. At the same time, Baldwin absolutely believes in his and any Black person's right to shape the laws that govern the United States. The law may not be able to deliver justice, but that does not mean Baldwin gives up on the possibility. And this is not a mere hypothetical or theoretical exercise for him.

To repeat, Baldwin theorizes this both/and through his abstraction vis-à-vis his embodied experience. Haptically knowing the police is a way for knowing the law, and insofar as the police are the embodiment of the law, Baldwin's knowledge of the law comes through violence. And philosophically, in the text of "The Fire Next Time," Blackness comes to know itself as produced by the law through violence. In this way, Baldwin severs the term *law* from the term *justice*, as any account of race and law in the United States must do.

But Baldwin refuses to only sever; he also sutures. In separating law from justice, he also attaches the former to the phenomenon of violence through the police officer's enforcement and the lived conditions of those he calls Negroes. "The Fire Next Time" thus highlights what would become a central question for Derrida in "Force of Law." In his extended essay, Derrida (1990: 925) occupies himself with thinking the seemingly simple truism that "there is no such thing as law that doesn't imply *in itself, a priori, in the analytic structure of its concept*, the possibility of being 'enforced,' applied by force." That is, the law means nothing if there is no capacity for making sure people follow what it says. The law can function only if it has as part of its structure the capacity to inflict violence. On a different register, Hartman (1997: 205) extends this through her analysis of police power, violence, the state, and the social as "the law's excess."[2] For Hartman, as with Baldwin, the law is that which maintains social order using force. On the one hand this sounds like a radical indictment of the law and its officers, but on the other hand it is basic social contract theory.

Without spending the time to close-read Locke, Hobbes, or Rousseau, or even John Rawls or Charles Mills or Carole Pateman—a worthy task that is beyond the scope of my present essay—one essential strand of mainstream social contract theory has been the state's monopoly on violence. Basically, citizens agree to cede their claims on means of violence to the state to be used to maintain order.

2. See chap. 6, "Instinct and Injury: Bodily Integrity, Natural Affinities, and the Constitution of Equality" in *Scenes* for an elaboration of the policing-state-violence-social nexus.

Put simply, I give up my right to bash your skull in for stealing my property in exchange to the police so that they can physically restrain (and injure and kill) people engaged in "criminal" activity as a way of preventing innocent folks from being harmed. So, the state has a monopoly on violence embodied by the police. The police patrol the borders of the law. Inside these borders are those who are members of the body politic, the citizens who have agreed on the social contract and are thus protected by it in the form of the violence of the law as embodied and performed by the police. Should any person break the social contract, they remove themselves to the outside of the law's protection from violence.[3] Once on the outside, they are subject to the (legal) violence of the police because they are beyond the law's protection.

Hartman observes that Black people in the United States are both inside and outside the law.[4] They are within the vision of the law as potential criminals subject to the law's punishments, but they are outside the law's reach of protection insofar as they are not counted as fully Human citizens that merit protection from violence. And so, extralegal violence against Black bodies is made legal in the sense that violence against a body outside the boundaries of the law, especially when enacted on a presumed criminal—and as Hartman (1997: 189) writes, "the slippage between being Black and a felon is quite remarkable in this punitive ontology of race"—is the legal violence of policing.

Here we have an account of the law's magic—the transubstantiation of extralegal violence into that which is necessary to maintain order. The policeman's badge—like the slave catcher's badge when he was operating in a Northern city after the Fugitive Slave Act—casts a spell that makes an illegal chokehold a mechanism of justice. It has always already been permissible, according to this account of American law, to violently attack Black subjects.

After invoking without fully unpacking this aspect of social contract theory, Derrida (1990: 927) asks, "What difference is there between, on the one hand, the force that can be just, or in any case deemed legitimate . . . and on the other hand the violence that one always deems unjust?" Derrida asks these questions in arguing that law comes into existence through a founding violence, and that this found-

3. This is of course more complicated because of the ways in which suspected criminals are guaranteed due process. Of course, convicted criminals then have rights and freedom of movement taken away, so on conviction this model of the criminal outside the boundaries of protection does seem to hold in the form of "civil death," about which Colin Dayan writes in *The Law Is a White Dog* (2011).

4. Hartman sustains this argument throughout her book, but to see it particularly lucidly illustrated, see the chapter "Seduction and the Ruses of Power," especially the opening and the section titled "The Violence of the Law."

ing violence is indistinguishable from the violence it requires of itself to enact in order to sustain its very existence. That is, the structural violence of the law inaugurated by the social contract is both that which births law as the "ordering" force of society and that which sustains law as the fabric keeping us all together.

It is at this point in "Force of Law" that it becomes most apparent why we ought to include Derrida in this constellation of thinkers through which we can read Baldwin on law. After all, the tension of indistinguishability between the "legitimate" force of law and the force "one always deems unjust," and the indistinguishability between the law's founding violence and its sustaining violence, are most apparent in the very structuring terms of Baldwin's thinking—the police. "But what today bears witness in an even more 'spectral' way in mixing the two forms of violence," Derrida (1990: 1005) writes, "*is the modern institution of the police*" (my emphasis).

Thinking Hartman and Derrida alongside Baldwin as a way of occupying what Matsuda identifies as the apparent lacuna of critical legal studies[5] engages the reasoning behind Baldwin's fundamental skepticism of the law. Black studies scholars like Hartman, Sharpe, Weheliye, Spillers, Wynter, Jared Sexton, Calvin Warren, and Fred Moten have been and are thinking in this gap between law's monopoly on violence and actual embodied conditions of possibility of the social contract written in the blood of Black people. They are seeking analyses of how the Black subject comes into being as the ground on which the law is erected while also exceeding and escaping the reach of the law.[6]

As already mentioned, even as he does so by way of everyday embodied experience, Baldwin theorizes the Negro as a conceptual figure brought into existence by the law through the violence of slavery. So when Baldwin claims "the Negro" as the figure that best describes his own existence in the mid-twentieth century, he is claiming a figure haunted by the pejorative contained in the capitalized letter *N* that begins its name and can never let go of the founding violence of the law. Thus, for Baldwin, no matter what the law does to claim a change in the position of the

---

5. This lacuna is admittedly less glaring today than it was when Matsuda first published "Looking to the Bottom."

6. Not that all Black studies scholars would agree, of course. Moten and Sharpe, for example, would certainly insist, in different ways, by different means, and to different degrees, that Blackness exceeds or escapes the reach of the law. For Moten Blackness indexes a kind of "fugitivity" even as white supremacy remains. On the other hand, Warren would insist that the question of escaping the law is nonsensical, since escaping is something a subject does, and there is no Black subject because Blackness has no ontological ground on which to assert axiological value. See Moten 2013, Sharpe 2016, and Warren 2018.

Negro, it is impossible to construct a "postslavery" Negro or a "post–civil rights" Negro. In Sharpe's (2016: 21) words, "the semiotics of the slave ship continue" in "the reappearances of the slave ship in everyday life in the form of the prison, the camp, and the school." The barrier that the law would erect between the founding violence of law that brings the Negro into existence as thing and the continued violence of law in the present that treats the Negro as object is revealed to be full of holes by the very concept the law inaugurates.

So if the construct of the Negro is produced through law, and the law is produced and maintained through violence, then the construct of the Negro is produced and maintained through violence. But Baldwin's insight is in the mutual imbrications and coconstitutive relationship of these inextricable concepts. Rather, if violence becomes the inaugurating condition of the law, then Blackness becomes a constituting force of law. He is anticipating Sexton (2011: 36), as, indeed, "the law is dependent on what it polices."

To return to Baldwin's pronouncement that to be a Negro in America is to be the descendant of enslaved Black people defined as property, as non-Human, as "flesh" in Spillers's (1987) words, and as not possessing rights that white people are bound to respect, to be a Negro in America, then, is to be a product of the law and the object against which the force of law acts in maintaining the law's very enforceability and therefore its very existence. Blackness thus does not merely exist in relation to law as that which is outside it and therefore oppressed by it, but Blackness is inscribed in the law as that other which receives the violence meted out by police that ensures the law's possibility. Thus to extricate Blackness from law is to tear apart the fabric of law—and, if we follow Hartman, the entire social world, and, if we follow Weheliye as we will below, the entire category of the Human as Man—itself.

Anti-Blackness as Both/Neither Legal and/nor Extralegal

Even after the signing of the Civil Rights and Voting Rights Acts and the immediate signs that such legislation is ultimately inadequate, Baldwin continues to write about the law, perhaps most directly in "No Name in the Street," an essay that began as a meditation on the lives and deaths of Martin Luther King, Jr., and Malcolm X. In this essay, the fact that the law is violence—made material in the form of police and prisons—becomes a given for Baldwin and thus no longer a point that needs to be argued but a point from which to argue.

Baldwin argues that the demarcation between that which is and those whom are inside and outside the law is based in appearance alone. This has two valences:

on one level, this means that actions that are supposedly within the scope of the law are not substantively different from actions ostensibly prohibited by the law; and on another level, this means that individuals who are supposedly embodiments of the law—that is, the police—are actually different from those who ostensibly embody the law's limits—that is, criminals—only in appearance, not in substance. In Baldwin's ([1972] 1998: 452) words, "It means nothing therefore, to say to so thoroughly insulated a people [as white and privileged Americans] that the forces of crime and the forces of law and order work hand in hand in the ghetto, bleeding it day and night. It means nothing to say that, in the eyes of the Black and the poor certainly, *the principle distinction between a policeman and a criminal is to be found in their attire*" (my emphasis). This emphasis on attire pushes Baldwin's argument beyond a simple (and still important) assertion that the justice system is racist by exploding the difference that defines justice in terms of legality.

The argument of "No Name in the Street" begins in France. In recalling the atmosphere in Paris during the early years of the Algerian War, Baldwin describes the precarity faced by anyone in Paris "who was not, resoundingly, from the north of Europe" when hailed by the Paris police officer (375). In one scene, Baldwin describes "two young Italians" who, "speeding merrily along on their Vespa, . . . failed to respond to a policeman's order to halt, whereupon the policeman fired, and [their] holiday came to a bloody end" (376). While this brief account lacks the venom of the passage in which Baldwin differentiates between the cop and the criminal based solely on appearance, it is appearance that emerges as the marker of the law in this (ocularcentric) earlier moment in "No Name."

Within the shades of whiteness that are visible in Europe, Italians can be identified against the French by perhaps being marked by a slightly darker, more Mediterranean hue. The policeman's visibility, in contrast, comes not through an ethnic identity readable in his skin color—during a time when skin color could ostensibly differentiate between enemies on opposite sides of a colonial war—but instead from his attire. He is dressed in the garb of the state and armed with the instrument of its monopoly on violence. The policeman is the embodiment of the (colonial) law, and the Italians embody the shades of the (colonized) criminals who exist outside that law in their failure to heed the law's hailing. Even though they are Italian and not Algerian, in appearance the darker-skinned Italians can be read by the eyes of the law as outside its arm of protection. In this French-Italian example, the borders of the law fall along national borders, highlighting what was perhaps only implicit in "The Fire Next Time." If the police are the embodiments of the violence that is the force of law (Baldwin and Derrida), and if the force of law is that which secretes the social as law's excess by enforcing a defined order on the people of a state (Baldwin and Hartman),[7] then Baldwin's analysis of the violence of policing is also an analysis of the violence of the liberal nation-state itself. Policing operates on anti-Black logic, and the nation-state is an anti-Black project.

It is important that this moment come early in Baldwin's essay, for it establishes the stakes of what is to come. What happens when legal agents of the state are granted the authority and means—the power—to end life? This question is given frightening inflection when brought back across the Atlantic Ocean to the United States, where the context of assumed inherent criminality shifts from colonial war to the specificity of anti-Blackness.

At one point, Baldwin recalls an encounter he had with "one of the most powerful men in one of the states [he] visited" (390). We don't learn exactly what this person's official position was, though it is not hard to imagine him as a senator, representative, governor, or other kind of government official. While the scene serves mainly as an occasion for Baldwin to offer complex meditations on power, sex, sexuality, and love, there is also an important moment when the mortal threat of policing rears its head: "This man, with a phone call, could prevent or provoke a lynching" (390). We don't know for sure if this man is indeed an employee of the state, but we do know that lynching can be interpreted as a kind of policing. And yet, it is definitively an extralegal means of policing, supposedly outside the realms of the law. But there is a possibility that this man could be a worker of the very law that precludes lynching from the legal means of its own enforcement. Thus Baldwin gives us two different forms of violence—legal, such as when a police officer shoots those who do not obey his hail, and extralegal, such as when a person is lynched—and brings them into a common space for interpretation.[8]

There is a literal common space for interpreting legal and extralegal vio-

7. From page 199 of Hartman's (1997) *Scenes*: "As Pasquale Pasquino notes, the exercise of police power constitutes the population as its object. The science of police constitutes and fashions the social body. The limitlessness or amorousness of this power, which is one of its defining characteristics, is evidenced in 'the plethora of petty details and minor consequences.' Key in thinking about the enactment of withholding by the state is Pasquino's observation that police powers are 'sort of spontaneous creations of law or rather of a demand for order which outreaches the law'. . . . What I am trying to detail here is the inventiveness of the law, the ambiguity that shrouds what is within and without the reach of the law, and the excess of the law and that which is in excess of the law."

8. For more on the distinction between legal and extralegal violence in terms of lynching and policing, see Bryan Wagner's *Disturbing the Peace: Black Culture and the Police Power after Slavery* and Jacqueline Goldsby's *Spectacular Secret: Lynching in American Life and Literature*. I have also written on this distinction regarding stop-and-frisk policing practices, racial profiling, and the history of lynching in a special issue of *CLA Journal* (Goldberg 2016).

lence within the geography of Baldwin's essay, and that is the American South itself; more specifically, it is the Jim Crow–segregated restaurant into which he accidently enters through the wrong door. He fails to be hailed correctly by the entrance signs. Like the case of the police officer's uniform, the law enters Baldwin's text in the form of a dressing, this time an ornament of a business establishment, and the danger of (extra)legal violence is presented when a Black person fails to heed the hailing of this instantiation of the law. In failing to be hailed, however, Baldwin enacts a mode of being in excess of the law precisely as his flesh is threatened with violence, if we follow Weheliye's (2014: 110) discourse on pornotroping when he writes, "Instead of emerging as an ontological condition, flesh comes into view as a series of desubjectivations, which are always already subjectivations, that hail the slave and the spectator in order to engrave upon him or her the hypervisible yet also illegible hieroglyphics of the flesh." Baldwin thus not only "fails" to move according to the hail; he moves, as (de)subjectivated flesh, in excess of the hail. His subjectivity is not destroyed, but the moment highlights "how violent political domination activates a fleshy surplus that simultaneously sustains and disfigures said brutality" (2).

While walking in a Southern town, Baldwin turns and enters a restaurant on a corner and is met with the paralyzing stares and deafening silence of an establishment full, at least visibly, with only white people. A woman eventually breaks the silence, barking, "What you want, boy?" Baldwin backs away and hears a voice behind him directing him to a separate entranceway. Upon turning around and seeing a white man, as Baldwin ([1972] 1998: 397–98) reflects, "This man thought that he was being kind; and he was, indeed, being as kind as can be expected from a guide in hell."

Baldwin goes around to the other entrance, fearing what confrontation could come if he were to answer back, especially given his northern accent. Indeed, there exists a script that these actors clothed in the color of their skins are expected to follow on the stage set by Jim Crow's dance. In this moment, the police officer's gun and the lynch mob's rope imagined in the earlier two scenarios come together, as Baldwin tells readers: "It was impossible to get anything but bourbon, and the very smell of bourbon is still associated in my mind with *the mean little eye of deputy sheriffs and the holster on the hip and the ominous trees which line the highways*" (400, my emphasis). Here in the American South, a Black "boy" could be shot by the gun on the hip of the sheriff's deputy and hanged from the tree on the side of the road by a lynch mob of respectable citizens. He is subject to both legal and extralegal violence as means of policing his subjectivity, so that the two forms of violence become indistinguishable.

The Black Panthers and Baldwin's Abolitionism

Since *Notes of a Native Son*, Baldwin has pointed out how whiteness has packed the potential for its own demise within its own means of control, its own weakness within its ostensible strength. This is no different in "No Name in the Street," since in this very moment of segregation, the potential for violent backlash against Jim Crow—the potential for self-defense—is made powerfully present.

After seating himself in the "colored" portion of the restaurant, Baldwin realizes, "I was nearly close enough to touch them, certainly close enough to touch her, close enough to kill them all, but they couldn't see me, either" (398). In this moment Baldwin embodies or, better, enfleshes Weheliye's concept of *habeas viscus*. The flesh, Weheliye (2014: 2) writes, "represents racializing assemblages of subjection that can never annihilate the lines of flight, freedom dreams, practices of liberation, and possibilities of other worlds." Baldwin seating himself at the segregated counter is not merely a defeat at the hands of the state, the law, and (the threat of) force. It is also in excess of the state, the law, and (the threat of) force that disfigures even as it sustains the social order.

In a scene that eerily mirrors Herman Melville's Babo holding a shaving razor in "Benito Cereno," in "No Name" Baldwin recalls a barber who refuses to register to vote in consideration of the threat of violence posed by his white customers. In his interaction with this barber, while it would seem that Baldwin would be displeased by the refusal to register to vote, the man's "response made it impossible to disagree with him: he may have been planning to cut a white man's throat one day. If I had been white, I certainly would never have allowed him anywhere near *me* with a razor in his hand" (392–93). Every stroke of that barber's blade on the soft flesh of a white man's exposed throat is the discourse-brushed flesh of the object of the law's force brushing back against the body of the state—its law. This is because, to follow Hartman (1997: 199) in her reading of *Plessy v. Ferguson*, "police power was little more than the benevolent articulation of state racism in the name of the public good. The identification of the state with its subjects was thus inseparable from the process of creating internal enemies against which the comfort and prosperity of the populace could be defended." Simply put, the Black barber, like Baldwin at the "colored" counter, is the internal enemy of the state against which police power is deployed to maintain the social order of the state's body politic. But, because the racialized assemblage produced by this objectification exceeds the force of law, it can retain the potential for an act of self-defense that would undo the social order being thus maintained by law's violence.

It is this potential for self-defense that frames Baldwin's ([1972] 1998: 454–55) advocacy for the politics of the Black Panther Party for Self-Defense. He describes their emergence as "inevitable":

> Yet the advent of the Panthers was as inevitable as the arrival of that day in Montgomery, Alabama, when Mrs. Rosa Parks refused to stand up on that bus and give up her seat to a white man. That day had been coming for a very long time; danger upon danger, and humiliation upon humiliation, had piled intolerably high and gave Mrs. Parks her platform. . . . Just so with the Panthers: it was inevitable that the fury would erupt, that a black man, openly, in the sight of all his fellows, should challenge the policeman's gun, and not only that, but the policeman's right to be in the ghetto at all.[9]

If Baldwin is aligning himself with the Panthers, who "are far from being an illegal or lawless organization" but instead are understood in "No Name" as "a great force for peace and stability" (455), then he is also aligning himself with the critique made by the very existence of the Panthers: the American legal system does not include Black people in its boundaries of protection, and yet it punishes these same people with its monopoly on violence.

Baldwin's theorizing is not only illuminated and enriched by theorists like Weheliye and Hartman, but Baldwin himself illuminates and enriches those theorists. Baldwin reads the Panthers as responding to the police as an embodied claim of the state's legitimacy. But he then articulates that the Panthers respond to the nonevent of emancipation by refusing to recognize the legitimacy of the law and its force. Thus the legal anti-Black violence of the police is rearticulated by Baldwin and other radical Black thinkers as "the violence which one always considers unjust." The system is established on the originary foundation of anti-Black violence, but survival must still be possible within that system's daily enactment of anti-Black violence that sustains the state's existence.

Simply put: the logic of policing in the United States is the logic of anti-Blackness. This logic dissolves the distinction between legal and extralegal violence directed at Black subjects; it is always unjust violence. This violence, which is both/neither legal and/nor extralegal is structurally inherent in the law as the necessary potential for the law's enforceability. This is the only way to make

---

9. This framing of the Panthers as both inevitable and an instantiation of the practice of self-defense takes as its assumption something like Sexton's (2007: 201–2) formulation in "Racial Profiling and the Societies of Control" that "the ethos of slavery—in other words, the lasting ideological and affective matrix of the white-supremacist project—admits no legitimate black self-defense, recognizes no legitimate assertions of black self-possession, privacy, or autonomy."

sense of New York Police Department officer Daniel Pantaleo's nonindictment in 2014 for killing Eric Garner. Because the system depends on the expendability of Black people, who are assumed as always already criminal and therefore beyond the law's protection, as the necessary objects of the violence that maintains the law, it is necessary by the law's own logic of policing that Pantaleo's violence not be deemed unjust. Policing in the United States is racist not merely because of individual prejudice but because it is inherently structured by racism as its founding and maintaining violence.

It may seem like there is no way out of this situation. But as Baldwin highlights in the scene with the Black barber holding his blade against the throats of white men, because of the dependent relationship between the law and its objects of violence, the law's ostensible monopoly on violence is constituted by vulnerability and thus is never truly a monopoly. The social structure as it is maintained by law is haunted by the very specter the law seeks to keep at bay: the Black revolution that would literally undo the world as it is known.

As Kaba (2017) notes, the system is working exactly as it is structured to work. But other ways of being are possible. Throughout her work, Kaba articulates how radically revisioning our notions of community and relationality in both philosophical and concrete ways is the work of abolition that not only seeks to tear down systems of oppression but also build up a life-sustaining network of accountability and care.

Here, too, the Panthers provide the best possible closing note. In their refusal of the state's legitimacy and their turn toward caring for their own vulnerable communities—think of the breakfast program as prominently as the armed patrolling of the police—the Panthers were wrestling with the questions Sharpe (2016: 101) articulates in *In the Wake* when she writes, "How are we beholden to and beholders of each other in ways that change across time and place and space and yet remain?" It is in this being beholden to each other, and in his reading of the Panthers' attempts at this beholding, that Baldwin's abolitionism emerges even if he never names it as such. What Baldwin's work dares to do is imagine that the world need not be the way it is. He is not merely describing the excesses of law's violence; he is theorizing the possibilities that exceed that violence. Because, in Sharpe's words, Black people "are constituted through and by continued vulnerability to overwhelming force though not *only* known to ourselves and each other *by* that force" (16), Black subjectivity, for Baldwin, is crafted by the force of law via the policeman's club and the slave master's whip, but it also lives beyond the reach of the club and whip. There are worlds within the world, and the Panthers are merely one vision on which Baldwin focuses in his gaze toward what Kaba calls "the horizon of abolition." Without ever leaving this world and all its terror, Baldwin theorizes another.

A world without prisons.

A world without police.

A world where Black people can breathe.

References

Baldwin, James. (1963) 1998. "The Fire Next Time." In *Baldwin: Collected Essays*, edited by Toni Morrison, 287–347. New York: The Library of America.

Baldwin, James. (1972) 1998. "No Name in the Street." In *Baldwin: Collected Essays*, edited by Toni Morrison, 349–475. New York: The Library of America.

Baptist, Edward. 2014. *The Half Has Never Been Told: Slavery and the Making of American Capitalism*. New York: Basic Books.

Benjamin, Walter. (1921) 1978. "Critique of Violence." In *Reflections: Aphorisms, Essays, Autobiographical Writings*, edited by Peter Demetz, 277–300. New York: Schocken Books.

Blackmon, Douglas A. 2009. *Slavery by Another Name: The Re-enslavement of African Americans from the Civil War to World War II*. New York: Penguin.

Dayan, Colin. 2011. *The Law Is a White Dog: How Legal Rituals Make and Unmake Persons*. Princeton, NJ: Princeton University Press.

Derrida, Jacques. 1990. "Force of Law: The "Mystical Foundations of Authority." *Cardozo Law Review* 11, nos. 5–6: 920–1045.

Goldberg, Jesse A. 2016. "Theorizing and Resisting the Violence of Stop and Frisk–Style Profiling." *CLA Journal* 58, no. 4: 256–76.

Goldsby, Jacqueline. 2006. *A Spectacular Secret: Lynching in American Life and Literature*. Chicago: University of Chicago Press.

Haley, Sarah. 2016. *No Mercy Here: Gender, Punishment, and the Making of Jim Crow Modernity*. Chapel Hill: University of North Carolina Press.

Hartman, Saidiya V. 1997. *Scenes of Subjection: Terror, Slavery, and Self-Making in Nineteenth-Century America*. New York: Oxford University Press.

Kaba, Mariame. 2017. "Towards the Horizon of Abolition: A Conversation with Mariame Kaba." Interview by John Duda, November 9. thenextsystem.org/learn/stories/towards-horizon-abolition-conversation-mariame-kaba.

Kendi, Ibram X. 2016. *Stamped from the Beginning: The Definitive History of Racist Ideas in America*. New York: Nation Books.

Matsuda, Mari. (1987) 1995. "Looking to the Bottom: Critical Legal Studies and Reparations." In *Critical Race Theory: The Critical Writings That Formed the Movement*, edited by Kimberlé Crenshaw, Neil Gotanda, Gary Peller, and Kendall Thomas, 63–79. New York: The New Press.

Morgan, Edmund S. 2003. *American Slavery, American Freedom*. New York: W.W. Norton.

Moten, Fred. 2013. "Blackness and Nothingness (Mysticism in the Flesh)." *South Atlantic Quarterly* 112, no. 4: 737–80.

Muhammad, Khalil G. 2011. *The Condemnation of Blackness: Race, Crime, and the Making of Modern Urban America*. Cambridge, MA: Harvard University Press.

Sexton, Jared. 2007. "Racial Profiling and the Societies of Control." *Warfare in the American Homeland: Policing and Prison in a Penal Democracy*, edited by Joy James, 197–218. Durham, NC: Duke University Press.

Sexton, Jared. 2011. "The Social Life of Social Death: On Afro-Pessimism and Black Optimism." *InTensions Journal* 5 (Fall/Winter): 1–47.

Sharpe, Christina. 2016. *In the Wake: On Blackness and Being*. Durham, NC: Duke University Press.

Smallwood, Stephanie. 2008. *Saltwater Slavery: A Middle Passage from Africa to American Diaspora*. Cambridge, MA: Harvard University Press.

Spillers, Hortense. 1987. "Mama's Baby, Papa's Maybe: An American Grammar Book." *Diacritics* 17, no. 2: 64–81.

Wagner, Bryan. *Disturbing the Peace: Black Culture and the Police Power after Slavery*. Cambridge, MA: Harvard University Press.

Warren, Calvin. 2018. *Ontological Terror: Blackness, Nihilism, and Emancipation*. Durham, NC: Duke University Press.

Weheliye, Alexander G. 2014. *Habeas Viscus: Racializing Assemblages, Biopolitics, and Black Feminist Theorizations of the Human*. Durham, NC: Duke University Press.

Jesse A. Goldberg completed his PhD at Cornell University and is currently visiting assistant professor of English at Longwood University, where he teaches courses on African American literature, carcerality studies, and Black studies. His writing appears in *Callaloo, MELUS, CLA Journal*, and the edited volumes *Toni Morrison on Mothers and Motherhood* (2017), *Against a Sharp White Background: Infrastructures of African American Print* (2019), and *Teaching Literature and Writing in Prisons* (2020).

The Police Are the Punishment

Didier Fassin

"It was not a desire for vengeance, but a desire for justice," the lawyer told the court at a trial I attended a few months before I started my ethnographic research on urban policing in the *banlieues* of Paris.[1] The defendants were seven police officers indicted for acts of violence that had occurred a year earlier. The photographs of the plaintiff, a man from Turkey, whose swollen and bruised face appeared on the front page of a Turkish monthly soon after the incident, left little doubt about the brutality he had endured at the hands of the law enforcement agents. Based on the complete case file given to me by the public prosecutor after a conversation we had later on, I could piece together the story of the unfortunate man.

On New Year's Eve, the local police station had received a phone call from the resident of a housing project who was reporting a scuffle that had started at a family party after intruders had tried to get into the community hall where it was held. It was late in the night. The officers on duty, who had been celebrating the holiday and were by then fairly intoxicated, rushed to the scene ten miles away, lights flashing and sirens wailing. More than two dozen agents from neighboring precincts hurriedly joined them. All were heavily equipped with riot gear, hel-

This essay is based on the keynote lecture that I gave at the conference "Policing the City: Violence, Visibility, and the Law," at Stanford University on March 30, 2017, but I have almost entirely rewritten it. I am thankful to Caren Kaplan and Andrea Miller for their helpful comments on an earlier version. I also express my gratitude to the commissioner of the precinct and the prosecutor of the jurisdiction for having facilitated the research on which this essay is based, the former by giving me permission to conduct fieldwork for fifteen months with the police of his district, the latter by providing me the hundreds of pages of the case file of the court case reported here. I finally want to manifest my appreciation to the officers for their patience and candor as they have accepted my presence with them on patrols during these many days and nights.

1. The trial and the events that led to the prosecution of the officers are narrated and analyzed in detail in *Enforcing Order: An Ethnography of Urban Policing* (Fassin 2013).

Public Culture 31:3   DOI 10.1215/08992363-7532691
Copyright 2019 by Duke University Press   **539**

mets, and batons. When they arrived on the premises, the project was calm, with only the distant voices of a group of people conversing near the place where the party had taken place. At the sight of the sudden and impressive deployment of the police force rushing into the alleys, these bystanders started to run away. They were immediately chased by the agents. After a few minutes of stampeding and shouting, which generated angry protests from inhabitants at the windows of their apartments, the meager prey was brought back to the cars and taken into custody: two men, one of Caribbean origin, the other from Turkey. The former was apparently walking away from the community hall, the latter was also quietly returning home after another family gathering. Both were badly hurt, the Turkish man being later diagnosed at the hospital with a perforation of the eardrum, periorbital hematomas, and acromioclavicular strain.

It appeared during the investigation conducted by a judge during the following months that the two men had experienced similar physical assaults. As they were trying to flee from the aggressive and inebriated officers, they were brutally stopped, pinned to the ground, beaten with batons and sprayed with tear gas. Even after they had been handcuffed, they continued to be roughed up, punched, and kicked, first in the street, then in the car, and eventually at the station. Rather than being taken to the hospital for a medical examination, they were initially held in custody. Only the following day were they permitted to see a physician, who wrote impressive forensic reports. The accusation of insulting an officer and resisting arrest that was filed against them should have led to an immediate appearance trial and a probable prison sentence, but, as the public prosecutor told me, because of the international resonance of the incident, the Ministry of Justice requested that, in contrast with what usually happens in similar situations, this case of police violence be treated in an exemplary manner by the judicial system. In fact, only the Turkish victim, supported by his community, lodged a complaint, the Caribbean man deciding to avoid the expenses and troubles of a lawsuit.

To affirm that the investigation was a model of fairness would be an overstatement, as all seventy-nine witnesses interviewed were police officers with the exception of a few firefighters; no one from the project was heard by the judge. During the trial, it was revealed that at the beginning of the intervention, the sergeant major had galvanized his troops with this conspicuous encouragement: "We lost the Algerian War. Forty years ago, we chickened out. We're not going to do it again today. Take no prisoners! It's no holds barred!" Despite this acknowledgment by the accused officers, the public prosecutor chose not to consider this cry to be an aggravating circumstance, which should have been invoked if it had been deemed racist or discriminatory. As he told me, the case would have been more difficult to establish in court, although the aggressive call by the officer in charge of the squad having been uttered as his men were bursting into a neighborhood whose residents were for the most part North and sub-Saharan Africans from former French colonies, its racist meaning and discriminatory implications were blatant.

Partly as a result of this choice, the verdict was lenient, as it is almost always the case when the police are indicted. One officer was acquitted. Six, who had acknowledged their involvement in the assaults, received four-month suspended prison sentences without mention in their criminal record, which meant that the punishment had no consequence on their future professional activity. They were also required to collectively pay twelve thousand euros to the victim for bodily injury and moral wrong. Three years later, however, the Turkish man had still not received one cent from his aggressors, who had in the meantime been posted in other precincts. When his lawyer inquired of the Ministry of the Interior where the officers were then working so as to be able to claim the payment of the damages, the official answer he got from the administration was . . . that it did not know.

In light of these well-documented events, the counsel's statement that the use of force by the officers expressed their "desire for justice" may sound surrealistic. One has to simply imagine the two men being beaten up during their arrest even after having been handcuffed and again roughed up while in custody, while there was absolutely no evidence of their involvement in any wrongdoing and while, moreover, it was not even clear from the testimonies collected on the spot that there had ever been more than a verbal altercation at the party. However, I want to take seriously the lawyer's claim or rather explore the possibility that such violence be thought as ordinary punishment, and therefore as a form of retributive justice.

In the present case, as in many others that I have witnessed or been told of, the punishment takes two forms: physical, with the thrashing in the street and at the station; and legal, with the initial accusation of insulting an officer and resisting arrest. It also often includes a moral dimension, via the debasement and humiliation of the individual arrested. My assertion undoubtedly goes against commonsense, according to which such acts are pure brutalization, although the officers' counsels pleaded that they should be excused in the allegedly warlike context of public housing, as well as against a long tradition of both legal theory and moral philosophy, whose definition of punishment precisely excludes these acts for being outside the judicial realm.

Against these views, I want to examine the retributive dimension of the exertion of violence in policing. Because it is a justified or justifiable practice in the eyes of many officers, because it is effectively protected by the institution, because it is treated with clemency by the judges, because it may even be encouraged by the state, and perhaps above all because it targets certain populations, namely, low-income categories belonging to ethno-racial minorities—all affirmations that I will develop—I argue that it should be regarded as a form of punishment. Far from being a deviant practice, it reveals that, for what concerns its lower segments, society delegates a significant part of the retributive justice process to the police. This shift of the perspective on punishment has major theoretical as well as political implications.

The Problem with the Dirty Harry Problem

Such argument is nevertheless not entirely new. If the word *punishment* does not appear as an entry in the indexes of most classics on the police written by criminologists, from William Westley, Jerome Skolnick, and James Q. Wilson to Peter Manning, Albert Reiss, and Jean-Paul Brodeur, the idea of punishment is sometimes present between the lines as a potential manifestation of the discretionary power of law enforcement agents, although it is generally presented as a moral justification of their seemingly deviant practices.

The best illustration of this indulgent interpretation is Carl Klockars's (1980) famous paper "The Dirty Harry Problem." It is inspired by Inspector Callahan, alias Dirty Harry, the hero played by Clint Eastwood in the eponymous 1971 crime thriller directed by Don Siegel. A man of few words and bad temper who has the reputation of dealing with difficult cases his own way, Callahan is involved in the case of a serial killer who terrorizes the city. As the justice system proves incapable of stopping the criminal from committing murders and even releases him because of procedural issues after he has been arrested, Callahan ends up substituting himself for it. Against his superiors' orders, he tails the criminal, at one point uses torture to have him confess where he is keeping a young woman who is later found dead, and finally, after an epic chase, as the man has taken a dozen children hostage in a school bus, shoots him dead. By executing the criminal in cold blood, he thus administers justice: he punishes the odious culprit.

For Klockars (1980: 33), the story illustrates a fundamental dilemma: "Policing constantly places its practitioners in situations in which good ends can be achieved by dirty means." In the film, this dilemma, the insolvability of which is epitomized in the last scene by Callahan throwing his badge into the water of the pond where the serial killer's dead body is sinking, takes an extreme and almost caricatured form as, on the one hand, the criminal is a dangerous and sadistic psychopath, and on the other hand, both law enforcement and judicial institutions prove to be impotent. Under these circumstances, the viewer is expected not only to feel sympathy for the solitary righter of wrongs but also to understand that the police need to use dirty means for good ends if they want to protect society from crime. Significantly, the more general questions raised by Klockars (39) on the basis of the story concern only the dirty means. Can they be justified as punishment? Should they in turn be punished? But he never challenges the good ends. Even in the less dramatic case of stops and frisks, for which racial profiling has long been documented, he finds arguments to exonerate the officers from their discriminatory practices: "Although the probability of coming upon a dangerous felon is extremely low, policemen quite reasonably take the possibility of doing so as a working assumption on the understandable premise that once is enough." There is no questioning of the real grounds of such practices, that is, the imposition of a social order targeting racial minorities belonging to disadvantaged neighborhoods. Instead, the official explanation provided by the agents is accepted. This interpretation of policing, based merely on the reproduction of the agents' justifications, is not infrequent in criminological writings, in particular in the literature on police culture.

Yet, in the fifteen months of my ethnographic research in the largest French police district, where crime rates were significantly higher than the national average, I have far more often observed dirty means for dirty ends, as was the case in the assaults against the Caribbean and Turkish men, than dirty means for good ends, as in *Dirty Harry*'s scenario.[2] But I contend that in both cases, from a sociological perspective, the violence perpetrated—on innocent passers-by or on the serial killer—should be regarded as a form of retribution. The argument that I want to make here is that in the eyes of law enforcement agents as well as, in many cases, from the perspective of their institution, the excessive use of force can find its justification as a legitimate, if not legal, way to dispense justice on the street.

2. The research was carried out from May 2005 to February 2006 and from February 2007 to June 2007 in a district of the Paris region with levels of poverty and unemployment, a proportion of foreign and immigrant populations, and crime rates all significantly above the national average. There were both middle-class residential areas and lower-class housing projects. As was the case in many urban districts, the police were composed of regular officers in uniform patrolling in marked vehicles and of special anticrime squads with plain-clothes officers driving unmarked cars. Although they had somewhat distinct missions, the former covering the entire range of law enforcement activities and the latter being specialized in red-handed arrests, they participated most of the time in the same operations, with the main difference being that the anticrime squad officers had the justified reputation of being more aggressive than their colleagues and also of being more effective in terms of arrest, not least because they provoked youths, especially those from an immigrant background.

In 1979, Malcolm Feeley (1992) published a book that had a profound influence on court studies and soon became a classic in the sociolegal field. *The Process Is the Punishment*, subtitled *Handling Cases in a Lower Criminal Court*, shows that, contrary to common representations of the administration of justice, in the great majority of cases, especially those regarding minor offenses, decisions are made and sentences imposed outside procedural justice. Only one-third of the defendants facing jail time have a counsel. Bails imposed on arbitrary criteria lead to defendants being detained before adjudication twice more often than as the consequence of jail sentences. Plea bargaining rather than adversarial confrontation with prosecutors results in the fact that only a minority of defendants have a fair trial. Costs, both direct, related to the bail, the lawyers' fees, and the court's procedures, and indirect, in terms of time spent within the judicial bureaucracy and risk of losing one's job, imply a profound inequality before the justice system. It should be noted that, the study having been conducted four decades ago, that is, before the hardening of the penal system, the enactment of mandatory sentencing laws, and the further pressure on defendants to accept to plead guilty rather than exercise their right to stand trial in court, most of its findings would look even more valid today.

The crucial conclusion drawn by Feeley is that the pretrial phase, which most of the time is paradoxically not even followed by a trial, is where justice is commonly dispensed, that multiple social factors unrelated to the case appear more determining than the alleged offense itself, and that the combination of these elements produces profound disparities. I want to extend these conclusions by showing that even before what Feeley calls "the process," with its attorneys and judges, bailiffs and sheriffs, bail bondsmen and bail commissioners, representatives of family relations and drug treatment programs (or the equivalent major players and supporting actors in other parts of the world), there are the police, which play a crucial role, in the street and at the precinct, as part of the punitive system. It is a sort of pre-pretrial, which may or may not precede a trial—or even a pretrial—and can be either a contributing factor to the judicial process (the framing of the person and/or his indictment) or entirely self-contained (a corporeal and/or moral chastisement). In other words, for many of those who, whether guilty or not, have regular encounters with them, the police are the punishment.

Bypassing the Definitional Stop

But what is punishment? To affirm that it is part of police practices, one has to circumscribe what it is. Legal theorists and moral philosophers have long attempted to give an answer to this question. The most widely accepted definition, that of H. L. A. Hart (1959), half a century ago, provides five decisive criteria. Punishment is (1) the infliction of a pain or of an unpleasant equivalent (2) to an actual or supposed offender (3) in response to an offense against legal rules (4) that are intentionally imposed by a legal authority and (5) administered by human beings with appropriate roles. Although the definition is said to be independent from any justification, it assumes that punishment is both legitimate, since it sanctions an offender for the offense he has committed, and legal, since it is applied for a violation of the law by appropriate means defined by the law. Under this normative definition (which describes not what punishment is, but what ought to be regarded as punishment), law enforcement has no place, except as the lawful provider of cases for the judicial system. The police are not supposed to inflict pain on individuals suspected of having committed a misdeed, and their legal authority does not imply that such would be an appropriate role for them.

But should we limit our inquiry to the verification of the matching of actual practices with the a priori definition? In fact, Hart himself insisted that one should never use what he called a "definitional stop"—allowing one to say whether a given action is or is not a punishment—to elude a more radical and critical questioning about the nature and rationale of the act of punishing. To avoid this pitfall, I will reverse the reasoning by approaching the delimitation of punishment not through an a priori definition but via an ex post facto reconstitution based on the observation of reality. I will not start with the ideal of what punishment ought to be but instead analyze actual scenes to try to apprehend what it is.

One late winter afternoon, in a middle-class neighborhood, two young men were coming home from a basketball game when they saw two of their friends being searched by two motorcycle officers on the side of the road. As they passed by, they greeted them jokingly with a "Salaam alaikum!" to which one of the law enforcement agents aggressively retorted, "We're in France here, we speak French." The two youths were indeed French and born in France, but their parents were Senegalese. They talked back to the officers, who insulted them in return, calling them "filthy apes" and "fucking niggers," to which the youngsters responded with "French assholes." At this point, the police jumped on their motorcycles, and the two boys ran off toward their home. A few minutes later, the one-level detached house where they had found refuge was surrounded by several police vehicles with flashing lights, which had been called in for reinforcement. Helmeted, batons in hand, the officers broke the front window and rushed into the living-room where the terrified mother of the two youngsters, trying to protect them, was thrown to the floor. They grabbed the boys, took them to the ground, and started to hit them while handcuffing them. The pastor, who belonged to an evangelical church in the United States, later told me that the assault was so violent that it reminded him of the infamous beating of Rodney King.

In the meantime, alerted by the cries, a crowd of local residents had gathered, indignantly protesting against the brutality of the officers. Several were in turn shoved aside and threatened to be apprehended. In the middle of the turmoil provoked by the intervention, the two youngsters were taken into the police station and kept in custody under the accusation of insulting an officer and resisting arrest. In the evening, the event was reported in the news on television, as a neighbor had filmed the scene on his telephone. The following day a demonstration against police violence took place in the center of the city, and three weeks later a meeting was held with inhabitants of the family's neighborhood, representatives of the municipal council, and religious leaders, but no one from the law enforcement agency attended. People declared that they had been particularly appalled by the racist slurs hurled by the officers not only at the youth but also at the neighbors, several of them belonging to ethnoracial minorities. The pastor told me that he had been all the more shocked since he knew the boys whom he described as well-educated and well-behaved students. The commissioner said to me that his men had simply reacted to the offensive attitude of the youngsters. As I was discussing the event with members of the anticrime squad, one of them commented that he had not been surprised by how the incident turned out, the motorcycle officer who was at the origin of the disorder being known to be "a crazy brute." The boys' parents filed a complaint against him and his colleagues. However, both charges against the youths for insulting an officer and resisting arrest and against the police for aggravated assault were abandoned a few months later after the agent who had been the most confrontational and brutal died in a traffic accident.

Such events were common during my research. Similar ones are regularly reported all over the country. They do not generally exceed a local confrontation with bruises, slurs, and arrests. They sometimes end in deaths, however, almost always of young men of color from disadvantaged environments, and lead to urban disorders.[3] This is how the 2005 riots started: a group of adolescents being chased by the police in a project for a theft they had not committed; three of them finding refuge in an electric transformer where two died while the third one was severely burnt; the police, although aware of the danger, deciding not to intervene; the gov-

3. A list of the individuals killed as a result of an interaction with the police between 2005 and 2015 has been established by Urgence-notre-police-assassine en toute impunité 2019. For the year 2017, nineteen persons died after having been shot by the police, and fifteen more casualties resulted from other circumstances (Jean-Marc B. 2018).

ernment, instead of expressing sympathy for the victims, defaming them as thugs. Fortunately, most of these incidents have less tragic outcomes and even remain ignored by the public, except in the neighborhoods where they have happened and whose inhabitants often remain traumatized. The originality of the present case is that the young men did not belong to the working class, did not live in a housing project, and were not school dropouts—hence the fact that they did not expect to be treated by the police as they were. But they were black. In a certain sense, the racial—and racist—dimension was pure, not mixed with the other two with which it is usually intertwined: the social and the spatial. Hence the consternation of the local residents who thought that upward mobility and neighborhood gentrification protected them from police mistreatment. They were proven wrong.

But should we consider the violence deployed by the police in this incident to be punishment? Is it not mere abuse of power, sheer domination, pure repression? And since it is in response to an alleged offense against the police, is it not simply reprisal? Let us examine these two interpretations. According to the first option—the violence hypothesis—such set of actions would simply be an excess in the use of force, which is how authorities often tend to minimize such incidents, or, in legal language, would be inappropriate and disproportionate use of coercion, which is what the defendants' lawyers try to dismiss. That there is brutality cannot definitely be doubted, but is it just that? According to the second option—the vengeance hypothesis—the operation is a mere retaliation by the police against the youths who have talked back to them. That the reactions of the officers be a form of reprisal leaves little doubt, but should we be satisfied with this analysis? My argument is that there is more to the incident than violence and retaliation. Revisiting the first hypothesis, we can affirm, in accordance with Egon Bittner (1980: 37), that "the police authorization" to use force is "essentially unrestricted," rendering the "talk about the lawful use of force practically meaningless." Second, in agreement with Émile Durkheim (1984: 47), we can state that "punishment has remained for us what it was for our predecessors," meaning that it is "an act of vengeance." In other words, the fact that, in the incident recounted, there be acts of brutality and a sense of revenge does not exclude the possibility that it is also a form of punishment, that is, the administration of a form of justice in the street meant to correct an alleged wrong. What evidence can we have of such intention? They are of two sorts: one, subjective, refers to the meaning given by the officers to their action; the other, objective, concerns the interpretation that we can make of the course of action. In the case of police abuse, both strongly speak in favor of punishment.

The Moral Argument for Police Abuse

From their subjective viewpoint, the agents themselves consider their violent verbal and physical practices to be just deserts. It is not only that they try to mask their reprehensible practices because they fear the consequences from their hierarchy or the judges. They do find moral justifications for their acts. These are of two kinds, having to do with their public and with the judges.

Officers view the lower classes, which constitute the main part of their public, as criminal, with little capacity of discernment when they deal with ethnoracial minorities, since they are "not attuned to the signs of respectability" within them, as Robert Reiner (2000: 93) writes. They know of course that not all the inhabitants of the projects commit crime, but they have a hard time differentiating among them those who should be deemed suspect, largely because of ethnoracial prejudices that are reinforced during their training in the academy and their socialization with older colleagues. Indeed, eight out of ten officers come from rural areas and small towns where they hardly ever have contact with anyone from immigrant origin and are all the same posted for their first position in urban districts with high proportions of minorities. "They are unable to recognize thugs from honest people," the commissioner told me. "They cannot imagine that a black guy with a hoodie can be a PhD student and not a hoodlum," the mayor observed in one of our conversations. Moreover, in their eyes, even when people from these neighborhoods have not done anything wrong, they are viewed either as potential criminals, who may not have been arrested for a previous offense, or as mute accomplices, who do not tell what they supposedly know. Their belief does not seem to be affected by the dual evidence that, on the one hand, the great majority of the inhabitants of the housing projects where they patrol have never had dealings with the police, and that, on the other hand, they receive calls and sometimes information from residents about local dealers or gangsters. But this confusion is effective in justifying that, even if they do not arrest the right person, those who are caught either have committed some offense for which they may not have been punished or have been aware of it without reporting it to the police. Like the wolf in La Fontaine's fable, replying to the lamb who protests his innocence, the officers could retort: "If not you, then your brother. All the worse . . ." Or "someone else in your clan. For to me you're all of you a curse." This representation of the lower classes as composed of actual criminals, potential criminals, and accomplices of criminals thus legitimizes the harsh treatment they received.

Such negative generalization is in line with the officers' view that the population in general is hostile. Despite opinion polls showing that they are the most appreciated civil servants, they remain convinced, or persuade themselves, that the public has no sympathy for them. This misperception is, again, differentiated: it mostly concerns the youths of immigrant origin, in particular those from disadvantaged neighborhoods. "They don't like us, the bastards," commented the chief of the anticrime squad as we were slowly driving by a group of African and Arab youths who were watching us. The term *bastard* was the common way of designating young people belonging to ethnoracial minorities that they dealt with. After a short pause, he added, "But we don't like them either." This imagined or actual antagonism serves two functions. First, it makes reciprocity reasonable, as the officers' animosity seems to them a relevant response to the population's animosity, the badges of the anticrime squads clearly attesting to their worldview: one of them depicts, against the background of the French national flag, the tall blocks of a stylized representation of a housing project seen through a gun sight, while another shows a spider trapping a complex of high buildings in its web. Second, it reinforces group solidarity and "esprit de corps," as officers consider that they have to defend themselves against these potential enemies, both when they confront them directly in the street and when they have to testify about the deviant acts committed by one of their colleagues. Seeing their publics as hostile definitely makes abuses easier to produce and cover.

Moreover, officers regard judges as too lenient toward the suspects they arrest, since "in their eyes their decision to lay a charge or charges deserves to be supported by judges by punishment that establishes the authority of the law enforcement machinery," as Richard Ericson (1982: 68) explains. "We arrest criminals and the next day they are outside again. The judges have freed them. One wonders what we work for." Such was the lament often heard during our patrols through the projects. Again, evidence contradicts this assertion. National statistics demonstrate that the justice system is particularly severe, that this toughness increases over the years, and that it focuses on petty crime. In fact, the reason the police believe that judges are sabotaging their work is that they often arrest suspects without minimal proof. As a sergeant told his men one evening: "There have been too many police abuses, we have taken too many liberties. It's like us with the youngsters: we don't trust them. Well, you know what? The judges feel the same way about us." But his call for probity could not be heard because the police's misrepresentation had an important social function: disqualifying the judges as merciful legitimizes their own eagerness to dispense justice in their stead.

As a result of their prejudices regarding both crime in the lower classes and clemency of the justice system, officers find a moral justification to what they deem just retribution toward individuals who, in their view, definitely deserve it

549

but might not be punished otherwise. This retribution can be inflicted on a suspect. But it often affects innocent people in two ways—randomly or collectively. Random punishment, exemplified by the Caribbean and Turkish men, means that anyone in the group, usually the slowest runner or the least lucky passer-by, gets beaten up, arrested, and indicted in place of the supposed culprit. It is blind justice. In these situations, the retribution can be both immediate and deferred. On the spot, individuals are roughed up as they try to run away or even simply happen to be present at the scene, with an outcome in some cases of severe injuries. Then, they can be taken in to the station where intimidation goes on with threats of being kept in custody and referred to the prosecutor. Generally, however, for lack of evidence of wrongdoing, they are released, as the officers are content with the distress caused by the handcuffing in front of friends, relatives, and neighbors and the questioning dotted with menaces. This daunting experience ends up with their being back in the street far from their home, sometimes in the middle of the night, a practice that has been denounced by a judges' union as a common form of iniquitous punishment. In other cases, especially when the individuals have been injured and might be tempted to file a complaint for police violence, the officers indict them for insulting an officer and resisting arrest, an offense that can lead to up to two years in prison and a thirty thousand euro fine. Such practice is doubly beneficial from the police's perspective, since punishment is inflicted firstly in the street, where the person has been thrashed, and secondly in court, where he faces serious consequences. Collective punishment consists in abusing the whole group, with its members being scared, reviled, pushed, thumped, and menaced with weapons, as was the case in the arrest of the two young men of Senegalese origin. A deputy commissioner told me that she was aware of the deleterious effects of such actions and often tried to avoid them, but she conceded that it was usually in vain, as her troops wanted immediate retribution. In fact, such brutal operations could further affect the assaulted neighborhood, by creating a breach of trust among the inhabitants, especially when it is a resident who calls the police in the first place.

Remarkably, whether it is targeted on a suspect, random or collective, such retribution selectively concerns youth from the working class belonging to ethnoracial minorities and living in public housing. This is why the subjective approach does not suffice to grasp the broader meaning of police abuse not as mere oppression or reprisal but also as punishment.

The Political Context of Policing Excesses

Indeed, on the objective side, the institution, the state, and, in the end, society as a whole participate in this idea that the police should be part of the punitive apparatus. Since the 1970s, the discourse of law and order has progressively swamped the public sphere and the political realm in France. The historic victory of the left in the general elections of 1981, after twenty-three years of conservative domination, led to the restructuring of the French political landscape, with the rapid rise of the far right and the weakening of the traditional right. The National Front based its success principally on two issues, immigration and security, often mingling them by presenting immigrants or their children as the major source of insecurity (Albertini and Doucet 2013). The response of conservatives was to radicalize their discourse, in their turn adopting xenophobic themes and producing alarmist statements. Two men, both ministers of the interior, were pivotal in this process: Charles Pasqua in the 1990s and Nicolas Sarkozy in the 2000s, the former having been the political mentor of the latter, who is remembered for having promised to "cleanse" the housing projects and having described their youths as "scum"—this was just before the 2005 riots. In hindsight, this strategy paid off in terms of electoral successes in the following three decades. In this context, the police benefited from expanded human and technical resources, with new so-called nonlethal but definitely maiming weapons such as Flash-balls and Tasers; special units, the anticrime squads in particular, were created in an increasing number of urban districts; and new prerogatives, notably in terms of stop and frisk as well as use of firearms, were added in the code of criminal procedure.

These policies were not meant to be implemented everywhere toward everyone. The *banlieues* with their housing projects were their main focus. Their residents, especially the working-class youth belonging to ethnic minorities, were their principal target. One night, as we were cruising in the city center, the sergeant major recognized an Arab man in his thirties in the street. Since his men had arrested him several weeks before, he manifested his surprise, but was told by his colleague that the man had received a suspended prison sentence: "Don't worry, he'll get it! We will have no problem finding something to make him break his suspension order. I tell you: he'll serve his time." Indeed, their interactions with these publics included various forms of provocation, either verbal, via racist slurs, or physical, via harsh treatment during stop and frisk. Such harassment sometimes led to responses from the youths who, under pressure, either talked back to the law enforcement agents or pushed them back, thus opening the way to the accusation of insulting an officer and resisting arrest.

This offense, which, as the officers themselves and their superiors admitted to me, was viewed as a situation much more revealing of police misconduct rather than of youth misbehavior, has skyrocketed in the past two decades. The institution has forcefully backed this practice as the Ministry of the Interior has encouraged its agents to file complaints and request financial compensation from the accused, even paying the fees of the officers' lawyers and requesting severity from prosecutors. One evening, in a conversation at the station, a young officer explained to his colleagues that he had found a decree, dating to the time when tuberculosis was endemic in the first half of the twentieth century, that imposed a fine for spitting in a public place. Excited at the idea of reviving this offense, he sardonically declared: "It's great. If I see anyone spitting, I slap a charge on him and with a bit of luck it'll end with resisting the police!" The agents never ran out of imagination in that regard. They knew they would be supported by their institution.

These punitive policies and practices of law enforcement selectively oriented against ethnoracial minorities evoke the punitive law enforcement policies and practices toward colonial subjects, in particular Algerians residing in France (Blanchard 2011). From 1925 to 1945, the North African Brigade of the Prefecture of Police exercised strict control of the Algerian population living in the metropole. It was part of the Service for the Surveillance and Protection of North African Natives, the actual work of which had more to do with surveillance than protection. The activity of the brigade was indeed mostly devoted to monitoring and suppressing nationalist aspirations, deviant acts, and even the simple fact of residing in the metropole. Accused of racism and violence as well as of complicity with the German occupier, the infamous unit was dissolved after the Second World War. Two factors played a major role in the aftermath of this conflict. The first one, on May 8, 1945, was the brutal repression of the riots of Sétif, Guelma, and Kherrata that broke out after the killing of a young man by the police during a demonstration celebrating the liberation of Paris (the massacre of several thousands of Algerians fueled the independence sentiment that later led to the insurrection against the colonial power). The second one, on September 20, 1947, was the enactment of a new statute for Algerians who were no longer "natives" but "French Muslims" (although a legal improvement, this statute gave them rights that were distinct from those of the "French non-Muslims" who resided in Algeria, making them second-class citizens). The two elements were linked, as the new statute was a concession after the massacres, but they revealed the increasing predicament that the French government was facing with its colonial subjects.

In this context, the political and social tensions were exacerbated in the metropole, and a special police unit called the Anti-Assault and Violence Brigade was created in 1953 after the deadly repression of a demonstration on the fourteenth of July in Paris. Composed of members of the earlier-dissolved brigade, it extensively and brutally practiced checks and searches, raids and arrests. Rather than containing crime as its mission was supposed to be, it punished not only the political activity but also the mere presence of a population often described as "undesirable." The culmination of this repression was the massacre that occurred on October 17, 1961, in Paris when thousands of peaceful Algerian demonstrators defying the curfew were arrested and kept in custody in an arena and a stadium while hundreds of others were thrown and drowned in the river Seine.[4] The prefect of the Paris police in command of this operation at the time was Maurice Papon, who had been responsible, as head of Bordeaux's police, for the deportation of hundreds of Jews to concentration camps during the Second World War and, as prefect of the Constantinois, for the torture of prisoners during the Algerian War.

Although it would be incorrect to establish a direct link between yesterday's Anti-Assault and Violence Brigade and today's anticrime squads, and more generally between police practices toward the so-called natives in the colonial period and toward the ethnoracial minorities in the present time, one cannot deny the existence of a pattern and a genealogy. A pattern, with the creation of special units with extended prerogatives, the targeting of populations and territories more than individuals, the discriminatory treatment of stigmatized groups, the abuses endorsed by the government, the mode of surveillance and intervention. And a genealogy, explicitly referred to by the sergeant's rallying cry in the episode evoked at the beginning, implied in the injunction and insults of the motorcycle officer, and more broadly present in the language commonly used by the police to speak of their public designated as "savages" or "apes" whose neighborhood was called a "jungle," as well as in the countersubversive strategies employed by officials for the control of riots.

The Banality of Extrajudicial Retribution

In light of the subjective and objective elements gathered to interpret the meaning of police violence, it is clear that it has multiple dimensions of retorsion, repres-

---

4. The exact number of deaths has never been acknowledged by the French state. According to Jean-Luc Einaudi (2001), 200 people died that night, while another 325 were killed by the police during the autumn of 1961.

sion, domination, and retribution, but that the latter occupies a central role as justification both at the level of the officers, who consider themselves to be entitled to dispense justice on the street or at the station, and at the level of the institution and the state, which protect them from legal actions and even facilitate judicial retaliation. Crime or even suspicion of crime is not even necessary when the mere presence of certain groups is deemed dubious or simply undesirable.

Apprehending police violence as a form of punishment has two important theoretical implications. First, rather than attempting to verify that facts match the definition, one should strive to adapt the latter to the former. Here, the meaning that the agents give to their acts and the analysis that one can make of what underlies them lead one to contest the criteria proposed by normative theorists. When a reality does not fit its definition, it is the definition that should be revised. Second, while it is conceptually relevant to try to separate definition from justification, as these scholars do, it is empirically difficult as well as politically problematic to do so. Officers and their institution do need arguments, albeit fallacious, to legitimize what would otherwise appear as deviance. It is not the task of the social scientist to help them in this endeavor. Both these theoretical implications were implicit in Hart's critique of the definitional stop.

Putting together the various pieces of the puzzle in light of the classical definition of punishment, one can see that such police operations are conducted by a legal institution that is not designed to punish but considers itself entitled and is incited by public authorities to do so; that the offenses sanctioned do not match the initial motive of the intervention and can even be fabricated so as to neutralize potential complaints; that in the absence of an identifiable or suspicious offender, retribution can translate into punitive expedition or random punishment; and that extralegal forms such as physical and moral abuse are adopted.

What I have analyzed about France is in no way specific. In recent years, law enforcement agencies have increasingly appeared, in various parts of the globe, as suppliers of extrajudicial punishment. In Brazil, human rights organizations calculated that more than five thousand people were killed by the police between 2005 and 2014 in Rio de Janeiro as part of the so-called pacification of the favelas. In the Philippines, official statistics reveal that just within the months of July and August 2016 more than eighteen hundred suspects were shot dead, including seven hundred by the police, as a result of the war on drugs declared by the newly elected president. In the United States, 1,134 deaths caused by the police were registered in 2015, that is, forty times more than those by capital punishment during the same period, and remarkably, the socioracial profile of victims is similar.[5] The local interpretation of these homicides as extrajudiciary punishments varies according to the context: in some cases, the statements made by politicians and the positive reactions from part of the population leave no doubt about the existence of what is often called penal populism; in others, the support of these practices by the authorities, their facilitation by the institution, the impunity they benefit from, and the complacent silence that accompanies them reveal latent or veiled expressions of this populism.

However, the punitive function of law enforcement should not be reduced to these extreme manifestations. On a daily basis, for many belonging to the most vulnerable groups, it translates into harassment, provocations, humiliations, racist slurs, undue stops, unjustified searches, abusive fines, painful handcuffing, groundless arrests, arbitrary custody, blows leaving no traces, and sometimes even torture—all forms of mistreatment that must be accepted without flinching, since any form of response or rebellion would immediately be punished physically and legally. If the Black Lives Matter movement started with the killings of African Americans by the police in the United States, it soon extended its denunciation to the ordinary forms of oppression of ethnoracial minorities rendered invisible to the mainstream population.

The trivialization and normalization of extrajudiciary punishment by the police are a major unrecognized fact in contemporary societies. In fact, this very trivialization and normalization as a form of punishment could even be deemed part of the judicial system. In the same way that the immense majority of people who are indicted are not sentenced in court by a judge or a jury but accept plea bargaining even if they are innocent, the immense majority of people from certain groups who have interactions with the police are punished in the street or at the precinct even when they are not guilty. The informal and even illegal judicial system is thus much more extended than the formal and legal one. But the two are not separated. By arresting people and handing them over to the prosecutor, that is, by selecting whom they decide to arrest under their discretionary power and by forging accusations to conceal their own misbehavior, the police participate in the judicial system, which, by giving precedence to the word of sworn-in officers over the word of suspects, grants them legitimacy.

5. Sources for these statistics are to be found in the following documents and articles: Anistia Internacional Brasil 2015; Lema 2016; *Guardian* 2015; Death Penalty Information Center 2019; Karabel 2014.

Beyond Philosophical Justifications

But why would the police punish? And why would society expect from them that they play this role?[6] Two theories of justification prevail in philosophical and legal literature. For utilitarians, following Jeremy Bentham, only consequences that punishment may have for society should be taken into account. It should therefore be justified if it contributes to a decline in crime either by incapacitating the criminal, by rehabilitating him, by deterring future crime, or by combining the three. For retributivists, after Immanuel Kant, only the act that has been committed should be taken into account, punishment being just deserts. It should only be justified if it causes pain to the offender so as to pay for his offense in a degree equivalent to the suffering he has caused. Focused on reducing crime, the utilitarians look toward the future. Concentrated on the atonement of the offense, the retributivists are mainly oriented toward the past. Is one of these justifications applicable in the case of the police?

Let us examine one of the various similar interactions that I witnessed or heard about during my fieldwork. Three adolescents are talking and laughing joyously in a small square near the hostel of the youth protection service where they stay. Like the other minors residing in the three-floor house, they have been placed in this institution by a juvenile judge either because they have committed a misdemeanor or because they are deemed endangered. The three teenagers are of African origin. Two police officers on patrol stop by and ask for their papers. Such a check is banal but illegal, since there is no indication of a crime being or having been committed and since it is moreover established that such a stop is often based on racial profiling. The adolescents present their travel passes, which are normally regarded as sufficient since it has their name and photograph. Not satisfied, the agents demand their identification cards. The adolescents, who do not have the documents with them, explain that they live in the hostel some fifty yards away and propose the officers accompany them to fetch them. The police ruthlessly refuse and threaten to take them into the precinct for further verification. Panicked at this prospect, one of the teenagers escapes, runs to his lodging, takes the requested card and swiftly returns to prove his good faith. But the reception is not what he expects. The officers scold him harshly, using racist slurs while slapping him. Alerted by the shouting, one of the social workers of the service comes out, only to hear one of the officers viciously threaten the boy: "I'm going to kneecap you!" and hurtfully yell at him: "You're a failure in your family! You're a failure

6. The discussion of the justifications for punishment and the presentation of the anecdote are developed in more detail in my Berkeley Tanner Lectures published as *The Will to Punish* (2018).

at school! You, little faggot!" Not without difficulty, the social worker interposes herself and finally manages to bring the adolescent back to the hostel. There, with the director of the institution, she tries to convince him to file a complaint against the agent, telling him how important it is to defend his rights. Still shaken and distressed by the aggressive and humiliating handling he just endured, the teenager keeps repeating in a low voice that it does not matter. Obviously, he knows how much weight the word of a black minor under the care of a youth protection service would carry when confronted with the word of two officers, how easily his complaint could be reversed into a case against him for insulting an officer and resisting arrest, and in the end how costly it could be to try to assert his rights. He impatiently returns to his room.

How to interpret this scene? Added to the socially and racially grounded hostility, which is commonly expressed in words and acts by the police toward adolescents with this profile, is in this case a moral aspect. Being under the supervision of the judicial institution, the teenagers have already had dealings with the penal system, either as delinquents or as victims or, more often than not, as both. Although the agents pretend to ignore that the boys live in the hostel, as they refuse to let them fetch their identity cards there, they evidently know where they come from, imagine what may have been their history, and mistreat them accordingly: hence the hassle about the documents, the threat to arrest them, the nasty comments, the slaps. It is hardly imaginable that such a scene could have happened in a residential area, for the simple reason that, as the head of the anticrime squad unit told me, they never went there, except in the very rare cases when a crime had been committed. Their activity was limited to certain territories and populations.

In the present incident, the level of violence is all the more remarkable in that there has been no wrongdoing: only messing around in a public space. In fact, the officers punish the adolescents not because of what they do but because of what they are or represent: lower-class black boys of migrant origin, moreover with probable dealings with the judicial system. This combination of social, racial, and moral attributes is sufficient to presume their culpability, or at least to assume that they deserve a lesson. The psychological harassment and physical abuse do not only allow the police to exert and display their discretionary power. They also serve to inculcate a hierarchical order, as the youths learn, through the repetition of such experiences, their inferior social, racial, and moral position. Neither the justifications proposed by philosophers and legal theorists nor the justifications provided by the police suffice to account for the scene. In the absence of offense committed, it is difficult to resort to the utilitarian and retributivist arguments, in a strict sense, to justify the punishment.

557

Even if the officers pretend that they are strictly enforcing the law by verifying the identity of individuals in public spaces and teaching them to abide by the rules, it is difficult to justify the verbal and physical violence in the interaction. One must resort to a more general interpretation considering the function that they are assigned by society, which consists in using their discretionary power to call to social order the purportedly dangerous classes. The adolescent understood it, and this is why, for him, it made no sense to file a complaint. With whom? With the very institution whose members harass him? To be adjudicated by whom? By a justice system in which the word of young men of color has no weight against the word of sworn-in officers? Schooled by an already long experience of interaction with law enforcement, the adolescent knew that he was "police property," in John Alan Lee's (1981: 53) words.

Yet, the analysis must go further. Rationality—that provided by the law, that offered by officers, that elaborated by social scientists—does not exhaust the reasons the police punish as they do. Indeed, as one can see in the case of this adolescent, punishment is always in excess of what it is supposed to be. But why is it the case? Why would officers purposely put handcuffs incorrectly on to suspects they have arrested so as to painfully twist their arms and make fun of their complaint while taking them into the precinct for questioning, sometimes causing nerve compression that can be irreversible? Why would they take them into custody in filthy and cold rooms without letting them go to the toilets, have something to eat, or even sometimes take their medicine? Why would they intentionally drive their vehicle in a rough way when they extradite prisoners to a faraway jurisdiction so as to have them bang around or get car sick? Why would they debase them with offensive remarks and threaten them with dismaying prospects? In the act of punishing, something resists rational analysis or, better said, resists being analyzed as rational. There is almost inexorably an emotional dimension, which Friedrich Nietzsche (1989: 5) describes as "the voluptuous pleasure *'de faire le mal pour le plaisir de le faire'*, the enjoyment of violation." To punish is to produce a gratuitous suffering, which adds to the retribution, for the mere satisfaction of knowing that the culprit—or the one presumed such— suffers. In the assimilation of punishment with pain and, even more, in the unnecessary torment that is added to it, one cannot not recognize the expression of cruelty.

Conclusion

On February 2, 2017, in a housing project outside Paris, a twenty-two-year-old local educator of Congolese origin was violently arrested for having interfered with the brutal stop and frisk of three of his friends who were simply hanging around in his neighborhood.[7] As he was resisting the handcuffing, he was pushed against a wall and hit from behind by one of the officers with an expandable baton. The blow caused a tear of the sphincter muscle of the anus, a four-inch-deep wound of the rectum, and a perforation of the intestine. The prosecutor opened a criminal investigation for "voluntary violence," and the investigating judge indicted the guilty officer for "rape." Police experts tried, however, to explain that the gesture was part of normal police practice "to create a physical destabilization and bring the recalcitrant under control." One year later, not being able to defecate, the young man still had a colostomy with a plastic bag to collect his waste. In the meantime, one learned that the commissioner of the same district had received a six-month suspended prison sentence for not having stopped one of his agents who was threatening to sodomize a man with a hubcap, and that in a neighboring town an officer was indicted for having caused with his baton a one-inch-long anal wound to an inebriated young man as he was pushing him into the police car whose back seat had been folded down so as to force him to bend forward as he was handcuffed.

There seems to be in these cases a common pattern of humiliation of young men, especially of color, through the negation of their masculinity by these specific forms of violence. In this sense, they can neither be reduced to deviant acts of sadistic officers nor interpreted as mere techniques of control. It is part and parcel of retribution. In fact, following Everett Hughes's (1962) disturbing but lucid observation, one can say that society delegates to certain institutions and professions, notably the police, the dirty work of punishing with the implicit permission to exceed the moral and legal limits of punishment.

References

Albertini, Dominique, and David Doucet. 2013. *Histoire du Front National*. Paris: Tallandier.

Anistia Internacional Brasil. 2015. *You Killed My Son: Homicides by Military Police in the City of Rio de Janeiro*. Rio de Janeiro: Amnesty International.

Bittner, Egon. 1980. *The Functions of the Police in Modern Society*. Cambridge, MA: Oelgeschlager, Gunn & Hain.

7. The so-called Théo Affair and its developments are discussed in various articles, including in Pascual 2018. The sentencing of the commissioner is described in *Le Monde* 2017. The little publicized case of the other young man wounded by an officer can be read in Saviana 2018.

Blanchard, Emmanuel. 2011. *La police française et les Algériens (1944–1962)*. Paris: Nouveau Monde Éditions.

Death Penalty Information Center. 2019. *Number of Executions since 1976*. www .deathpenaltyinfo.org/executions-year (accessed February 18, 2019).

Durkheim, Émile. 1984. *The Division of Labor in Society*, translated by W. D. Halls. New York: Free Press.

Einaudi, Jean-Luc. 2001. *Octobre 1961: Un massacre à Paris*. Paris: Fayard.

Ericson, Richard. 1982. *Reproducing Order: A Study of Police Patrol Work*. Toronto: University of Toronto Press.

Fassin, Didier. 2013. *Enforcing Order: An Ethnography of Urban Policing*, translated by Rachel Gomme. Cambridge: Polity.

Fassin, Didier. 2018. *The Will to Punish*, edited by Christopher Kutz. Oxford: Oxford University Press.

Feeley, Malcolm. 1992. *The Process Is the Punishment: Handling Cases in a Lower Criminal Court*. New York: The Russell Sage Foundation.

The Guardian. 2015. "The Guardian View on Killings by US Police: Why We Must Keep Counting." December 31.

Hart, H. L. A. 1959. "The Presidential Address: Prolegomenon to the Principles of Punishment." *Proceedings of the Aristotelian Society* 60: 1–26.

Hughes, Everett. 1962. "Good People and Dirty Work." *Social Problems* 10, no. 1: 3–11.

Jean-Marc B. 2018. "Les policiers français ont abattu 18 personnes en 2017." *Mediapart*, January 11. blogs.mediapart.fr/jean-marc-b/blog/100118/les -policiers-francais-ont-abattu-18-personnes-en-2017.

Karabel, Jerome. 2014. "The Other Capital Punishment." *Huffpost Politics*, December 10.

Klockars, Carl. 1980. "The Dirty Harry Problem." *Annals of the American Academy of Political Science* 452, no. 1: 33–47.

Lee, John Alan. 1981. "Some Structural Aspects of Police Deviance in Relations with Minority Groups." In *Organizational Police Deviance: Its Structure and Control*, edited by Clifford Schearing, 49–82. Toronto: Butterworths.

Lema, Karen. 2016. "Philippines Drug War Deaths Climb to 1,800; U.S. Deeply Concerned." *Reuters*, August 22. www.reuters.com/article/us-philippines -duterte-un-killings-idUSKCN10X0IS.

Le Monde. 2017. "Le passé du commissaire de police d'Aulnay-sous-Bois refait surface." February 14.

Nietzsche, Friedrich. 1989. *On the Genealogy of Morals*, translated by Walter Kaufmann. New York: Vintage Books.

Pascual, Julia. 2018. "Affaire Théo L.: Des images de vidéosurveillance montrent l'interpellation du jeune homme." *Le Monde*, January 29.

Reiner, Robert. 2000. *The Politics of the Police*. Oxford: Oxford University Press.

Saviana, Alexandra. 2018. "L'autre affaire Théo: Alexandre attend que sa blessure anale par un policier soit requalifiée en viol." *Marianne*, February 21.

Urgence-notre-police-assassine en toute impunité. 2019. http://www.urgence -notre-police-assassine.fr/123663553 (accessed February 18, 2019).

Didier Fassin is James D. Wolfensohn Professor at the Institute for Advanced Study and Director of Studies at the École des Hautes Études en Sciences Sociales. Anthropologist, sociologist, and physician, he has conducted research in Senegal, South Africa, Ecuador, and France. Author of sixteen books, he was awarded a gold medal in anthropology at the Swedish Royal Academy of Arts and Sciences in 2016, and in 2018 he was the first social scientist to receive the Nomis Distinguished Scientist Award. His current work is on crises, their construction, their meaning, and the responses they generate.

Elimination Politics: Punishment and Imprisonment in Palestine

Ilana Feldman

"We have the honour to congratulate His Majesty's Empire for the decisive victory which His Forces has recently achieved." So opened a May 1945 petition to the High Commissioner for Palestine from three Palestinians requesting clemency. They had, they said, been banished from their village of Beit Daras to Khan Yunis "for political doubts." These political doubts almost certainly meant presumed participation in the Palestinian struggle for self-determination—a goal that required the end of both British Mandate rule and Zionist settlement in Palestine. Saying that they considered themselves subjects of the king, that they wished to "feel some of the happiness of such a great victory," and furthermore that no crime had been proved against them, the men asked that the banishment order be canceled to let them "feel free under the recent victory, to return to our families and to be more loyal."[1] The charge against them was that they were oppositional political actors. Their petition tried to reject that categorization, asking that they be viewed instead as loyal, docile, and, therefore, free subjects. The fate of these individuals is not recorded in the file, but the punishment of Palestinians for political activity and the concomitant effort to render them docile subjects have been at the center of the now hundred-year-long settler-colonial condition in the country.

Patrick Wolfe (2006: 388) has famously argued that the "elimination of the native" is a central aim of settler colonialism, and he further underscores that colonial invasion is a "structure rather than an event." As he explains, elimination entails the dissolution of native societies and their replacement by a new colonial

---

1. Israel State Archives (ISA), RG 2 O/72/45, Petition to High Commissioner, May 18, 1945.

Public Culture 31:3 DOI 10.1215/08992363-7532655
Copyright 2019 by Duke University Press

society. This replacement is sometimes accomplished through genocide, but it also occurs through a range of other techniques that destroy communities. Banishment (as described in the petition) and imprisonment have been key tactics for separating people from their homes and communities. In the case of colonial rule and anticolonial rebellion, of occupation and resistance to it, the prison and the imprisoned subject are at the center of a contest within politics. The struggle over elimination in Palestine has been ongoing for one hundred years. It has continued through multiple changes in governing regimes and across territorial reconfigurations. The different tactics deployed against Palestinians over these decades are a product both of these changes and of the continuing Palestinian refusal to acquiesce to their elimination.

A double move has been central to this project—an attempt to deny or destroy Palestinian political community, while simultaneously identifying Palestinians as political actors, specifically as bad actors. This double move seeks to undermine Palestinian political capacity by disrupting connection and organizing, while still deploying the weapon of categorizing Palestinians, individually and collectively, as enemies—under labels such as insurgents, terrorists, and enemy combatants. Such efforts to simultaneously destroy and weaponize the political have not, though, succeeded in ending resistance to the settler-colonial project in Palestine. As J. Kehaulani Kauanui (2016) puts it, indigeneity "endures." Repeated attacks on Palestinians, and modifications in tactics deployed against them, reflect the failure to complete the elimination project. But the fact that Palestinians have not been eliminated—either as a community or as a population—does not mean that they have not been grievously harmed by the century-long effort to make them choose between docility and expulsion.

Violence directed against Palestinians takes many forms—including military assault, bureaucratic torture (Lavie 2018), and dispossession. This essay focuses on punishment and imprisonment, which also take multiple forms. Imprisonment includes both formal incarceration in prisons and confinement in place. In addition to punitive imprisonment—meting out harsh sentences for criminal acts to punish nearby political activity—punishments directed at Palestinians have included destruction of property, material deprivation, and collective punishments of various kinds. Forms of punishment and categories of imprisonment clearly reveal the two-pronged attack on politics. As Palestinians have struggled against different forms of colonial occupation and for control over their political destiny for over a century, confinement has been a central weapon in the arsenal deployed against them. Palestine is by no means the only place where imprisonment is a tactic of elimination. The "carceral condition" (Fassin 2017) is global. Working in another settler-colonial space, Kelly Lytle Hernández (2017: 1) has shown that "incarceration operates as a means of purging, removing, caging, containing, erasing, disappearing, and eliminating targeted populations from land, life, and society in the United States."

The importance of locating Palestine in a settler-colonial paradigm has been increasingly recognized. Following this move, and its insistence on the importance of avoiding the analytic and political traps of both exceptionalism (in which Palestine appears sui generis and utterly incomparable to any place else) and localism (where different Palestinian populations are considered entirely separately) (Salamanca et al. 2012), this essay considers imprisonment in three periods of Palestinian history, and in three overlapping, yet distinctive, geographies of Palestinian experience. Each is part of the long history of colonial dispossession and ongoing efforts toward the elimination of the native in Palestine. These periods—the British Mandate over Palestine (1922–48), the Israeli occupation of the West Bank and Gaza (1967–), and the period since the pullout of Israeli settlers from the Gaza Strip (2005–)—illuminate related but distinctive use of punishment and imprisonment in this effort (Khalili 2013).

Like other aspects of policing, imprisonment is a work of sorting. It sorts licit from illicit, legal from illegal, public morality from social impropriety, obedience from dissidence. The distinctions of imprisonment are not just between the jailed and the free but also among different sorts of prisoners. The categorization of crimes (and therefore of prisoners) as either "ordinary" criminality or political action is an obvious way in which authorities claim to mark the boundaries of politics, but these categorizations are themselves deeply political. Furthermore, the proliferation of prisoner and punishment categories is not only or always a mechanism of distinction. Policing also operates through indistinction (Feldman 2007, 2015b), by making it difficult for people to know precisely where they stand in relation to the line of illegality, guilt, and, even, proper politics. Prisoner of war, security detainee, and unlawful enemy combatant are all political detention categories, but they reflect different judgments about the meaning of the politics they punish. The enduring importance of collective punishment in the effort to put down political unrest in Palestine makes clear that even as Palestinian political community may be denied, collective Palestinian culpability for the actions of individual "bad actors" is continually asserted.

Intercessions on behalf of prisoners—sometimes from the detained themselves, as in the petition described above, and sometimes from family members or organizations—engage the punishment categories of governments and also try to give weight to other, sometimes competing, ways of describing prisoners.

Categories that are used by international observers—such as protected persons or even victims—try to situate prison categories within a broader field of humanity law (Teitel 2011). Palestinians engage with all these categories—demanding recognition as political prisoners, seeking sympathy as victims. They also identify prisoners as national subjects and national heroes. In so doing, Palestinians not only identify prisoners as good political actors, they locate them as central to Palestinian political community.

On the Subject of Palestine

The British Mandate for Palestine (1922–48) was an instance of late colonialism, internationally sanctioned through the League of Nations. The terms of the Mandate committed the British government to supporting settler-colonialism by promoting the development of a Jewish national home in Palestine. In this effort, "nothing should be done which might prejudice the civil and religious rights of existing non-Jewish communities in Palestine" (Palestine Mandate 2019). Notably absent from this formulation was a recognition of a Palestinian national community with political rights. The Mandate itself, therefore, was structured toward the political elimination of the Palestinian native by the a priori disavowal of the existence of such a political community. The Zionist settlement project worked not only toward usurping the Palestinian place in Palestine but also toward occupying the position of the native in this territory.

In 1948 Palestine was divided, not according to the terms proposed by the United Nations (UN), which offered 56 percent of the territory to a Jewish state, but along the armistice lines that marked the end of fighting between Zionist (and after May 15 Israeli) forces and Arab armies. The majority of the native population was displaced, many people becoming refugees in nearby countries. The parts of Palestine that became the West Bank and Gaza Strip came under Jordanian and Egyptian control respectively, the former annexed to Jordan. Even as the *nakba* (catastrophe) marked the end, thus far, of a Palestinian political entity, it did not in fact mean the end of Palestinian political community, which became, if anything, more vibrant in exile.

In 1967, when Israel occupied the West Bank and Gaza Strip, along with the Sinai and the Golan Heights, the territory of historic Palestine came once again under a single ruler. But Palestinians who lived in different parts of this territory were governed differently. Some lived as second-class citizens—those who resided inside the Green Line and were Israeli citizens—and more were governed as an occupied population. For Israel the occupation entailed a reencounter with the native—now more politically organized and primed to resist. The occupation also brought a new phase in territorial elimination. Confiscation of land for Israeli settlement in the West Bank and Gaza and for military installations began shortly after the occupation (Weizman 2017; Pappe 2016). The infrastructure required to sustain and protect these settlements took still more land. This process has expanded and intensified as the years have passed.

The different parts of Palestine remain divided—by their territorial status, by the treatment of their population, and, as the years have gone by, increasingly by checkpoints, walls, and a permit system. It is these developments that Achille Mbembe (2003: 27) references when he describes the Israeli occupation of the West Bank and Gaza as the site of the "most accomplished form of necropower." Since the signing of the Oslo Accords, which brought a measure of autonomy to Palestinian population centers under the Palestinian Authority, the West Bank and Gaza have been further separated. And Palestinian movement between these territories has been increasingly disallowed. In 2005 Israel removed its settlers and soldiers from Gaza, changing the nature of occupation from the clear settler-colonial model still pursued in the West Bank to one in which this occupied area was declared "enemy territory." For the past ten years Gaza has been subjected to a punishing blockade. The siege on Gaza represents the widest generalization of imprisonment. It has gone from a punishment to which some persons are subjected to a condition under which the entire population lives. And it represents the latest phase in elimination—in which livability itself is targeted for destruction.

Mandate Punishment

Even as the denial of native Palestinian political community was built into the Mandate, British rule in Palestine was underpinned by the conviction—despite persistent evidence to the contrary—that Mandate governance could inculcate a shared political community between the native population and Zionist settlers, thus enabling Mandatory authorities to fulfill their contradictory obligations. This belief was repeatedly shattered by the outbreaks of violence in the country, including riots in 1921, 1929, 1933, and full-scale rebellion in 1936–39 (by Arabs) and 1946 (by Jews). Even as this ongoing opposition challenged the fictions of Mandate rule, it was not until the end of the Mandate that its lessons were recognized. In the face of this recognition, the British basically gave up, handing the Palestine matter to the United Nations.

Since Palestinians did not acquiesce to the elimination of their political community, denial had to be repeated throughout the Mandate. Palestine was thus a particular instance of a broader colonial dynamic. Repeated efforts by colonized populations to liberate themselves from colonialism put a lie to the pretense that natives can be convinced that governing themselves is beyond their capabilities and not in their interest. Hence counterinsurgency is often at the center of colonial rule. Police responses to Palestinian anticolonial resistance showcase the variety of forms of denial. Refusing to acknowledge resistance *as* resistance, as organized political action by a collectivity, was an instance of denial. So too was the considerable indistinction in categories of imprisonment.

Mandate officials also failed to recognize the actual impossibility of eliminating Palestinian political community simply by repeatedly denying its existence. The response of police personnel when faced with political violence is a case in point. The Palestine Police were composed of a relatively small British section and a much larger Palestinian contingent, mostly Arab. Outbreaks of violence were nearly always followed by investigations and recommendations for reorganization of the force. These reports were devastating in their evaluation of the existing state of things, forcing Mandate officials to acknowledge that the police had not yet been able to transcend their positions as members of communities in conflict and act for the general public good. Plans for reform were based, though, on the continued belief that this purpose could be produced in and for the future.

When the 1936–39 Palestinian uprising—the most sustained resistance to British rule—confirmed the continued failure to develop a "professional" police force that would rise above the national politics in which police officers were personally immersed, the British response was to deploy an increasingly militarized form of policing. There was no formal imposition of martial law, but British military personnel were engaged in quelling the revolt. Collective punishment, execution, and imprisonment were all used in this effort. Collective punishment was sanctioned by Mandate ordinances and incorporated into the instructions provided to soldiers (Hughes 2009: 317). Tens of thousands of Palestinian Arabs were detained (Khalili 2010: 423). The categorical terms of imprisonment reflect the British refusal to acknowledge the nature of the uprising. Matthew Hughes (2009: 318) indicates that Britain "classified the Arab revolt as an internal insurrection and not an international war and so denied POW status to Arab fighters. Thus it treated captured Arab guerrillas as civilian criminals subject to the ordinary civil law modified by any conditions of martial law, such as the death penalty for carrying ammunition or a firearm, and for whom international law did not apply."

British denial of internationally recognized and, therefore, protected status to Palestinian fighters was part of the project of elimination through denial of political community. This denial did not mean that Palestinians were not recognized as political actors, but that their politics was deemed improper. Treating fighters as individual bad actors and categorizing them as "civilian criminals" had the further effect of also rendering criminality politically suspect. Evidence of this effect can be found in many petitions submitted to the Mandate government by family members seeking clemency for their imprisoned relatives. Often these prisoners appear to have, in fact, been ordinary criminals whose punishment was caught up in the politics of Palestine. Not only did the boundary between civil crime and political action become increasingly murky as the Mandate went on, but the use of collective punishment further ensured that, even as collectivity in the form of political community was denied, Palestinians as a whole were deemed responsible for the political actions of particular individuals.

Among the petition files from this period are many requests for clemency for people convicted of weapons possession charges. Weapons possession was a crime adjudicated by a military court, even if the possession and/or use of the weapon was not evidently political. The wife of a prisoner from Isdud, a village in southern Palestine, sent two petitions in 1945. Her husband had been convicted by a military court, but his apparent purpose in possessing the firearm was robbery. The other crime for which he was convicted was housebreaking. The petition asked for compassion for the all-female household left behind: "Our present state of living deserves your sympathy as it is misery,"[2] and "we all become destitute and our living conditions are getting worse from one day to the other owing to the absence of our supporter, my husband, in whose absence we find no body to look after us and cultivate his lands from which he used to maintain us."[3] Clemency was not granted. Rejection appears to have been the most common response to such petitions. Whatever the result, these cases confirm that possession of a weapon was politically relevant, no matter the intent behind it. This absorption of criminality into the domain of the political was part of the wider denial that Palestinian politics was proper politics.

In 1945 village leaders from Iraq al-Manshiyya asked for clemency for a village resident who was halfway through a ten-year sentence for "intimidation and looting."[4] Asserting that the prisoner was innocent and a "straight-forward man and of good character," they asked for pardon on compassionate grounds. The petition stated that he had been convicted by a military court, but notations on the documents by Mandate officials indicate that this was not in fact the case. The crime was not political—it was an attempted theft through intimidation—but the

2. ISA, RG 2 346, OP/39/46, Petition for clemency, December 29, 1945.
3. ISA, RG 2 346, OP/39/46, Petition for clemency, May 4, 1945.
4. ISA RG 2 345, OP/8/46, Petition for clemency, n.d.

politics of Palestine entered into the deliberations about a possible release. This was a case not only of political considerations affecting the punishment of criminality but of the radiating effects of collective punishment. The district commissioner initially recommended against release because "Iraq el Manshiya village had a bad record during the disturbances [when the crime occurred] and has lately been showing signs of renewed unrest."[5]

The attorney general then commented, "I cannot help by feeling that the sentence would have been much lighter but for the fact that the offence was committed at the time of the disturbances." Acknowledging the district commissioner's judgment of the village as a site of "unrest," he went on, "be that as it may, I think that the six years odd which the prisoner has served is sufficient punishment and he should be released."[6] This argument ultimately convinced the relevant persons (including the district commissioner), and the prisoner was released in March 1946. Even as this prisoner found an escape from the matrix of a simultaneous denial of Palestinian political community and the expanding identification of Palestinians as improper political actors, the two-pronged counterinsurgency survived. And it continued beyond the end of the Mandate.

Occupation Imprisonment

The legal apparatus established during the Mandate was never overturned in any of the territories of historic Palestine. For two decades after 1948, Israel, Jordan, and Egypt each made slightly different use of these colonial mechanisms in the parts of Palestine they controlled. The results of the June 1967 war brought all of historic Palestine under Israeli control. And it brought governance of this territory into contested relation with international law. Israel argued that the West Bank and Gaza Strip were not "occupied territories" in a legal sense and that, therefore, Article 4 of the 1949 Geneva Conventions, which governs the management of such territories, did not apply (Aruri 1978). Occupation denial—an ongoing feature of occupation governance (Shafir 2017)—both rests on and furthers the project of eliminating Palestinian political community.

Central to the Israeli argument that the territories are not occupied is the claim that they were not part of an independent (Palestinian) state and therefore had no recognized political status. In a world made up of nation-states, territorial control

5. ISA RG 2 345, OP/8/46, from District Commissioner, Gaza, to Commissioner of Prisons, January 1, 1946.
6. ISA RG 2 345, OP/8/46, from Chief Secretary to District Commissioner, Gaza, February 15, 1946.

is closely connected to recognition of political status. There is circularity in this argument. The West Bank and Gaza Strip should not be viewed as occupied territories because Palestinians did not exercise sovereignty over these lands. And Palestinians are not a political community, in part, because they did not have sovereignty over territory. The effects of efforts to eliminate Palestinian presence are presented as evidence of their political absence. But just as the British Mandate could not, in fact, eliminate Palestinian political community by denying its existence, the denialist Israeli position neither dissolved the occupation as a category through which Palestinians and international observers understood Israeli rule in the territories nor dissipated Palestinian politics. The persistence of Palestinian politics is one reason that Israel turned toward increased repression, what Baruch Kimmerling (2003) terms "politicide."

Denial of occupation and refusal of international legal authority shaped the forms of punishment and confinement Israel used in governance of the territories. As Lisa Hajjar (2005: 54–55) explains, the Israeli government indicated that they would respect the "humanitarian provisions" of the Convention, but they did not specify what they viewed those to be. As Hajjar further notes, the International Committee of the Red Cross (ICRC) views the conventions in their entirety as humanitarian. One outcome of the Israeli stance was its "refusal to receive any international commission to investigate the conditions of the inhabitants of the occupied territories or allow an Israeli investigation with an international observer" (Aruri 1978: 52). During the occupation incarceration became a central feature of the Palestinian experience, as did the radiating effects of imprisonment on families and communities. The close connection between forms of territorial control and categories of imprisonment was evident in the first years of the occupation, as Israeli officials staked out their position, often in confrontation with international organizations such as the ICRC. And prisoners have been key subjects in the contest between Israel and the occupied population over proper political life for Palestinians.

The ICRC never accepted the Israeli position about the status of the territories and continued to seek acknowledgment of the authority of international law. The specific issues that the ICRC brought up repeatedly with Israeli government officials included expulsions of people from the territories, destruction of houses, conditions of detention, and recognition of the ICRC as a substitute protective power. Expulsion from the country of people "suspected of activities detrimental to state security"[7] and destruction of houses as a form of collective punishment were both

7. International Committee of the Red Cross archives (ICRC), B AG 202 139 036, letter from Marcel Naville to Golda Meir, February 24, 1971.

tools in the eliminationist project of occupation. The ICRC complained about each practice. In an April 1971 letter to Prime Minister Golda Meir, the president of the ICRC expressed his concern about reports that 140 houses had been destroyed in the territories. The ICRC, he said, "considers itself duty bound to address to your Government a further pressing appeal to abandon this method of combat against subversive activities." Acknowledging the "humanitarian" decision of the Israeli government not to apply capital punishment for security offenses, he went on to say, "We wish to point out that such collective punishment as the destruction of houses is a serious infringement of the principles of humanity and justice to which the Israeli government has often demonstrated its adherence and which it has actively supported in other circumstances."[8]

The Israeli response to this missive, and to similar letters about other matters, was to insist on both the legality and the righteousness of its actions: "The measures referred to are based on and are in conformity with the local law as laid down in the Defence (Emergency) Regulations of 1945. . . . The Regulations permit penal sanctions against any house or structure situated in any area where acts of terror or violence have been perpetrated."[9] Israeli discourse and practice confirm that even as international law was not fully applied to the occupied territories, colonial law certainly was. Meir rejected the argument that Israel's house demolitions constituted collective punishment under the terms of international law. She insisted that even as "regrettably such measures affect also members of the criminal's family," the fact that the houses demolished were the homes of perpetrators made the punishment specific. She further averred that they "have proved their value in combatting indiscriminate acts of murder and outrage perpetrated against the civilian population and members of the armed forces."

The terms of both the practice and the defense of home demolitions shed additional light on the two-pronged eliminationist project. Meir's letter indicated that demolitions were intended to punish "acts of terror and murder" that were designed to "undermine secure and normal life in the areas concerned." She continued, "The suffering this would involve for innocent, women, and children requires no emphasis." Foregrounding the claimed Israeli concern for the suffering of Palestinians at the hands of other Palestinians (a trope that has continued through the years), the Israeli position denies the existence of a Palestinian community engaged in resistance to Israeli occupation, identifying only Palestinian terrorists seeking to harm innocent Palestinians and Israelis. But even as com-

8. ICRC, B AG 202 139 036, letter from Marcel Naville to Golda Meir, April 30, 1971.
9. ICRC, B AG 202 139 036, letter from Golda Meir to Marcel Naville, August 20, 1971.

munity is denied, relatives of these "bad actors" had to, however "regrettably," shoulder responsibility.

Another key provision of the Mandate-era Emergency Law provided for "administrative detention" of designated security risks without charge and for an indefinite period of time (generally in six-month increments). Facing a politicized, organized, and actively resisting population in the occupied territories, Israel has made significant use of this provision—along with a military court system that has handed down long prison sentences for a wide array of political activities. Despite the political reasons for mass imprisonment, Palestinian prisoners were often not recognized as political prisoners. As Naseer Aruri (1978: 61) described, "No distinction is made between common criminals and civilians detained for political or 'security' offences." Aruri further described systematic discrimination between Arab and Jewish prisoners. Both equal treatment and recognition of their political status have been demands of prisoners undertaking hunger strikes over the years.

The ICRC, for its part, was concerned to have information about and access to Palestinians held in Israeli prisons. Even if agreement could not be reached on the framework for governance in the territories (Article 4) or the status of the ICRC (as possible substitute protective power), the ICRC continued to seek "pragmatic" implementation of international humanitarian law provisions. In a 1972 memo to Israeli officials with the subject heading "various tasks the ICRC would undertake following the new practical approach of the Israeli Authorities towards its humanitarian mission," it laid out its expectations in regard to "protected persons," a category that included prisoners. When and how would the ICRC be notified of detentions? Where are they detained? With what charges and what status? The memo went on to note that "at the moment, the ICRC does not carry out any significant activity in the judicial field, except for visits to detainees after a certain period of time" and expressed hope that this situation could change.[10] In its negotiations with Israeli authorities, the ICRC tried to politely insist on maintaining regular lines of communication for "security detainees," as Israel refers to Palestinian political prisoners (Latte Abdallah 2015: 39). The ICRC stressed the "preventive and not punitive motives of administrative detention"[11] and underscored that "the basic principles for the treatment of non-criminal and non-convicted detainees is that their relationships with the exterior [visits with

10. ICRC, B AG 202 139 036, letter from Guy Deluz to General Gazit, January 16, 1972.
11. ICRC, B AG 219 102-012, letter to General Gazit from ICRC, June 2, 1969.

friends and family] should be enlarged."[12] Even as the ICRC complained about certain policies—such as a refusal to allow prisoners to serve as interpreters for each other, meaning that ICRC delegations could meet only with English-speaking detainees—it expressed its "satisfaction over the frank and constructive working relationship we have established."[13]

At stake in these negotiations were the categorization and related treatment of prisoners. The above correspondence was about the category of administrative/security detainee. Israel also held prisoners of war, even if, like the British before, it did not always acknowledge them as such. After the battle of Karameh in 1968, the ICRC immediately asked that Israel grant the Fatah prisoners it had captured prisoner-of-war status.[14] The Israeli government refused, saying that it "cannot grant the thousands of members of Palestinian Terrorist organizations whom it has captured the status of prisoners of war. . . . They are not official members of any Arab State's army."[15] This position repeats the claim that without sovereignty there is no political community. The ICRC continued to press the matter of these prisoners. In a letter to General Gazit the following year, the head of the ICRC delegation summarized their recent conversation: "Upon my request that the Israeli authorities take a decision on the status of the 66 'Karameh prisoners' in Jenin you explained why this was not possible at present. The politico-military situation does not allow Israel to liberate potential fighters and—in your opinion—times are not yet 'ripe' for a break up of their group into different categories of detainees, allowing some of them to be liberated. I expressed the hope that our intervention would accelerate the 'ripening' process in cause."[16]

This dispute between Israel and the ICRC about prisoner status was not the only clash over categories. Palestinians have also engaged these categories, insisting on the recognition of detainees as political prisoners. Protests around official categories of imprisonment take place both inside prisons, often in the form of hunger strikes, and outside. Beyond contests about categories, Palestinians have also identified prisoners through their own terms—viewing them as central actors and heroes in the national community and in its struggle. Imprisonment—its net-

12. ICRC, B AG 219 102-012, letter from ICRC to General Gazit, April 27, 1969.
13. ICRC, B AG 219 102-012, letter from ICRC to General Gazit, April 27, 1969.
14. ICRC, B AG 219 102-012, letter from ICRC to Jordanian Red Crescent Society, May 20, 1968. The battle of Karameh, in which the Israeli military encountered unexpectedly strong resistance from Palestinian *fedayeen* (guerillas) when it attacked their base in the Jordan valley, is remembered as an important event in Palestinian national history.
15. ICRC, B AG 219 102-012, AFP Telex of April 30, 1968.
16. ICRC, B AG 219 102-012, letter from ICRC to General Gazit, May 9, 1969.

works, educational apparatus, and community building—has been a key part of Palestinian politics and political subjectivity under occupation (Bornstein 2001). As Esmail Nashif (2008: 9) puts it, prison has been a "social space for building a Palestinian national community" (see also Rosenfeld 2011). The effects of detention extend far beyond the walls of the prison. Rita Giacaman and Penny Johnson (2013) call attention to the gendered features of the radiating prison experience (see also Segal 2016). Wives and mothers of prisoners are the principle navigators of the carceral terrain that links, and separates, Palestinian prisoners and their communities.

By 1989, in the middle of the first intifada, the number of Palestinian prisoners held by Israel reached a peak of thirteen thousand (Latte Abdallah 2015: 40). As part of the Oslo Accords, and the subsequent establishment of the Palestinian Authority in the West Bank and Gaza, most Palestinian prisoners were released in the late 1990s. With the outbreak of the second intifada in 2000, the number of prisoners began to tick up again, but it has never quite reached its pre-Oslo level. During the Oslo years Israel moved almost all Palestinian political prisoners from prisons in the occupied territories to prisons inside Israel. Giacaman and Johnson note that this move contravenes international law. It is a further tactic in the disruption of community that is key to elimination. With the Green Line (the boundary between Israel and the occupied territories), the separation barrier, numerous checkpoints, and a complicated permit regime now lying between prisoners and their family, prisoners' "relationships with the exterior"[17] are impeded not only by the prison and its regulations but also by the restrictions on mobility to which all Palestinians are subjected. The Israeli closure policy creates barriers to family visits, as it disrupts most aspects of Palestinian life. For Palestinians such conditions only underscore the centrality of the prisoner as a political figure.

Collective Punishment Expands

The Israeli relationship to the territory of the Gaza Strip changed with the 2005 pullout of soldiers and settlers. And Israeli categories of imprisonment changed as well. Gazan prisoners were henceforth designated "unlawful enemy combatants." According to Stephanie Latte Abdallah (2015: 45), Israel first applied this categorization (one widely familiar to anyone who has followed the US "war on terror" since 2001) to Lebanese Hizbullah fighters in 2002. After the 2005 pullout, it declared the occupation over—a view not shared by the United Nations

---

17. ICRC, B AG 219 102-012, letter from ICRC to General Gazit, April 27, 1969.

575

and other international observers—and Gaza's population therefore residents of a "foreign country." A number of Gazans who were in Israeli prisons as administrative detainees were placed under new detention orders in the category of unlawful combatant. In response to a challenge to this categorization, in 2008 the Israeli Supreme Court upheld the Israeli government's position: "In view of the fact that the Gaza Strip is no longer under the effective control of the State of Israel, we are drawn to the conclusion that the inhabitants of the Gaza Strip constitute foreign parties who may be subject to the Internment of Unlawful Combatants Law in view of the nature and purpose of this law."[18]

Along with the development of new prisoner categories, a different sort of imprisonment has gained renewed prominence in Israeli practice since the outbreak of the second intifada: the confinement of the entire population. Population-level confinement is not a new tactic deployed against Palestinians. It was central to Israeli rule over Palestinians who remained in Israel after 1948, who were subjected to military rule for twenty years (Robinson 2013). Today confinement is deployed in both the West Bank and Gaza Strip. The closure policy that first began in the 1990s has been significantly expanded. Palestinian movement across the Green Line requires a permit, increasingly few of which are granted (Berda 2017). Checkpoints and road closures have regularly and significantly restricted movement inside the territories.

In the Gaza Strip confinement has been taken to new heights over the past decade. The 2005 pullout initially created freer movement within Gaza, even as movement across its borders was evermore restricted. After Hamas's victory in national parliamentary elections in 2006, followed by its assumption of full control of Gaza in 2007, Israel declared Gaza an "enemy entity" and imposed a siege on the Strip. The blockade bans the import of a wide array of goods and further restricts movement. Along with the siege, the last decade has witnessed three devastating assaults on the territory, each marked by further confinements—as parts of the Strip are declared "no-go zones" by the Israeli military (Smith and Isleen 2017)—and a persisting problem of the inability to rebuild, per the above-mentioned blockade.

The conditions that have obtained in Gaza over the past decade did not mark the beginning of talk of Gaza as an "open air prison," but they have certainly confirmed the aptness of this appellation (Feldman 2015a). They take collective punishment far beyond what was imagined by British Mandate ordinances, and

18. Supreme Court of Israel, Iyad v. State of Israel,[1] CrimA 6659/06, June 11, 2008. casebook .icrc.org/case-study/israel-detention-unlawful-combatants (accessed July 26, 2017).

also beyond how Israel used shared culpability to underwrite house demolitions in an earlier stage of occupation. The docile Palestinian subject that was envisioned in the Mandate and earlier in the occupation presumed that even if many Palestinians were "bad actors," some Palestinians could disassociate themselves from this category—whether by announcing themselves as loyal subjects, as with the petitioners with whom this essay opened, or by acting as civilians interested only in "seeking a livelihood for themselves and their families,"[19] as Israel described those Palestinians it claimed to defend through house demolitions. The blockade on Gaza envisions no such separation. Even as they are still denied recognition as a political community, all Gazans are deemed part of a mass of enemies.

What are the consequences of imprisoning not just a segment of a population but its entirety? The United Nations (2017: 7) has objected that "these measures are contrary to international law in that they penalize the entire population of Gaza, without regard to individual responsibility and thus amount to collective punishment." In addition to encompassing the entire population, today's collective punishment extends far beyond the destruction of houses and targets the entire sphere of livability: shelter, livelihood, water, and electricity. A UN report issued in July 2017 described the effects of ten years of siege on all aspects of life: "Gaza has been facing a downward spiral of de-development, while the people in Gaza are caught in a cycle of humanitarian need and perpetual aid dependency" (28). About the restrictions on movement it notes, "The effect of not having contact with people outside of Gaza has significant social, economic and even psychological consequences as the population remains essentially cut off from the rest of the world" (9).

Israel targets livability to affect Palestinian politics. And in so doing it identifies Palestinian politics—whether voting for Hamas, pursuing nonviolent resistance, or engaging in armed struggle—as a punishable act. The UN response to Israel's brutal imprisonment of Gaza's population, and sometimes the Palestinian response as well, have been to highlight its devastating humanitarian effects. Part of the discursive struggle that has occurred around the Gaza blockade has been about into what categories Palestinians in Gaza fit. Are they bad political actors—terrorists, jihadists, and enemy combatants—per Israel and its supporters? Or should they be seen as humanitarian subjects—victims, "'regular' citizens" (as the UN report puts it [2]), and humans? But a decision about whether they are viewed as political or humanitarian subjects is not a real choice for Palestinians. As I have explored elsewhere (Feldman 2009), and as the Mandate-era

19. ICRC, B AG 202 139 036, letter from Golda Meir to Marcel Naville, August 20, 1971.

petition with which this essay opened also shows, it is nearly impossible for Palestinians to disavow their status as political subjects even if they wanted to. The Palestinian struggle—their ongoing fight against elimination—is instead to have their status as political actors be recognized as proper. Resolution of their situation demands recognition of both political subjectivity and political community.

References

Aruri, Naseer. 1978. "Resistance and Repression: Political Prisoners in Israeli Occupied Territories." *Journal of Palestine Studies* 7, no. 4: 48–66.

Berda, Yael. 2017. *Living Emergency: Israel's Permit Regime in the Occupied West Bank.* Stanford, CA: Stanford University Press.

Bornstein, Avram. 2001. "Ethnography and the Politics of Prisoners in Palestine-Israel." *Journal of Contemporary Ethnography* 30, no. 5: 546–74.

Fassin, Didier. 2017. *Prison Worlds: An Ethnography of the Carceral Condition.* New York: Polity.

Feldman, Ilana. 2007. "Observing the Everyday: Policing and the Conditions of Possibility in Gaza (1948–67)." *Interventions: International Journal of Postcolonial Studies* 9, no. 3: 414–33.

Feldman, Ilana. 2009. "Gaza's Humanitarianism Problem." *Journal of Palestine Studies* 38, no. 3: 22–37.

Feldman, Ilana. 2015a. "Gaza as an Open-Air Prison." *Middle East Report* 275 (Summer).

Feldman, Ilana. 2015b. *Police Encounters: Security and Surveillance in Gaza under Egyptian Rule.* Stanford, CA: Stanford University Press.

Giacaman, Rita, and Penny Johnson. 2013. "'Our Life Is Prison': The Triple Captivity of Wives and Mothers of Palestinian Political Prisoners." *Journal of Middle East Women's Studies* 9, no. 3: 54–80.

Hajjar, Lisa. 2005. *Courting Conflict: The Israeli Military Court System in the West Bank and Gaza.* Berkeley: University of California Press.

Hernández, Kelly Lytle. 2017. *City of Inmates: Conquest, Rebellion, and the Rise of Human Caging in Los Angeles, 1771–1965.* Chapel Hill: University of North Carolina Press.

Hughes, Matthew. 2009. "The Banality of Brutality: British Armed Forces and the Repression of the Arab Revolt in Palestine, 1936–39." *English Historical Review* 124, no. 507: 313–54.

Kauanui, J. Kehaulani. 2016. "'A Structure, Not an Event': Settler Colonialism and Enduring Indigeneity." *Lateral* 5, no. 1.

Khalili, Laleh. 2010. "The Location of Palestine in Global Counterinsurgencies." *International Journal of Middle East Studies* 42, no. 3: 413–33.

Khalili, Laleh. 2013. *Time in the Shadows: Confinement in Counterinsurgencies.* Stanford, CA: Stanford University Press.

Kimmerling, Baruch. 2003. *Politicide: Ariel Sharon's War against the Palestinians.* New York: Verso.

Latte Abdallah, Stephanie. 2015. "Denial of Borders: The *Prison Web* and the Management of Palestinian Political Prisoners after the Oslo Accords (1993–2015)." In *Israelis and Palestinians in the Shadows of the Wall*, edited by Stephanie Latte Adbdallah and Cedric Parizot, 39–55. London: Ashgate.

Lavie, Smadar. 2018. *Wrapped in the Flag of Israel: Mizrahi Single Mothers and Bureaucratic Torture.* Lincoln: University of Nebraska Press.

Mbembe, Achille. 2003. "Necropolitics." *Public Culture* 15, no. 1: 11–40.

Nashif, Esmail. 2008. *Palestinian Political Prisoners: Identity and Community.* London: Routledge.

The Palestine Mandate. 2019. The Avalon Project: Documents in Law, History, and Diplomacy. Lillian Goldman Law Library, Yale Law School. avalon.law.yale.edu/20th_century/palmanda.asp (accessed February 15, 2019).

Pappe, Ilan. 2016. *The Biggest Prison on Earth: A History of the Occupied Territories.* New York: One World Books.

Robinson, Shira. 2013. *Citizen Strangers: Palestinians and the Birth of Israel's Liberal Settler State.* Stanford, CA: Stanford University Press.

Rosenfeld, Maya. 2011. "The Centrality of the Prisoners' Movement to the Palestinian Struggle against the Israeli Occupation: A Historical Perspective." In *Threat: Palestinian Political Prisoners in Israel*, edited by Abeer Baker and Anat Matar, 3-24. London: Pluto.

Salamanca, Omar Jabary, Mezna Qato, Kareem Rabie, and Sobhi Samour. 2012. "Past Is Present: Settler Colonialism in Palestine." *Settler Colonial Studies* 2, no. 1: 1–8.

Segal, Lotte Buch. 2016. *No Place for Grief: Martyrs, Prisoners, and Mourning in Contemporary Palestine.* Philadelphia: University of Pennsylvania Press.

Shafir, Gershon. 2017. *A Half Century of Occupation: Israel, Palestine, and the World's Most Intractable Conflict.* Berkeley: University of California Press.

Smith, Ron, and Martin Isleen. 2017 "Farming the Front Line." *City* 21, nos. 3–4: 448–65.

Supreme Court of Israel, Iyad v. State of Israel,[1] CrimA 6659/06, June 11, 2008. casebook.icrc.org/case-study/israel-detention-unlawful-combatants (accessed July 26, 2017).

Teitel, Ruti. 2011. *Humanity's Law*. New York: Oxford University Press.

United Nations. 2017. *Gaza: Ten Years Later*. unsco.unmissions.org/sites/default/files/gaza_10_years_later_-_11_july_2017.pdf.

Weizman, Eyal. 2017. *Hollow Land: Israel's Architecture of Occupation*. New York: Verso.

Wolfe, Patrick. 2006. "Settler Colonialism and the Elimination of the Native." *Journal of Genocide Research* 8, no. 4: 387–409.

Ilana Feldman is professor of anthropology, history, and international affairs at George Washington University. She is the author of *Governing Gaza: Bureaucracy, Authority, and the Work of Rule, 1917–67* (2008), *Police Encounters: Security and Surveillance in Gaza under Egyptian Rule* (2015), *Life Lived in Relief: Humanitarian Predicaments and Palestinian Refugee Politics* (2018), and coeditor (with Miriam Ticktin) of *In the Name of Humanity: The Government of Threat and Care* (2010).

Carceral Oversight: Force-Feeding and Visuality at Guantánamo Bay Detention Camp

Michelle C. Velasquez-Potts

In May 2014, lawyers from the London-based international nonprofit organization Reprieve filed a motion on behalf of Guantánamo Bay Detention Camp prisoner Abu Wa'el (Jihad) Dhiab to produce thirty-two videotapes of Dhiab being forcibly extracted from his cell and force-fed in a restraint chair. Dhiab's lawyer described his force-feedings as being administered so incorrectly that he vomited repeatedly and lost consciousness. As a consequence, he suffered a chest infection, and his nostrils and throat were so raw that he had difficulty breathing. Then in 2015, the US government turned over, under seal, eight of the thirty-two videos with the voices and faces of Guantánamo workers redacted. The Justice Department contends that releasing the videotapes would compromise national security, "spurring extremist attacks against US personnel or encouraging resistance by Guantánamo detainees," and argues that the footage might provide too much visualization of "prison infrastructure" (Hsu 2015) or set an example for how other prisoners might best refuse their own force-feedings. The case came to a close in 2017, when a three-judge panel of the Circuit Court of Washington, DC, ruled that the videotapes would remain under seal and not made public (see Worthington 2017).

The state's refusal to release the video footage illustrates the ways that geopolitics and race are mobilized to propagate a xenophobic panic that reauthorizes

Many thanks to Samera Esmeir, Keith Feldman, Michael Mascuch, and Juana María Rodríguez for their generous engagement with drafts of this essay. I'm also grateful for Kel Montalvo-Quiñones and Emily O'Rourke's comments and support at various stages of this project. My writing and thinking benefited greatly from the Violence and Policing Conference at Columbia University. Thank you to everyone involved with the workshop for the thoughtful feedback and suggestions.

Public Culture 31:3 DOI 10.1215/08992363-7532727
Copyright 2019 by Duke University Press

indefinite detention at the naval base. It is precisely indefinite detention that has motivated the staging of individual and collective hunger strikes throughout the camps since 2002. Hunger striking necessarily prioritizes the life of a cause over the integrity of the body. As Banu Bargu (2010: 254) argues in her work on the Turkish death fast of the early 2000s, hunger striking resists the "hegemonic allure based on 'mak[ing] live.'" This rupture to the biopolitical functioning of the state destabilizes modern sovereignty, the legitimacy of which "is built on the idea of individual preservation" (254). As such, camp protocol that authorizes the force-feeding of prisoners who, for example, have only refused meals for days or weeks "long before their lives were in danger" (254) points to the state's mobilization of biological life as a means by which to counter political opposition at the camp. Indeed, the state and its subjects are constantly negotiating the parameters of what constitutes corporeal sovereignty, and what constitutes a just measure of life.

Critiques of force-feeding rely in large part on narratives detailing the administration of the procedure. To shift the public's perception toward the elimination of force-feeding, the practice must be made visible as the state's exercise of biopolitical authority. To make visible the racial and religious othering practiced by the state, one must resort to "facts" but also the more affective and relational approaches to pain and suffering that are induced by force-feeding and confinement. In Samir Naji al Hasan Moqbel's (2013) widely circulated *New York Times* testimonial of the pain he endured from being forcibly fed, he insists that the spectator both listen *and* look at his suffering, concluding his testimony with a plea: "I just hope that because of the pain we are suffering, the eyes of the world will once again look to Guantánamo before it is too late." Following Moqbel's embodied approach to witnessing, this essay argues that pain becomes the basis of not only political subjectivity but also relationality between those held captive and the spectator.

As A. Naomi Paik (2016: 17) comments, "Testimonies of rightlessness contest the nationalism and racism behind camp-thinking." Prisoner testimonials in response to force-feeding attest to the violence of "camp-thinking" and, importantly, to the desire for corporeal sovereignty. The sovereignty of the prisoner relies on others to witness the suffering induced by state practices by "build[ing] a link between the speakers and us (the rightless and the relatively rightful), to reach beyond the camp's boundaries and connect their world to us" (15). Indeed, suffering, for Moqbel, isn't that which numbs the spectator but what is capable of jolting one out of complacency. In what follows, I consider Moqbel's plea and what it might mean to be an ethical witness. To do so, I consider how the metrics of force-feeding suspends political life—that is, the right to protest the conditions of one's confinement through hunger striking and other acts of self-harm. Such metrics are undoubtedly displayed in the videos of Dhiab's cell extractions and force-feedings, but without access to the footage one must turn to other forms of knowledge that aren't solely visual, but sonic and felt.

By examining Moqbel's testimony; Joint Task Force Guantánamo Bay's *Medical Management of Detainees on Hunger Strike*, a thirty-page document detailing the standard operating procedures for force-feeding; and a video project by human rights organization Reprieve featuring artist Yasiin Bey simulating the "proper" techniques for force-feeding, this essay maintains that the verbal and embodied modes by which prisoners and activists resist the state's framing of force-feeding as ethical obligation exposes how such a medical procedure is, in fact, torture. Here, testimony is crucial in that it places the spectator in a certain proximity to the men held captive, allowing for the felt pain of force-feeding to travel outside the detention camp and take on an expression of recognizability.

Witnessing and a Responsibility to Look

Moqbel (2013) begins his testimony by describing the first time he was force-fed at Guantánamo: "I will never forget the first time they passed the feeding tube up my nose. I can't describe how painful it is to be force-fed this way. As it was thrust in, it made me feel like throwing up. I wanted to vomit, but I couldn't. There was agony in my chest, throat and stomach. I had never experienced such pain before. I would not wish this cruel punishment upon anyone."

Moqbel's narrative, and the many other testimonies by prisoners that bear witness to force-feeding, opens up the possibility for pain to be more than an experience felt in isolation, but rather an experience shared with a public. Talal Asad (2003: 85) writes that "as a social relationship pain is more than an experience. It is part of what creates the conditions of action and experience." Indeed, the legal battle that started in 2013 to end force-feeding at Guantánamo depends on the narratives from prisoners such as Moqbel to incite legal and public outrage against the pain that they insist force-feeding causes. The state must exercise its authority over life without causing pain, or at the very least there must be a clear penological purpose behind the cause of pain. The military at Guantánamo Bay claim that the feeding process is safe. The denial of the adverse health effects caused by force-feeding relies on a logic that considers Moqbel's pain unverifiable.

The state's refusal to see or feel the pain that these prisoners testify to, I argue, is what makes it unverifiable. The unverifiability of pain is documented well in Elaine Scarry's *The Body in Pain*. Scarry (1987: 4) stresses the curious nature of physical pain to oscillate back and forth between being that which "cannot be denied and that which cannot be confirmed." There is something about pain, for Scarry, which is beyond representation and resists language. It is true that there are cultural and communal ways of registering pain. The sounds and words emanating from the subject help communicate, convey, or expose pain, but, ultimately, the central problem remains that pain's "resistance to language is not simply one of its incidental or accidental attributes but is essential to what it is" (5). Scarry argues that physical pain is an exceptional interior state precisely because it is "not *of* or *for* anything. . . . It is precisely because it takes no object that it, more than any other phenomenon, resists objectification in language" (5, emphasis in original). In Scarry's account of pain, the subject can lose recourse to speech and, as such, relies on outside actors to speak on their behalf. Inherent to the verbal strategies of speaking on behalf of pain is doubt: "To have pain is to have *certainty*; to hear about pain is to have *doubt*" (13, emphasis in original). Ultimately, pain is individually experienced, lacks precision of language, and is always at risk of being appropriated.

Litigation, in turn, attempts to remedy the gap between language and experience. The motion to produce video footage of Dhiab being force-fed is an example of a human rights demand at making public pain and injury. In May 2014, Judge Gladys Kessler ordered that the thirty-two videos showing the forcible feeding of Dhiab be turned over to his lawyers but that the content of each was not to be commented on publicly. However, only eight redacted videotapes were given to Dhiab's defense team, and in 2017 the district court in Washington, DC, ruled that the videos would remain classified. The emphasis on acquiring filmic evidence acknowledges the instability of mere descriptions of suffering. What would the video footage of Dhiab's forcible cell extraction and tube feedings tell us that Moqbel's narrative doesn't? And what of the power of the visual to interrupt the reality that the authorities at Guantánamo have constructed concerning new force-feeding procedures, such as the restraint chair featured in the footage of Dhiab? Ultimately, it is not just litigation or advocates who fill the gap between language and experience but also the prisoners themselves who represent their own pain to the world. Indeed, the prisoners speak for themselves, even as the state refuses to listen.

Thinking of pain as relational takes us in a different direction than Scarry's account—one more concerned with what Asad understands as the agentive possibilities generated by the articulation of pain. There will always be certain aspects of pain that cannot be fully conveyed to an observer and will thus remain to some degree unintelligible. There is no way to experience the exact pain that Moqbel felt as the feeding tube was thrust up his nose, but, as Asad argues, this needn't be the point of sharing one's pain with others. "Sufferers are also social persons (animals)," he writes, "and their suffering is partly constituted by the way they inhabit, or are constituted to inhabit, their relationships with others" (2003: 85). Importantly, there is a power dynamic involved in assuming we can feel another's pain, as we end up substituting our own body for that of the sufferer. Pain here, however, is more than simply an experience that may or may not be verifiable but is instead the means by which relations are mediated. This is not to say that there is something inherently good about the experience of pain, but that contrary to pain being viewed as passive and commensurable only by the subject experiencing it, pain is actually active and capable of recognition.

If we take Moqbel's pain as something more than a private event and rather something relational, then perhaps a space of plurality might be opened where the spectator feels called to take part in "new conditions for moral action" (Azoulay 2008: 144). This call is not abstract; indeed, contemporary visual culture around human rights takes what Ariella Azoulay (2008: 287) calls the "active gaze" quite seriously. This gaze necessitates an extreme attention to the image at hand and destabilizes any presumption of vision as transparent. Such a gaze, Azoulay writes (287), "holds itself humble before the image, recognizes the fact that not every-thing can be seen or shown, knows that removing the social prohibition of the vis-ible will not lead to full visibility, and understands that not only is such visibility impossible, but that the passion for such visibility is precisely what thwarts the eye from seeing what is visible on the surface."

Here a spectator must decide how to decipher images of violence and which images should and must be made public. As such, to extend the active gaze to Moqbel's verbal testimony isn't counterintuitive but a means by which to reorga-nize what is meant by the category of what Azoulay calls "authentic documenta-tion" (421). This is to say that a multitude of textual elements are essential to one's recognition of the visible. Embedded in Moqbel's testimony is an opportunity to listen and imagine what we are barred from seeing. This is what it means to recon-struct and fabricate images from testimony that are spoken or written down. But, despite this gap we continue to look. Moreover, as Azoulay argues, we *must* look, for there is a responsibility inherent to the witnessing of the image.

Moqbel's insistence on not only his own pain but also public acknowledgment of that pain resists the prison's control over what audiences will have access to concerning the detention camp. After all, vision is regulated inside the camps but outside as well, through the control of what information is made public concerning hunger striking and force-feeding. Camp oversight takes the form of panoptical surveillance at the same time that it hides or prevents certain forms of life from being made visible. The sealed videotapes documenting how punishment is medicalized at the camp is one such instance of obfuscation, as is the detention camp's decision in 2013 to no longer report to the public the number of men hunger striking. Indeed, camp officials understand that violence done to the self for the self is a powerful demonstration of sovereignty that pushes up against the state's emphasis on biological life/existence.

The military task force that runs the facility based at Naval Station Guantánamo Bay has established itself as the authority of not only what can be said but also what can be seen. Militarization at the detention camp authorizes its own authority through methods of classification and organization of the men held captive, deciding what information does or doesn't serve "operational purpose." Moreover, this relation between authority and visibility is an unstable one in constant need of rearticulation. In the following section, I consider how the state frames force-feeding as ethical medical care to cover over or hide what is in fact a regime of compulsory visibility within the field of authority, power, and punishment. I ask: How does the state frame medical ethics inside the camps and documents such as the *Medical Management of Detainees on Hunger Strike*? How does the state's emphasis on care obfuscate not only the demands of the prisoners but also the feeding tube as carceral technology?

The Standard Operating Procedures of Authority

In 2013 *Al Jazeera* asked to see *Medical Management of Detainees on Hunger Strike*, the document outlining the standard operating procedures (SOP) for force-feeding. The request was granted. Originally written in 2003, but updated in 2005, the SOP was designed to serve as a policy manual in the event of hunger striking at the camps. In 2013 the manual was revised again with the intention of preventing another mass hunger strike like the one that took place in 2005 (see Leopold 2013). It was put into effect on March 5 and, unlike previous versions, released without redactions.[1]

Unique to the 2013 manual is that it directs staff in how to handle prisoner resistance to the feeding tube itself. The introduction states that "just as battlefield tactics change throughout the course of a conflict, the medical response to GTMO detainees who hunger strike has evolved with time" (JTF 2013: 1). Here the evo-

1. It's unclear when the SOP was declassified. *Al Jazeera* reports that the Pentagon declassified the manual several years prior to its public release in 2013, but that that version still contained redactions. In this essay, I quote from the 2013 version (see Leopold 2013).

lution of tactics is synonymous with the alteration of medical technology and procedure—hunger strikers are no longer simply nasally fed but strapped down to restraint chairs and forcibly fed several times a day, and it is the commander—not the certified physician—who has final say over whether a prisoner is forcibly fed (see Stafford Smith 2007). The thirty-page document details twelve categories of medical management, some of which include evaluation and assessment sheets, medical equations, calculations, and electrolyte deficiency management. These categories, taken together, make up the "General Algorithm for a Hunger Strike," a worksheet that is also included within the report. Staff use the algorithm as a guide in the event of a hunger strike to enact "involuntary enteral feeding" of prisoners who "[are] at a weight less than 85% of the calculated Ideal Body Weight" or suffering from other adverse health effects, such as seizures, muscle wasting, and significant weakness as a consequence of the prolonged refusal of food and water. The SOP guidelines also mobilize visual techniques of oversight, such as observation, examination, and documentation, in an attempt to "rehabilitate" the prisoner into a docile and normalized subject who eats rather than hunger strikes, concedes rather than objects.

The language of the report is medicalized, referring to prisoners on strike as "patients" and enteral feedings as "procedures," as if it is a surgical operation that the prisoner has consented to. Enteral feeding is the continuous administration of nutrients to the digestive system using a tube. Intermittent feedings, in contrast, are feedings that take place at different times throughout the day. When not quoting the report, I have chosen to refer to enteral feedings as "force-feedings." This term both highlights the coercion and abuse on the part of the state as well as respects how prisoners themselves have chosen to describe what has been done to them in response to hunger striking. The SOP's "Policy" section specifies that it is a nasogastric tube (NGT) used to administer enteral feedings. Once admitted to the detention hospital (DH) the prisoner is administered a 10 French or 12 French (this is the diameter, or size) tube, which is inserted through the stomach, all the way down to the small intestine.

The state's term *involuntary* already gestures toward a lack of autonomy for prisoners, but the use of the feeding tube at the detention camp should also be situated within a longer history of carceral punishment, where force-feeding has been used as a tactic of incapacitation meant to immobilize and stifle political defiance within the prison regime.[2] This is not to say that the authority of JTF at

2. Notable examples include the force-feeding of incarcerated British suffragettes and Irish Republicans during the early 1900s, but force-feeding also has roots in psychiatric hospitals and on the experimentation of animals.

the detention camp is totalizing. Rather, as Lorna Rhodes (1998) warns in "Pan-optical Intimacies," although disciplinary spaces of confinement are contingent on transparency of panoptical vision, they also

> invite and magnify disorder, pollution, and noise. While vision is certainly central to the effect of transparency, inmates and prison workers attest that the senses of smell and hearing predominate in some of the more aversive prison experiences and can be deployed to interfere with the pan-optical mechanism and challenge the notion of a transparent society free of zones of darkness. Their experiences serve to remind us that the visual emphasis both of the panopticon and of our use of it as a figure of modern discipline . . . is an "optical" illusion that minimizes the material, felt body even as it highlights the body as the mediator of projects of docility. (Rhodes 1998: 288)

Indeed, the restraint chair and feeding tube as instruments of discipline produce suffering in the prisoner but also resistance and strategy. The felt experiences of pain, such as lacerations in the back of the throat, trouble swallowing, and the discomfort of tape used on the face to secure the feeding tube, should not be ignored, for they demonstrate the disconnect between the SOP as policy manual and the lived experience of the prisoner who chooses to hunger strike. By biting and swallowing the tube, prisoners resist the camp's medicalization of punishment, and incapacitation, but at the cost of physical discomfort and suffering. Pain, then, becomes one such zone of darkness that escapes the detention camp's complex of visuality predicated on oversight and surveillance (see Mirzoeff 2011).

Surveillance and Control

The SOP document instructs staff to surveil prisoners' bodies, recording heart rate, blood pressure, and weight. As an authoritative document, surveillance and management are legitimated through the coupling of care with the preservation of life. Medical personnel are constructed as the technicians of carceral oversight, and force-feeding as the technology of health and nutrition that most efficiently protects, preserves, and promotes life at the camp. Here life is purely biological and takes precedence over political life. As a policy manual, the SOP document focuses not on medical ethics but on targeting, disciplining, and surveilling the captive's body with the objective of eliminating political opposition.

The SOP makes clear the centrality of isolation and immobility to incarceration: "In event of a mass hunger strike, isolating hunger striking patients from each other is vital to prevent them from achieving solidarity" (JTF 2013: 6). The medical evaluation and subsequent punishment begins by closely monitoring and recording prisoner meals. The Joint Detention Group security force notifies medical personnel of any prisoner appearing to be hunger striking, and a daily list of those perceived to be striking is sent out to "key leadership" in Joint Task Force Guantánamo. Once it is determined that a prisoner is on hunger strike, then a medical provider counsels him on the health risks of going without food and/or water for prolonged periods of time. The "Hunger Striker Medical Evaluation Sheet" documents whether the prisoner is drinking fluids, the number of meals that have been missed, and the reason for the hunger strike. It also records a full physical assessment that consists of documentation of the prisoner's weight. Weight plays an important role on this sheet, with specifications needed for the "in processing weight," "pre-hunger strike weight," "current weight," and "weight loss."

The preoccupation with weight at the detention camp has been described by Sami al-Haj, who was released in 2008, as the only concern of physicians. He states, "All they care about is the prisoner's weight. . . . 'Are you sick? Are you in pain?' Who cares? It is all about the number on the scale" (Worthington 2008). For al-Haj, a side effect of force-feeding was bloating, resulting in the impression of legitimate weight gain whenever he was made to step on the scale. Indeed, the importance of recording weight at the naval base cannot be understated, and the public release of the measurements and weight of prisoners has been used to give the illusion that the majority of the men held captive are not only healthy but also not participating in the hunger strikes (see Worthington 2009).

A behavioral assessment follows weight intake to determine the exact reasons behind the prisoner's decision to hunger strike. Following the assessment, the prisoner is evaluated daily using the "Hunger Striker Medical Flow Sheet," used to keep track of the prisoner's heart rate, blood pressure, fluid intake, whether he is eating, the caloric intake of the enteral feed, weight, and comments concerning the prisoner's mental health. All counseling efforts and treatments are recorded in the prisoner's medical record. If it is determined that medical intervention is necessary, the prisoner will be admitted to the DH or transferred to a designated feeding block to be force-fed. The various disciplinary techniques surrounding force-feeding, such as the algorithm, medical evaluation sheet, and flow chart, keep the prisoner constantly within a line of sight, with the intention of correcting the prisoner's behavior. The ultimate goal is that the prisoner terminate his hunger strike and return to "oral nutrition." Staff management of hunger striking at the camp normalizes, attempting to unify behavior while also observing, judging, and making visible differences. This "normalizing gaze" is what both subjects and objectifies those being examined (Foucault 1977: 184).

However, just as Rhodes cautions against believing disciplinary spaces to be transparent, force-feeding at the detention camp is more opaque than other forms of discipline administered, both hiding and making visible its intentions. One example of this is the way in which the SOP prevents the hunger striker's own knowledge about the health and status of the body itself in the form of concealing measurements such as weight loss or weight gain. In his testimonial, Moqbel notes that at least one month passed before he was updated on how much he weighed. And Dhiab is quoted, along with several others, in litigation as being certain that the medication Reglan is being administered without their consent. The drug is used to treat nausea and vomiting, but prolonged usage has been linked to a neurological disorder called tardive dyskinesia—the involuntary movements of the tongue, lips, face, and extremities.[3] Other complications that can arise when tube feedings are administered poorly are diarrhea; dehydration; aspiration pneumonia, which is the inflammation of lung due to the entrance of food; and a number of gastrointestinal disturbances (see Plumner 1983). Prisoners reported to their attorneys that it was pointless to resist tube feedings. Regardless of whether they cooperated, the tubes only got bigger, and both insertion and removal were equally painful, causing the men "to urinate and defecate on themselves" (White 2006). These testimonials are in stark contrast to Guantánamo officials' assertion that "medical personnel do not insert nasogastric tubes in a manner intentionally designed to inflict pain" (Rose 2006). Yet the protocol for intermittent "enteral feedings" administered in restraint chairs suggests otherwise.

Restraint chairs were introduced to the detention camp in 2005 after a psychiatrist, accompanied by three consultants from the Federal Bureau of Prisons, visited the camp. It was suggested that the SOP be revised to include the use of restraint in managing hunger strikers. The chair is described by the Constitution Project (2013: 229) as a technology that "completely immobilizes a person strapped into it, using a lap belt and straps that immobilize the head as well as wrist and ankle restraints." The use of the chair is also described in the SOP where the guard

> shackles [the] detainee and a mask is placed over the detainee's mouth
> to prevent spitting and biting . . . the detainee is escorted to the chair
> restraint system and is appropriately restrained by the guard force . . .
> upon completion of the nutrient infusion and removal of the feeding tube,
> the detainee is removed from the restraint chair and placed in a 'dry
> cell.' . . . The guard force will observe the detainee for 45–60 minutes
> for any indications of vomiting or attempts to induce vomiting. . . . If

3. Shaker Abdurraheem Aamer et al. v. Barack Obama, 742 F.3d 1023 (D.C. Cir. 2014).

the detainee vomits or attempts to induce vomiting in the 'dry cell' his participation in the dry cell protocol will be revoked and he will remain in the restraint chair for the entire observation time period during subsequent feedings. (JTF 2013: 7)

The will of the prisoner here is trapped, and his movements are constricted. The feeding tube both maintains biological life at the same time that it kills political life. We can also think of this in terms of the living or social death of the prisoner, or what legal scholar Colin Dayan (2013: 70) calls "soul death." For Dayan, the prisoner is one who possesses a natural life but whose loss of civil rights illustrates how the law can make one dead in life. If, as Dayan also suggests, confinement offers prescriptions and treatments for those constructed as criminal, what kind of treatment, then, is force-feeding? The SOP illustrates how force-feeding aims for the incapacitation of the body at the same time that it keeps the prisoner alive, fulfilling Michel Foucault's (1999: 241) definition of biopower as the power to "make live or let die."

Biopower, the introduction of life into power, names the techniques for achieving the subjection of bodies and the control of populations. Both the terms *control* and *population* become significant, as the necessary precursor for control of a subject is life. Force-feeding presents a paradox that is at once emblematic of Foucault's biopower while also functioning as incapacitating technique. For Foucault, at issue are two different populations: the one that will die and the one that will live a healthier life. In the case of the hunger striker, the paradox is found within the same figure. The same figure who is to be saved is also incapacitated. I name this paradox "suspended animation," for it gets at the ways that confinement and captivity produce in subjects a state that is neither dead nor alive.

Suspended animation, itself a medical term, is a process that replaces the body's blood with cold saline, dropping one's temperature to 10°C, making almost all cellular activity stop. In 2014, surgeons at University of Pittsburgh Medical Center Presbyterian Hospital conducted a trial using suspended animation on gunshot victims. A doctor working on the trial clarified to a reporter that "we are suspending life, but we don't like to call it suspended animation because it sounds like science fiction. . . . So we call it emergency preservation and resuscitation" (see Yang 2014). Although toward very different ends, the SOP, too, articulates force-feeding as emergency preservation, a procedure that in its vitalism rehabilitates the body to its proper weight and physiological functions. However, terminology aside, what is it if not the suspension of life, which is to say the suspension of one's right to protest, an end to indefinite detention predicated on religious othering, xenophobia, and racism?

The SOP for force-feeding and the use of the restraint chair, described by one prisoner, Nabil Hadarab, as an execution chair, calls to mind Foucault's (1977: 204) notion of the panopticon as a laboratory of power, a "privileged place for experiments on men, and for analyzing with complete certainty the transformations that may be obtained from them." Indeed, the restraint chair has remained a powerful image in the popular imaginary for the medicalization of punishment at the detention camp. Physicians and military officials meld into one in this imaginary, and the DH becomes synonymous with a cell—or a laboratory.

The Visible/Nonvisible

The Guantánamo Bay hunger strikes offer a counternarrative to the authority of the SOP. The prisoners' resistance to being force-fed is an attempt at reclaiming political and corporeal autonomy. The SOP points to such embodied forms of resistance: "On occasion, a detainee undergoing enteral feeding will attempt to bite the tube in an attempt to swallow the feeding tube. . . . The detainee may attempt to bite the portion of the tube outside the nose by turning his head and snaring the tube with his mouth, or may attempt to regurgitate the tube partially into the oral cavity and attempt to sever the tube covertly without opening his mouth" (JTF 2013: 12). Here we see the prisoner resisting incapacitation by attempting to bite or swallow the feeding tube. We can read this resistance as not only struggling against the administration of force-feeding but also opposing the feeding tube itself as medical apparatus. The feeding tube, as Patrick Anderson (2005: 6) asserts, "represents and facilitates the enforcement of normative alimentary exchange by the institutional apparatuses of the State—for example, clinic and prison." Indeed, medical personnel in the clinic are cleared to restrain the prisoner in instances of resistance:

> If a particular detainee displays repeated attempts to bite the tube, a weighted 10 ft tube shall be used. . . . If the detainee is able to gain the tube between his teeth, the nurse will: 1. Simultaneously turn off feed and, immediately stabilize the distal end of the tube and pull the tube from the detainee's nose. 2. Maintain traction on the proximal portion of the tube until the detainee releases the tube from between his teeth. This may take considerable time. . . . If the detainee refuses, the RN shall immediately remove the tube, inspect it for damage, and re-insert it. (JTF 2013: 29)

How are we to understand the biting and attempts at swallowing the tube? Important is the repetition of the feeding. No matter the amount of resistance or pain on the part of the prisoner, the feeding does not cease; rather, its administration intensifies through its repeated insertion.

Similarly, Sami al-Hajj, a journalist for *Al Jazeera* who was held at the detention camp for seven years and whose hunger strike lasted 480 days, describes force-feeding in terms of its repetition:

> They're supposed to feed you [with] two cans, small cans . . . but they feed us 24 cans and 24 bottle[s] of water, continuous. And we [were] throwing up, it continues and we throwing up and it continues. This is one feeding; [it] would take 8 hours like that, you are in chair. Until your cell become full of [vomit]. And after that, when they come and [remove the feeding tube from the esophagus], they [would grab the tube and just walk away with it]. Then there was blood coming. And [the guard] takes it from you and he goes to another [detainee] directly and [inserts it] . . . without cleaning. (Constitution Project 2013: 227)

Such repetition is precisely what transforms enteral feeding into force-feeding and the "preservation of life" into torture. The death of spirit caused by confinement, for Dayan, is akin to suspended animation. Indeed, the feeding tube, like solitary confinement, keeps the mind and body technically whole, but at the cost of the spirit, which will deteriorate in the restraint chair or cell. Yet the suspended animation of force-feeding doesn't completely foreclose embodied forms of opposition. Similarly, Dayan (2001: 28) argues that prisoners who self-mutilate while in solitary confinement make visible what the law seeks to mask. What do the prisoners of Guantánamo make visible about not only the law but, more specifically, the militarization of medicine? The self-inflicted pain of the hunger striker works to communicate not only the pain induced by force-feeding but confinement itself. In the next section, I turn to one of the ways in which the public has responded to force-feeding and how video and performance come to play a role in the ethics of witnessing.

Reframing Force-Feeding

On July 8, 2013, in response to the first litigation filed concerning the force-feeding of Dhiab and several other prisoners, Judge Kessler concluded that although there was sufficient evidence to suggest that force-feeding is torture, the court nonetheless lacked the jurisdiction to grant the injunction. On the same day, the human rights organization Reprieve launched a campaign in solidarity with prisoners on hunger strike, releasing a nearly five-minute video, directed by BAFTA (British Academy of Film and Television Arts) award winner Asif Kapadia, featuring the artist Yasiin Bey (formerly known as Mos Def) being force-fed according to Guantánamo's SOP (Kapadia 2013). In July 2013 the *Guardian* newspaper released the video, which has over 7 million views on YouTube. By creating this video, Reprieve aimed to create public outrage and pressure President Barack Obama to close the military prison.

The video begins with a caption stating that 120 prisoners are hunger striking at Guantánamo Bay and forty-four of them are being force-fed. Yasiin Bey then enters an empty white room furnished with a feeding restraint chair, two cameras, an IV, and a table with the feeding supplies. He introduces himself and calls what we are about to see a "demonstration of the standard operating procedures for force-feeding." The camera focuses on Bey's attire, lingering on his expensive-looking jacket, pants, and shoes. The next shot is of him in an orange prison jumpsuit and in shackles, as his hands, feet, and head are strapped down into the feeding chair. As the procedure is about to begin, "Standard Operating Procedure: Medical Management of Detainees on Hunger Strike" appears on the frame. While the doctor, a British physician, lubricates the nasogastric tube, Bey's eyes shift back and forth nervously. The physician proceeds to insert the tube into Bey's nose. Bey immediately begins to physically struggle, coughing, moaning, and grunting. At this point, actors in black T-shirts enter the room to restrain Bey; the doctor removes the tube from Bey's nose and begins to lubricate it again, restarting the procedure. As the doctor attempts to reinsert the tube, Bey becomes significantly more agitated and, at this point, begins to resist; he must be restrained at the head and neck. Bey cries toward the end of the video, "No, please, stop, stop it please, this is me, I can't do it anymore." He puts his head in his hands and begins to cry. The captions tell us that at Guantánamo the full procedure is carried out twice a day and typically takes two hours to complete. The video ends with Bey describing the tube being inserted into his nasal cavity as having caused a burning sensation—a feeling he describes as unbearable that goes into his brain, reaching the back of his throat to the point that he really couldn't take it.

A criticism of the above simulation is Bey's ability—his agency—to stop the feeding and demand that the tube be removed. Here, Moqbel's and Dhiab's testimonies are a sharp contrast, in which they, too, begged that the feeding stop, but to no relief. "It was so painful," writes Moqbel (2013), "that I begged them to stop feeding me. The nurse refused to stop feeding me. As they were finishing, some of the 'food' spilled on my clothes. I asked them to change my clothes, but the guard refused to allow me to hold on to this last shred of my dignity." While Bey expressed gratitude at being asked to participate in the simulation,

Moqbel remained indefinitely detained, suffering for exercising his right to protest. If Bey's simulation pales in comparison to what happens when prisoners are force-fed at the detention camp, what, then, is the utility of Bey's representation of force-feeding? After all, what is necessarily hidden from the frame are the dozens of men unable to escape the restraint chair and feeding tube. Looking relies on not only an exchange of gazes but also the visual degradation of the other, or misrecognition of the other. Bey's failed simulation, and by failed, I mean that he stopped the feeding before its completion, speaks to this, then, in that it moves away from the insistence that representation can successfully reproduce reality. The video neither fails nor succeeds at reproducing the SOP; instead it derives its force from highlighting the pain authorized by the SOP and the practice of force-feeding itself.

Bey's performance deflects from the subject to orient the viewer to the felt experience of pain and the technology responsible for producing that pain. Indeed, the camera makes a point to linger on all medical technology present: the positioning and lubrication of the tube and the IV drip, both against a white backdrop.[4] I would caution against any interpretation of Bey's performance in the video as emancipatory, but I deem it important to highlight his interruption of the simulation when he pleads, "No, please, stop, stop it please, this is me, I can't do it anymore." His refusal to continue bars the viewer from continuing to witness his suffering and, as such, pushes against a gaze that has already naturalized the pain and suffering of the captive body. This is to say, Bey doesn't equate his own pain with that of Moqbel, Dhiab, or any of the other men who have been forcibly fed. Rather, Bey's participation responds to Moqbel's call to once again look toward the detention camp. This simulation, or what I would like to call Bey's embodied looking, centralizes pain and suffering in such a way that what began at the start of the video as, in the language of the SOP, a "medical procedure" becomes a torture session. The feeding tube is thus transformed from medical instrument that "makes live" to carceral technology that inflicts unnecessary pain and suffering.

Reprieve's video of Bey demonstrating Guantánamo's feeding procedures builds

---

4. This is not to say that Bey's own embodiment can or should be ignored. Bey's lived reality as a Black man and practicing Muslim is made all the more visible as he replaces his own clothing for the orange jumpsuit. Whether Reprieve consciously sought to draw a parallel between the captivity of Black men within the US prison regime and the racialized men held captive at Guantánamo is unclear. Indeed, one might argue that Bey's blackness here is exploited to make translatable the suffering taking place, in that, as Saidiya Hartman's *Scenes of Subjection* (1997) argues, blackness always already marks a social relationship of dominance and abjection. Yet she also makes clear that blackness marks the potential for redress and emancipation.

on the relationality between the subject in pain and the spectator watching. The video is an example of framing that provides a visualization of the punitive use of force-feeding that is otherwise offered solely through testimonials and human rights reporting. Framing is first and foremost about presentation, but also about boundaries. In other words, the frame is a boundary to the image but is also itself that which structures the image (see Butler 2010: 63–100).[5] The camera's gaze frames the feeding tube as a weapon against Bey and those being force-fed at Guantánamo. The feeding tube, here, comes to signify and critique the state's emphasis on life, and the perceived necessary management of the captive in the service of US security. Reprieve's video is a tactic that has the potential to reverse the authority of the state by wresting control of the gaze. This reversal of the gaze whereby documentation is used to respond back to authority by using the state's own standard operating procedures mobilizes pain in the service of drawing visibility around the medicalization of punishment at the camp.

Reprieve's campaign accompanying the video encouraged members of the public to undertake short-term hunger strikes in addition to drawing awareness to Guantánamo Bay with their political representatives (see Reprieve 2013). It's unclear just how many participated in the campaign, and, ultimately, President Obama was unable to close the detention camp (see Savage and Davis 2016). However, accessing the success of Reprieve's campaign is less of interest to me than how the video competes against the state's refusal to release video documentation of Dhiab's force-feedings. In doing so, the reenactment of the SOP makes pain as public as possible instead of relegating it solely to inside the detention camp where the state frames the procedure as medically sound. Although the state denies the pain it subjects onto prisoners, the video demands that Bey's pain be seen as real by attempting to "resituate the terms of which reality is understood" (Mirzoeff 2011: 28). This resituating of reality attempted by Bey can also be likened to a reframing of the field of representation, forcing us to look at the "image outside the scene of its production" (Butler 2010: 100) where its interpretation is no longer solely controlled by the norms of the state. Our attention as spectators is turned toward the functioning of the feeding tube as a prosthetic capable of administering a pain that is authorized by the state. The video, then, is a simulation of the prisoner's struggle for corporeal autonomy but also a demand for transparency and accountability. Bey—as both spectator and performer—provides a mode of

5. Butler, in *Frames of War* (2010), argues that framing, affect, and interpretation extend beyond the viewer to the camera itself. Indeed, if the presence of the camera is understood as some form of enhancement, then the photograph builds and augments an event. Thus, for Butler, both seeing and photographing are shaped by norms that frame which life is rendered destitute and abject.

visibility for the zone of darkness that is the detention camp, and the moans of suffering from the men held captive there. What we see in Reprieve's video is Bey's ability to interrupt being force-fed through his verbal commands "please stop, please . . ." but also through the sonic substance of his moans (Moten 2003).[6] Bey's attempt at simulating the SOP of force-feeding ultimately uses representation as a way by which to impose form onto the sealed videos, the absence of Dhiab's recorded, yet sealed cries.

Reframing the Archive

This essay has argued that inherent to the punitive use of force-feeding at Guantánamo Bay is the compulsory visibility of the prisoner's body inside the detention camp. In its attempts to normalize the hunger striker's embodied defiance and behaviors, the SOP guidelines ultimately highlight the struggle intrinsic to state authority and the corporeal modes of resistance that are ongoing by Dhiab and those remaining at the detention camp. Integral to this struggle is the question of the visual, and the power of the state to control what information and images can be made public. The SOP of force-feeding and Dhiab's missing video footage are central archives of visuality in that they not only further the investigation of how force-feeding has become a medicalized technique of punishment but also expose the aggressivity essential to contemporary tactics of surveillance, tactics that literally violate the corporeal integrity of the body.

Dhiab was released from Guantánamo Bay to Montevideo, Uruguay, in 2014 (see Goodman 2016). He has yet to be reunited with his family and began hunger striking in 2016 to protest his detainment in South America. His most recent hunger strike began around the same time as a nationwide US prison strike started at California's Pelican Bay State Prison. On September 9, 2016, incarcerated people across the United States began hunger striking in protest of long-term solitary confinement (see Vongkiatkajorn 2016). Such ongoing political struggles remind one that to engage with archives of suffering and pain is to necessarily engage in its constant repetition. However, confronting pain and its visual and sonic representations can provide us with an affective engagement with images, one that urges a more relational approach during times of war and incarceration.

With the ruling against making public Dhiab's video footage, we must look toward alternative archives of evidence not authorized by the state. The SOP and

---

6. Here I am indebted to Fred Moten's (2003) idea of the phonic substance of mourning imbued in the photographic encounter.

Dhiab's court litigation, for that matter, are certainly central to this archive, but part of what this essay has attempted to do is to locate more affective resources by which to bear witness to the pain and suffering of those held captive and subjected to various techniques of power. Moqbel's testimony, although one of many, presents an opportunity to not only look but also listen to the sounds of suffering generated by force-feeding. This phonic substance is embedded within any representation of violence and, indeed, we ought to consider both Moqbel's statement and Bey's enactment of the SOP as simultaneously aesthetic and political, which can be just another way to think about representation itself (Moten 2003). And if representation always already signifies an absence, as we've seen throughout this essay, then what I would like to propose is that within this absence is the condition of possibility for imagining a new ethics of seeing, acting, and feeling. It remains unclear what Moqbel wishes us to do once we have again wrested our gaze toward Guantánamo. Perhaps here, then, the power of looking hinges not on an ideal ethical witness but a gesture of defiance that resists transnational carceral enterprises such as Guantánamo Bay and the US supermax prison, both of whose objective is, ultimately, to disappear its subjects.

References

Anderson, Patrick. 2005. "On Feeding Tubes." *Drama Review* 49, no. 3: 5–9.

Asad, Talal. 2003. *Formations of the Secular: Christianity, Islam, Modernity.* Stanford, CA: Stanford University Press.

Azoulay, Ariella. 2008. *The Civil Contract of Photography.* New York: Zone Books.

Bargu, Banu. 2010. "Spectacles of Death: Dignity, Dissent, and Sacrifice in Turkey's Prisons." In *Policing and Prisons in the Middle East: Formations of Coercion*, edited Laleh Khalili and Jillian Schwedler, 241–61. New York: Columbia University Press.

Butler, Judith. 2010. *Frames of War: When Is Life Grievable?* New York: Verso Books.

Constitution Project. 2013. *The Report of the Constitution Project's Task Force on Detainee Treatment.* The Constitution Project, April 16. detaineetaskforce.org /report/?utm_source=News%3A+Task+Force+2nd+Anniversary&utm_campaign =News%3A+TF+2nd+Anniv&utm_medium=email.

Dayan, Colin. 2001. "Legal Slaves and Civil Bodies." *Nepantla: Views from the South* 2, no. 1: 3–39.

Dayan, Colin. 2013. *The Law Is a White Dog: How Legal Rituals Make and Unmake Persons.* Princeton, NJ: Princeton University Press.

Foucault, Michel. 1977. *Discipline and Punish: The Birth of the Prison*, translated by Alan Sheridan. New York: Vintage.

Foucault, Michel. 1999. *An Introduction*. Vol. 1 of *The History of Sexuality*, translated by Robert Hurley. New York: Vintage.

Goodman, Amy. 2016. "Freed Gitmo Prisoner Jihad Abu Wa'el Dhiab Speaks as Pres. Candidates to Debate Terrorism." *Democracy Now*, September 26. www .democracynow.org/2016/9/26/exclusive_freed_gitmo_prisoner_jihad_abu.

Hartman, Saidiya V. 1997. *Scenes of Subjection: Terror, Slavery, and Self-Making in Nineteenth-Century America*. New York: Oxford University Press.

Hsu, S. Spender. 2015. "Judge Again Orders U.S. to Release Guantanamo Bay Force-Feeding Videos." *Washington Post*, October 27. www.washingtonpost .com/local/public. safety/judge-again-orders-us-to-release-guantanamo-bay -force-feeding-videos/2015/10/27/6b46bfc8-7cd5-11e5-beba-927fd8634498 _story.html.

JTF (Joint Task Force) Guantanamo Bay, Cuba, Joint Medical Group. 2013. *Medical Management of Detainees on Hunger Strike*, SOP: JTF–JMG.

Kapadia, Asif. 2013. "Yasiin Bey (aka Mos Def) Force-Fed under Standard Guantanamo Bay Procedure—Video." *Guardian*, July 8. www.theguardian.com /world/video/2013/jul/08/mos-def-force-fed-Guantanamo-bay-video.

Leopold, Jason. 2013. "Revised Guantanamo Force-Feed Policy Exposed." *Al Jazeera*, May 13. www.aljazeera.com/humanrights/2013/05/201358152317 954140.html.

Mirzoeff, Nicholas. 2011. *The Right to Look: A Counterhistory of Visuality*. Durham, NC: Duke University Press.

Moqbel, Samir Naji al Hasan. 2013. "Gitmo Is Killing Me." *New York Times*, April 14. www.nytimes.com/2013/04/15/opinion/hunger-striking-at-guanta namo-bay.html.

Moten, Fred. 2003. "Black Mo'nin'." In *Loss: The Politics of Mourning*, edited by David L. Eng and David Kazanjian, 59–76. Berkeley: University of California Press.

Paik, A. Naomi. 2016. *Rightlessness*: *Testimony and Redress in U.S. Prison Camps since World War II*. Chapel Hill: University of North Carolina Press.

Plumner, Nancy R. N. 1983. *Tube Feedings*. Indianapolis, IN: Vocational Educational Services.

Reprieve. 2013. "Yasiin Bey Force-Feeding Video Launches Campaign to Support Guantanamo Hunger-Strikers." Reprieve, July 8. reprieve.org.uk/press /2013_07_08_guantanamo_force_feeding_yasiin_bey/.

Rhodes, Lorna. 1998. "Panoptical Intimacies." *Public Culture* 10, no. 2: 285–311.

Rose, David. 2006. "The Scandal of Force-Fed Prisoners." *Guardian*, January 7. www.theguardian.com/world/2006/jan/08/usa.Guantánamo.

Savage, Charlie, and Julie Hirschfeld Davis. 2016. "Obama Sends Plan to Close Guantánamo to Congress." *New York Times,* February 23. www.nytimes.com /2016/02/24/us/politics/obama-guantanamo-bay.html.

Scarry, Elaine. 1987. *The Body in Pain: The Making and Unmaking of the World*. New York: Oxford University Press.

Smith, Clive Stafford. 2007. "Gitmo: America's Black Hole." *Los Angeles Times*, October 5. www.latimes.com/news/la-oe-smith5oct05-story.html.

Vongkiatkajorn, Kanyakrit. 2016. "Why Prisoners across the County Have Gone on Strike." *Mother Jones*, September 19. www.motherjones.com/politics /2016/09/prison-strike-inmate-labor-work.

White, Josh. 2006. "Guantánamo Force-Feeding Tactics Are Called Torture." *Washington Post*, March 1. www.washingtonpost.com/wp-dyn/content /article/2006/02/28/AR2006022801344.html.

Worthington, Andy. 2008. "Sami al-Haj: The Banned Torture Pictures of a Journalist in Guantanamo." Andy Worthington, April 13. www.andyworthington .co.uk/2008/04/13/sami-al-haj-the-banned-torture-pictures-of-a-journalist-in -guantanamo/.

Worthington, Andy. 2009. "Guantanamo's Hidden History: Shocking Statistics of Starvation." Andy Worthington, October 6. www.andyworthington.co.uk /2009/06/10/guantanamos-hidden-history-shocking-statistics-of-starvation/.

Worthington, Andy. 2017. "After Four-Year Legal Struggle, Judges Support Government Claims that Videotapes of Force-Feeding at Guantanamo Must Remain Secret." Andy Worthington, February 4. www.andyworthington .co.uk/2017/04/02/after-four-year-legal-struggle-judges-support-government -claims-that-videotapes-of-force-feeding-at-guantanamo-must-remain-secret/.

Yang, Ina. 2014. "How It Works: Putting Humans in Suspended Animation." *Popular Science*, June 3. www.popsci.com/article/science/how-it-works-putting -humans-suspended-animation.

....

Michelle C. Velasquez-Potts is a doctoral candidate in the Department of Rhetoric at University of California, Berkeley. Her dissertation, "Technologies of Incapacitation: US Torture Regimes and the Captive Body," studies the medicalization of punishment, and in particular the rise of force-feeding post-9/11. Her writing appears in the anthology *Captive Genders: Trans Embodiment and the Prison Industrial Complex* (2011) and the journal *Women and Performance*.

To Protect and Serve Themselves: Police in US Politics since the 1960s

Stuart Schrader

"**W**ho do you protect? Who do you serve?" You could hear this chant frequently at protests in recent years, directed at lines of grim-faced cops across the United States. Modifying a common police tagline, the chant raised the possibility that the aggressive police management of Occupy Wall Street and Black Lives Matter street protests was not simply about maintaining the peace but rather about a more sinister effort to maintain the racial capitalist status quo. But the chant also raises a challenging sociological question about the purpose or function of police and how that has changed over time. How does the internal organization of law enforcement as an institution interact with the external role of law enforcement to enact authorized state violence? To ask such a question is to inquire into the organizational sociology of police, a topic typically analyzed to understand outward effects of police activity.[1] Instead, I am interested in the inward effects of police activity, particularly in the realm of formal politics. Changing internal organization, I argue, affects what police activity looks like on the streets. This article examines how that internal organization has shifted over the past five decades since the 1960s.

In the United States, the notion that police serve the citizenry and impartially enforce the law is relatively new. To win widespread belief in this notion was a political achievement of a coterie of mid-twentieth-century police professionals

Thanks to Tyler Wall for helpful advice on an early version of this article. I am grateful to fellow authors in this issue for their feedback, particularly Graham Denyer Willis. I would also like to thank Shamus Khan and Madiha Tahir for their support of this publication and their innovative, collaborative approach to review and revision.

1. Among the most important such studies are Armenta, *Protect, Serve, and Deport* (2017); Brown, *Working the Street* (1988); Fassin, *Enforcing Order* (2013); Herbert, *Policing Space* (1996); and Peirson, "Introductory Study of Institutional Racism" (1977).

Public Culture 31:3 DOI 10.1215/08992363-7532667
Copyright 2019 by Duke University Press

who felt they had to stamp out voluminous evidence to the contrary in many Americans' everyday lives. According to widely accepted periodizations, US police underwent a transformation across the twentieth century. In the first part of the century, police officers were largely the foot soldiers of partisan political machines. They had little formal training. Political loyalty was the primary job requisite. The machines were engines of state formation, with police violence protecting business interests and assuring racial and ethnic order. Police directly served powerful political bosses and enforced loyalty with their nightsticks. Once entrenched, however, these very engines of state formation proved incapable of ensuring state legitimacy. Cruel violence and clear partisanship, along with class and racial selectivity, imperiled the ability of the state to govern without serious challenge from social movements. Police professionalization was one major response. This effort had two peaks, one in the 1920s and one in the 1960s, with the first originating within policing and the second imposed more directly by social-movement and other public pressures in the high era of civil rights struggles. Professionalization disentangled cops from political machines, raised standards of training, increased pay, and formalized procedures. Entry-level educational requirements increased, reliance on technological innovations intensified, and rigorous divisions of labor within police forces emerged. Instead of a haphazard and purely reactive stance toward crime and emergency response, the mark of professionalized policing was to be methodical planning. Prestige and political independence were the goals. Now police would better serve to legitimize the liberal state by enacting violence, or its threat, with fairness and without bigotry. That project was never completed, but it was the dominant approach among police for decades. It remains the dream of many police leaders today.[2]

Yet since the 1970s another period in the evolution of policing has been upon us, one that scholars have yet to identify and name. If professionalization entailed the extraction of police from political control of partisan machines so that they might act as independent executors of law and order, a peculiar result followed. Once freed of political requirements, police were able to organize themselves as coherent and semiautonomous political actors with their own interests. This new purpose and function is inwardly directed, as police have come to protect neither party machines nor the legitimacy of the state but, rather, themselves. Police assert political autonomy while also making demands on the state for resources. With crime as a key campaign issue, and with bipartisan calls for its reduction, elected

2. One classic account is Fogelson, *Big-City Police* (1977).

officials entrusted police to fulfill their political promises. Professionalization, moreover, conferred on police a monopoly of expertise in the particular social region of crime control. This situation created a structural trap: police gained more resources and ideological support even when they could not or did not curtail crime because officials had made campaign promises that assumed police would succeed and officials were thus loath to criticize their failures. Police gained prodigious political power in the process, touted for isolated successes and fiscally rewarded because of the mistaken belief that more resources would finally turn the tide in the fight against crime.

Rather than elected officials demanding loyalty from police, as was the case during the partisan era, today police demand fealty of elected officials. At the same time, police continually expand their capital-intensive repertoires. In this way, as fiscal Electroluxes sucking up every last penny they can find, the police of today might be best characterized not as partisan or professional but as profiteering. The internal logic of police has shifted. This perspective suggests that activist appeals for fairness and procedural reform in the wake of police killings of unarmed Black people are asking for a return to a bygone internal logic of police, one that itself gave rise to the conditions of the present.

To analyze the changing organizational sociology of police, this article examines the International Association of Chiefs of Police (IACP), a membership organization composed of police executives from across the United States and beyond. The IACP got its start in the nineteenth century and has counted among its members many important figures in the history of US law enforcement. It became the locus of police professionalization in the 1950s, aiming to sever cops from political machines once and for all. In this article, I show how the IACP renovated itself under the leadership of former high-ranking FBI agent Quinn Tamm in the 1960s to become a key supporter of what became President Lyndon Johnson's "war on crime," building on the organization's experience in assisting the federal government in the Cold War effort to raise policing standards and introduce professionalism in "Third World" countries considered at risk of communist subversion. At home, the federal government waged war on crime by providing money and technical assistance to states and municipalities, as well as private organizations, research firms, and academics. The Office of Law Enforcement Assistance (OLEA), created in 1965, and the much larger Law Enforcement Assistance Administration (LEAA), which replaced it in 1968, were the vehicles for the war on crime. This effort marked the apogee of professionalization and set into motion processes that would usher in the next era of policing, characterized by a strong rift opening up between professionalizing police executives and rank-and-file officers. After explaining the IACP role in the development of the war on crime, I examine an episode from the 1980s that revealed this rift. I then turn to how the IACP attempted to continue to spearhead the self-conscious organization of police as a political force throughout the 1990s, when it provided key support for President Bill Clinton's anticrime efforts. The IACP has been the crucible and catalyst for the shifting institutional logic of police, while reaping material benefits from policies it has advocated.

Territorialism and Scales

Police protect and enforce social boundaries. Through professionalization, this boundary work became a key part of how police approached themselves, orienting officers' accountability mainly to professional standards rather than to broader social forces, actors, and institutions. The police came to protect the boundaries of their profession by orienting expenditure of political capital inward, rather than using it on behalf of a broader project of securing the legitimacy of elected officials or governing regimes.[3] Notably, a catalyst for this disposition was itself a territorial border-crossing effort, as explained below, to impart US-style professionalism to police from other countries, which changed the IACP's relationship with the federal government. If professionalism was supposed to tame some of the wild and brutal characteristics of policing, then its unexpected effect was to allow police to take on a political life of their own.

What professionalism enables has been mutating, particularly as crime rates have fallen and urban economies and municipal tax bases have metamorphosed. These transformations did not occur in a vacuum. From the 1960s to the present, intragovernmental fiscal relations have undergone rescaling processes affecting police. The war on crime itself rescaled federal-state-municipal relations. It aimed to help jurisdictions with limited fiscal capacity to improve law enforcement by funneling federal dollars to them, even as other federal funding tightened.[4] Yet it is important to pay attention to actors beyond administrative and elected bodies. Organizations like the IACP act nationally or even internationally but are composed of place-bound member police executives. These members, through these organizations, can "jump scales" to address legislative bodies and audiences

3. The classic sociological text on professionalization is Abbott, *System of Professions* (1988).
4. The war on crime has been unfortunately ignored in the literature on state-spatial rescaling: Cox 2009; Brenner 2009a.

outside their jurisdictions.[5] At the same time, state- and municipal-level organizations, including unions or union-like entities that engage in formal or informal collective bargaining, are vehicles for pressing sector-wide demands introduced to the national agenda by lobbying of the IACP and other organizations but in distinctly geographically bounded forms. National executive organizations like the IACP and rank-and-file unions converge on the expansion of resources for police but differ on how best to use police legitimacy and professional autonomy. The conflict between them can be characterized by looking at the perspectives each brings to the internal organization of policing. Executives answer to elected officials, but rank-and-file police answer to the internal police hierarchy. This article focuses on the efforts of executives and their organizational cohesion, rather than the rank and file and the effects of unionization. For executives organized extrajurisdictionally, professionalism enables political autonomy. For rank-and-file officers, political autonomy enables professional insulation.

Internal conflict and variegation within police, however, must further be analyzed in terms of macro-level changes in political economy. A key component of the rescaling processes shaping urban finances and governance in the period under examination has been what David Harvey (1989) characterized as the shift from managerialism to entrepreneurialism. US police organizations have also been caught in this shift. Political demands for crime control in this period have had great affinities with the economic turn toward urban entrepreneurialism, as city governments compete with each other, using crime rates as proxies for consumer desirability. But less appreciated has been the way that this condition has pushed police departments to become entrepreneurs themselves. They have advocated for their own interests, within a matrix of urban competitiveness shaped by racialized fears of crime. At the national scale, organizations like the IACP have pushed for greater sector-wide fiscal endowments. At state and local scales, police departments have competed with each other and competed with other administrative state agencies for resources. This intrastate competition is nestled within locational competition among municipalities for mobile capital investment. If neoliberalization has entailed concomitant "rollback" and "rollout" moments, interagency competition has meant fiscal rollback for some agencies and fiscal rollout for others (Peck 2012). Police have frequently won this competition, which helps

5. In the literature on scale, "scale jumping" has typically been considered the activity of social movements. Here I suggest that it is also a key activity of actors within the state, particularly in the specific situation of US federalism. At the same time, I recognize the analytic problems of such a metaphor, which reifies and hierarchizes scales as external to social processes that are better understood as "scaled." See Brenner 2009b and Miller 2009.

explain why fiscal austerity has not been applied uniformly within and among the fifty states and their municipalities.

Policing Theories of the State

This research reveals the surprising convergence between orthodox Marxist and liberal theoretical approaches to police. Both remain ahistorical and inattentive to the shifts across the twentieth century in policing charted here. Both often fail to grasp the state itself as complex and contradictory, presuming rather than demonstrating that state legitimacy is achieved and uniformly shared across state apparatuses. Neither theorizes how actors within the state instrumentalize legitimacy for their own purposes. The orthodox Marxist approach posits the police as an instrument of class rule, a conduit for exogenous forces to impinge, mainly through coercion, upon exogenous objects, from dominating to dominated. Police exist for the "rationalization of social relations," which remains a key analytic and political insight, though it cannot explain what police achieve at scales beyond the street stop or even the factory picket line (Spitzer 1993).[6] In such theoretical accounts, class struggle occurs outside the police. The police consistently aid class rule by acting according to external dictates transmitted from an often monolithic-seeming capitalist class. Similarly, liberal accounts, which focus on procedural fairness, or lack thereof, in police activity, posit a neutral institution as the goal (President's Task Force 2015). Again, class and other forms of conflict occur outside the police, but occasionally police take a (predictable) side. If the police can devise procedures that enable them not to take a side, then their neutrality will be preserved, and fairness will be within reach.

The alternative approach developed here understands the police as possessing a specific institutional materiality and a scale-selective mode of operations. Building on the insight of Nicos Poulantzas that the state is a social relation—a material condensation of a balance of forces expressed in a specific form—the police too might be understood as a social relation, in addition to the rationalizer of social relations that exist beyond them. The state, for Poulantzas, comprises social relations expressing and realizing dominant and subordinate forces through specific agencies or branches. These branches contend strategically with each other within the state for ideological and resource primacy. Policing is also an internally con-

6. Sidney L. Harring (1983) offers the best account of the orthodox Marxist view, while also suggesting a route out from it that remains within a Marxian theoretical project. He argues that police do not exist outside class struggle, but he nonetheless insists that the "form" of police has not changed in over one hundred years. See also Walker 1977.

tested field, but police are endowed with material interests and political where-withal to realize those interests. Such inwardly directed action is semiautonomous from what police outwardly do to secure the conditions for capital accumulation and enforce and perpetuate racial inequality. Police are not neutral or frictionless vessels that transmit exogenous forces. Nor are police the thin blue line, as they have historically understood themselves: the bearers of reason and virtue, against the chaos of civil society. Rather, police are institutionally striated, with officers and units channeled in competing directions (technoscience is one, manual labor is another). Police self-organize according to this contestation, with capital-intensive professionalization as one expression. Police professionalization was, to repurpose the words of Poulantzas ([1978] 2000: 184), "imposed on the State by the struggle of the dominated classes," who became fed up with the conduct of police, particularly after World War II. But police action in the current era represents not simply the reassertion of the power of the dominating classes but the police acting as a type of dominating class for itself, inscribing its power on the state and civil society. Police action to rationalize social relations is their downscaling prerogative of governance; police action to endow themselves with resources and institutional autonomy from onerous oversight is their upscaling prerogative. This perspective suggests a superordinate unity behind contending popular understandings of the current era of policing, such as militarized, order maintenance, data driven, or community policing. All entail organized police activity to bolster their own power, independence, and resources, conditioned by a macro-level political economy of interjurisdictional and intrajurisdictional competitiveness.

Professionalization and Its Discontents

The conditions of the current moment of politically self-interested advocacy by police grew out of contradictions of the earlier professionalization moment. The IACP has been at the center of both. Police have never spoken with a unified voice. Leaders of the IACP, however, attempted to speak on behalf of the profession. This move was successful in creating institutional, if not ideological, coherence among police, even as it created new divisions and challenges for purposeful and unified action. As a private, membership-based organization and publisher of a major magazine, *The Police Chief*, the IACP advocated on behalf of police as a whole. Yet it did not actually represent them because it was not a democratically accountable organization. The IACP successfully pushed for two main goals that secured its status as a representative of law enforcement's cutting edge: first, for the creation of a federal program that would enlarge the amount of resources available to police, and second, for a professionalization and reform program that would result from this expanded pool of resources.

The IACP's efforts in the 1960s to garner resources for police opened a Pandora's box. In general, police have been happy to accept the resources since the 1960s but have been less willing to accept the demand for professionalization. In effect, a divide opened between the top echelon of police executives and the rank and file. It was not new but became exacerbated as leaders tried to insist that their officers undertake new approaches to patrol, investigation, and emergency and special-event preparedness. The rank and file saw professionalizing reforms as a form of undue control over them. These cops used the newfound legitimacy of police to make fiscal demands on the state. The push to delink the quest for resources from the quest for reform has been largely successful. Resources flowed, but the money was not conditional on reforms IACP leaders also wanted, thanks to the design of the funding infrastructure and to long-standing conservative nostrums, as well as the architecture of federalism. The IACP's influence over policing did not diminish greatly, but other contenders, including representatives of rank-and-file police who felt no compunction to advocate reform, took advantage of the new discursive and ideological space the IACP had created by turning police into political actors.

Two major impediments to the organization of police as a coherent political force have characterized the decades since the 1960s. The first preexisted the era of professionalization: geographic unevenness. Compared to big-city police executives, small-city and rural police executives faced dramatically different social situations, crime profiles, demographics, and, most importantly, resource availability. Further, small-city chiefs have long tended to be more politically conservative and beholden to local political interests than big-city chiefs, especially after the IACP in the 1960s and 1970s successfully advocated new hiring practices for police chiefs that would enable the appointment of individuals who had not risen through the ranks of a given force he or she was to oversee. As mentioned, the war on crime's availability of funding for police through the LEAA, and its successors, combined with state increases in anticrime budget appropriations, was one major effort to decrease fiscal unevenness across the United States. To lessen the impediment of unevenness was a target of the very political intervention that ushered in the war on crime. It was a struggle to garner greater shares of the fiscal pie for law enforcement. Still, the objectives of the war on crime's fiscal instruments were innovation and reform. Lawmakers designated how LEAA funding could be used and kept it from offering direct infusions of cash to pay full salaries of new police hires, buy new equipment, or purchase land for building new facilities. Police chiefs may have desired such infusions in the 1960s, but Congress did not allow such federal funding until the 1994 Violent Crime Control and Law Enforcement Act. By this time, chiefs' fears that such subventions might come with conditional strings attached had largely been assuaged—because by then police chiefs were speaking with a more unified voice. Geographic unevenness was not impervious to federal outlays.

In contrast, a divide between police chiefs and rank-and-file officers, also pre-existing, grew as professionalization became dominant. In general, the leading professionalizers of the mid-twentieth century saw the route to reform and modernization of policing as the institutionalization of a more military-like hierarchy, with greater controls on the activities of patrol officers. These controls would be ensured not only by more extensive training requirements but also by explicit procedural codes. The particular modality of the war on crime, which made most funding contingent on innovative research-intensive measures, heightened hierarchical tensions. These measures often required new everyday routines among officers. Many chafed at such requirements. Moreover, this division overlapped with geographic unevenness, as few small-city chiefs were deeply interested in innovation, though some realized that innovative and experimental reforms might raise their own professional profiles while additionally garnering new revenue streams (Schrader 2017). Perceived as limitations on the sacrosanct and racially selective discretion of individual rank-and-file police officers, professionalization fostered a backlash that took two forms: first, a rumbling labor revolt that persists to the present (outside the scope of this article), and second, an effort among police scientists to create a new police orthodoxy that reasserted the individual officer's discretion. This new orthodoxy has earned a range of labels. The most common and misleading is "community policing," which makes it seem like this approach is exogenously directed when in fact it is endogenously directed toward the work routines, rhythms, and requisites of "the job." Notably, the intellectuals who have pushed this new orthodoxy all took advantage of the platforms and funding structures that professionalization created, from professional magazines to LEAA and Police Foundation grants (Kelling and Kliesmet 1971; Wilson and Kelling 1982). Some of them would resist the form professionalization took.

Professionalization was supposed to claim external legitimacy, but this organizing principle corroded from the inside. The generation of police leaders associated with professionalization was aging out over the course of the 1960s (Bittner 1978). By the beginning of the 1970s an upstart generation was challenging it, including academic figures like George Kelling and police executives like Daryl Gates of Los Angeles and Clarence Kelley of Kansas City (Tafoya 1990). The fiscal infrastructure to at last achieve professionalization came into being in 1965 with the commencement of the federal war on crime and the creation of the OLEA. At this moment, professionalizers were accomplishing their goal of political independence for police, in reaction to the preceding politicized version of policing. Yet political independence was not enough because police legitimacy was fragile. Protests against racialized injustice, including police killings of Black people, spurred nearly all the civil unrest of the 1960s. These destructive events troubled the hope for slow but steady achievement of professionalism, and persistent corruption in many big-city forces seemed impervious to professionalization. For police executives, professionalization would help bolster legitimacy, but the demands it placed on rank-and-file officers were high. Routinization, methodical planning, and military-like adherence to standards, which professionalizers ordered, provoked rank-and-file revolt. For its part, the LEAA funded research, including by the IACP, on how chiefs could protect against such revolt.[7] Professionalization alone did create political independence for police, but police officers transformed independence into self-interest.

Fiscal austerity, shrinking union density, and the political popularity of "law and order" appeals have coincided in the decades since Richard Nixon's election to president in 1968. These conditions created the structural context for police to embody a new type of authoritative political actor. In the period while fiscal austerity shaped government budgets across the United States and union density shrank, police in most locales managed to buck these two major trends, in part because union or union-like activity dovetailed with police-managerial efforts to resist austerity even as rank-and-file demands clashed with managerial efforts to reform work routines. In the contemporary moment of precipitously declining crime rates in most areas of the United States, the capacities police developed in their entrepreneurial or rollout efforts have now become surplus. Rather than allow these capacities to evaporate, police protect them. Police have become unwilling to let go of their competitively realized gains, placing their self-interested advocacy at an increasing distance from achieving their nominal mission of crime control.

International Associations

The initial impetus for police to issue greater demands on the federal government had an unlikely origin: a forgotten Cold War effort to prevent communist revolution across the globe. From 1955 through 1962, the IACP held a contract

---

7. The LEAA issued a grant of over $160,000 to the IACP for research on strike activity among police in the 1970s, resulting in William D. Gentel and Martha L. Handman's *Police Strikes* (1980).

with US foreign aid agencies to coordinate training of police executives from the "developing" world in the United States. Police from Iran, South Vietnam, Somalia, Chile, and many other countries visited stationhouses in US cities and towns, as well as a range of other destinations, including colleges, manufacturers of technical policing implements, military bases, prisons, and so on. The idea was to demonstrate the US model of professional policing, as well as to cultivate relationships between these police officials and US intelligence agencies. At its peak, the program brought upward of three hundred foreign police officials to the United States annually. Although the IACP admitted there were inefficiencies in its coordination of the program, the program still entailed a lot of work. Around sixty thousand days of local police work went into hosting, orienting, and training visiting police officials. Many US chiefs, though they felt honored to be included, did find the visits burdensome. And neither the IACP nor Washington reimbursed them for the effort and time their officers expended, beyond direct costs for the visit. The rewards were intangible: playing a key role in facilitating the prosecution of the Cold War in "Third World" countries conferred a sense of purpose and belonging on underresourced US police.

Changes within the IACP were afoot. The new executive director and editor of *The Police Chief*, Quinn Tamm, was responsible for the IACP's shifting posture. He believed there was an opportunity for the IACP, and its member police chiefs around the country, to accelerate the movement to professionalize policing. The IACP was relocating to a new building in Washington, DC, and its leaders had developed plans to create an international police college, along with other training initiatives. Such growth could allow it to spearhead all training of police officials visiting from overseas. A new contract that might expand the IACP role in national security efforts could provide more money for other IACP programming, while also bolstering the organization's credibility as the leading voice of police professionals. And, most importantly, Tamm, who had once been close to J. Edgar Hoover, was trying to assert independence from the FBI director, raise his own prominence nationally, and give the IACP a unique institutional identity.[8]

In 1962, the newly formed Agency for International Development (AID) decided not to renew the existing contract with the IACP to maintain the training program. IACP officials were infuriated. The contract's cancellation seemed to

8. Director, IACP Training Division to Chief, Public Safety Division. September 13, 1961, IACP Move to New Headquarters Building, entry 29, box 8, RG 286, National Archives and Records Administration (hereafter NARA); Edward C. Kennelly, Memo for the Record, December 29, 1962; Quinn Tamm to Fowler Hamilton, February 2, 1962; Edward C. Kennelly, Memo for the Record, March 9, 1962, IACP 1962, entry 29, box 1, RG 286, NARA. Caplan 1973; Schrader 2019.

be a setback for the organization at a crucial moment. AID had decided to build its own International Police Academy, rendering the IACP's planned international police college superfluous. The response of Tamm and the IACP's Training Division to the cancellation was petty. The IACP returned file cabinets to AID without the files in them, for example, claiming the files were now IACP property. Tamm sent letters to colleagues imploring them to support him and even interfere with future AID efforts. And he demanded a public explanation and apology from AID. Once the bitterness subsided, however, the experience proved useful. It turned out to be a rehearsal.[9]

Tamm's Take-Home Lessons

The abrupt cancellation of the IACP's contract to facilitate foreign police training planted seeds that would blossom in the federal war on crime. Tamm, already deeply knowledgeable about law enforcement, gained experience in negotiating with intricate federal bureaucracies. Three aspects of the unraveling of the AID-IACP relationship stuck with him to shape how the IACP would advocate for the war on crime. First was the avoidance of external control. Tamm worried that AID might disburse funding to other institutions instead of the IACP, which could place civilians without policing expertise in positions to exercise influence over police. That never happened, but Tamm repeated this very concern a few years later when advocating federal anticrime legislation. Similarly, he and other IACP officials continually denounced civilian review boards (*Police Chief* 1963b, 1964; Murdy 1965). Deeply conservative senators who supported the legislation concurred with this inclination. North Carolina's Sam Ervin insisted to Tamm that a key legislative goal was avoiding a "federally directed and federally implemented program."[10] One way to do so was not to give a direct oversight role to Attorney General Ramsey Clark, whom conservatives in Congress distrusted. Tamm himself made just such a request, despite his own politically cautious support of the administration.[11] The cops' demand to avoid external control of policing produced

9. Sixth Meeting of the Interdepartmental Subcommittee on Police Advisory Assistance Programs, May 11, 1962; Johnson F. Munroe to Daniel Van Buskirk, March 19, 1963; Quinn Tamm to Ralph A. Butchers, January 11, 1963; Edward C. Kennelly to Byron Engle, March 4, 1963; Quinn Tamm to Byron Engle, December 17, 1962, IACP 1963, entry 29, box 1, RG 286, NARA.

10. US Senate, Hearings before a Subcommittee of the Committee on the Judiciary, July 22, 23, and 30, 1965, 89th Cong., 1st sess. (Washington, DC: Government Printing Office, 1965), 90.

11. Clark turned out to be in agreement with Tamm on the need to "rely on the expertise and the needs of the states and local communities," which "bear the heaviest burden of law enforcement." Tamm told President Johnson's aides that Clark was "the most sincere, the most intelligent and the

the peculiar shape of the Omnibus Crime Control and Safe Streets Act of 1968, which created state planning agencies to determine how block grants would be distributed. The legislation empowered governors, who had not exhibited much desire to be so empowered and were even more susceptible to complaints from police than congressional representatives. Keeping federal oversight or democratic control out of the legislation would ultimately be gravely consequential for the transformation charted here. The protection of local autonomy and sanctioning of patrol discretion led to a lack of accountability that emboldened police politically.

Second, Tamm recognized the power of Washington's purse. During the seven years of the IACP program for foreign police, multiple prominent policing experts realized that money from Washington might be a useful stimulant to local law enforcement, long hamstrung by the limited fiscal capacities of states and municipalities. Among these men—they were all men—were reformist chiefs with whom Tamm collaborated, including members of the executive board of the IACP. Herbert Jenkins of Atlanta, for example, was the most nationally prominent police chief from a southern state, and he became an important ally of the Johnson administration in its anticrime efforts. Jenkins had urged the IACP to complain up the AID ladder about the contract's cancellation, unaware that the foreign police assistance program was not answerable to the AID hierarchy but was nearly autonomous owing to its unique national security role. Nonetheless, this disposition suggests that the chiefs were becoming aware of their own leverage, political capacity, and power, particularly as elected officials across the political spectrum deemed police to be a bulwark against ongoing civil unrest among minoritized peoples.[12]

Third, beyond Washington, police executives recognized that private foundations could be useful in transforming policing. Already by 1959, policing experts working in networks affected by or adjacent to the AID-IACP relationship discussed ways to garner funding for the modernization of US policing that did not necessarily entail any foreign-affairs entanglement, such as from the Ford Founda-

---

most helpful toward local law enforcement" of the many attorneys general he had known in his thirty-seven-year career. Still, Tamm specifically asked Congress in open session to ensure that the attorney general "have the benefit and counsel of professional state and local police executives." Horace Busby to Marvin Watson, February 1, 1968, FG 135; White House Central File, box 186, Lyndon Baines Johnson Presidential Library, Austin, TX (LBJL); Department of Justice, *Law Enforcement Assistance, Part V*, Administrative History, box 3, LBJL, 4.

12. Excerpt from Minutes of the Meeting of the Board of Officers of the IACP, September 18, 1962, IACP 1963, entry 29, box 1, RG 286, NARA.

tion. Shortly, exactly this type of foundation funding started to become available, with Ford granting $1.46 million to the IACP, the Southern Police Institute, and two law schools. Ford and the IACP cosponsored a 1963 conference titled "Police Responsibility in Race Tension and Conflict," attended by police administrators from across the South. It included addresses by African American leaders Roy Wilkins and James Farmer along with several prominent law-enforcement figures. The IACP under Tamm's guidance led the charge to pursue private funding. In 1973, the Ford Foundation provided the seed funding for the Police Foundation, which became a competitor with the IACP that was not beholden to the demands of the chiefs and could focus solely on innovative research, some of which undermined reigning orthodoxies of the era of professionalization (Ford Foundation 1964; *Detroit Tribune* 1964; *Police Chief* 1963a; Murakawa 2014: 74–75; Schrader 2019). Altogether, avoiding external control, drawing on the federal purse, and relying on foundations would all become key planks of the war on crime. They also empowered police to become self-interested.

Crime Bills

Although the 1960s closed with the election of a new president on a platform of "law and order," Richard Nixon's predecessor's support for a war on crime surprised many police themselves. Once active, this war effort created new opportunities for police to act in self-interested ways. At the decade's outset, few cops or legislators thought federal intervention into policing would be possible. Police were wary of change. They were skeptical of federal action, even in the name of improving the policeman's lot. Many police officers could not easily disentangle new civil rights legislation, which seemed to intrude on local prerogative, from other forms of attention from liberals in Washington. Nevertheless, under the sway of prominent social scientists and jet-setting police reformers, the Johnson administration (1963–69) was poised to act. Urban unrest in northern cities in the summer of 1964 proved the necessity of upgrading police capabilities (Hinton 2016). But on what terms? The IACP's membership "wanted more men and equipment—not studies and innovative programs." Members even criticized the new Law Enforcement Assistance Act by issuing a resolution because the federal government seemed to be going too far, placing its coarse hands on the shoulders of municipal cops (ACIR 1977: 10). Tamm saw things differently. In the pages of *The Police Chief*, he rebuked the membership for passing this resolution. Soon the OLEA awarded the IACP $800,000 in grants ($6.4 million in 2018), with more to come. Tamm knew he had made the right decision.

The availability of federal money changed the attitudes of IACP members. The OLEA in effect created a constituency that would defend federal funding for law enforcement, even though the legislation was designed to foster research and reform. IACP leaders were genuine in their belief that funding for research and reform would diminish crime and raise the stature of the police. But that was beside the point. The incentive to support federal funding now existed, regardless of its use. When Congress lessened appropriations for the OLEA in 1966, Tamm used his acid tongue, usually reserved for supposed communists, to attack legislators for their malfeasance (Lewis 1965; *New York Times* 1966; Caplan 1973). He hoped a much bigger anticrime bill was in the works. To indicate the two-way, mutually beneficial relationship between Johnson's anticrime push and the IACP's demands, the president spoke at the IACP annual meeting in 1967. Within a year, Congress passed a bill that used block grants and lodged control of the LEAA's planning dimensions with state-level agencies controlled by governors. It was an inefficient system. But the IACP came to benefit from discretionary spending in Washington, under the Safe Streets Act's provisions.

Becoming voracious, the IACP continued to lobby. The effort was not without dangers. The organization risked its own tax-exempt status through aggressive lobbying at a time when such activity was considered unseemly for nonprofit entities. By accepting the risk and winning its actual demands, the IACP helped pave a path toward such self-interested lobbying by other similar organizations. When funding for the LEAA came up for renewal in 1970, again Tamm and the IACP were ready to offer "strong support" for the federal effort. This support helped dramatically expand a program that was widely considered in Washington not to have gotten off to an efficacious start. Notably, Tamm did not agree with prevailing criticisms of the LEAA, which pointed to the inefficiencies of the block grant system and the tendency of this system to shower funding on areas outside the major cities, away from the hotspots of crime. Instead, he savvily concurred with the thrust of the block grant system by arguing that a modification that might direct funds toward the big cities in a more focused manner would only "dislocate" crime from "the central city into the suburban environs."[13] Not only did this argument resonate with racist fears of Black crime spreading from beyond cities into growing white-flight bedroom communities, it tried to ensure that small-town IACP-member chiefs would still have a shot at securing some funding from

13. Statement of Quinn Tamm, Executive Director, IACP, March 17, 1970; Hearings before Subcommittee No. 5 of the Committee on the Judiciary, House of Representatives, 91st Cong., 2nd sess., 820–21.

LEAA grants, particularly if they were proactive and innovative. Most importantly, Tamm also asked Congress to rewrite the law to allow discretionary LEAA funding to be awarded to private-sector projects directly so that private nonprofit organizations like the IACP might be able to win such funding without subcontracting through a public unit. It was an arcane request that was not fulfilled until the 1973 renewal of the legislation. Previously, private organizations needed to be included in state-level criminal-justice planning grants or they could be awarded funds through the LEAA's in-house research institute. As the amount of money the LEAA distributed on a discretionary basis grew, from $4.35 million in 1969 to $87.9 million in 1973, the range of recipients expanded (LEAA 1973). J. Edgar Hoover's death in 1972, moreover, created new breathing room and possibilities within law enforcement nationally. With legislative change, the door opened to a much greater private-sector role in expanding the criminal-justice sector, effectively creating a self-interested lobby that worked parallel to law-enforcement officials in government. It was also independent from the direct police function of the state. A revolving door opened, as the ideological and practical valorization of the private sector gained a foothold within the criminal-justice system.

Chief versus Chiefs

By the early 1980s, the criminal-justice landscape was shifting. The new, internally directed logic of policing had not quite coalesced, but the professionalizer generation of the 1960s was being eclipsed. Tamm had retired from his position with the IACP. The LEAA was on life support by the end of President Jimmy Carter's administration (1977–81), with some modifications to the governing legislation under his watch but no radical shifts. Congress finally pulled the plug in 1982. Crime remained a pressing political problem at local levels, but because Carter rarely spoke of it, his administration lavished little attention on federal anticrime efforts. President Ronald Reagan (1981–89) addressed the IACP annual meeting in 1981, and high-level officials from his administration tried to draw attention to the problem of drugs at the next year's annual meeting. With the support of the IACP, Reagan exercised a pocket veto of crime-related legislation passed by Congress in 1982 that, among other goals, was to create a new federal "drug czar." (In 1988 he signed legislation that did create a drug czar position.)

Meanwhile, a dispute roiled police executives. Although not a fight between executives and rank and file, it emblematized the division between proactive professionalizers and those who wanted to be left alone, simmering since the 1960s. At its center was Patrick V. Murphy, a top OLEA official in the 1960s and then the commissioner of the New York Police Department. In 1973, Murphy became the president of the Police Foundation. This organization funded disruptive research and questioned prevailing orthodoxies. Although Murphy was a consummate reformer and professionalizer, the Police Foundation's research, such as the well-known Kansas City Patrol Experiment, overseen by George Kelling, came to upend shibboleths of professionalized policing. Murphy publicly criticized racism among police officers, and under his leadership the Police Foundation helped create additional professional organizations, like the Police Executive Research Forum and the National Organization of Black Law Enforcement Executives. The former was a top-echelon advisory group of law-enforcement elites that would come to have the ear of policy makers, without any accountability to a membership. These moves heightened tensions within the profession.

Murphy's outspoken approach earned him enemies. In New York City, as commissioner, he faced a five-day wildcat strike by as much as 85 percent of the force in January 1971. In August 1972, he instituted a new policy on the use of deadly force only in defensive situations, which was supposed to replace the customary fleeing felon posture—which allowed police to shoot suspects in the back. In 1980, he attempted to get the IACP to adopt an analogous defensive policy. He failed miserably. The membership reaffirmed its commitment to the outdated fleeing felon approach.[14] Already in 1978 Murphy had excoriated the "stranglehold" of small-town chiefs on the IACP, complaining that their "needs, fears and level of attainment and education . . . predominate in setting" its "priorities and tone" (Henry 1978). How to divvy LEAA funds was the question. The IACP, in his view, pushed for too much money to go to relatively pacific small towns. Murphy's Police Foundation, like the Police Executive Research Forum that he was addressing, was not beholden to conservative small-town chiefs. But these comments came back to haunt him, not only derailing his attempt to get the IACP on board with a global limit on discretionary use of deadly force, but in 1982 leading the censorious IACP to expel him from its member rolls.

This expulsion indicated how both Tamm and Murphy—and, by extension the professionalizers—were losing their grip on the profession. The two had been allies for over a decade. Tamm defended Murphy, calling the episode "shabby" and "outrageous" (UPI 1982; Herbers 1982). He also decried the attempt to impose "conformity" among IACP members—exactly what he had tried to do a decade and a half earlier in the effort to push passage of federal anticrime legislation.

14. The Supreme Court's 1985 decision in *Tennessee v. Garner* held that deadly force cannot be used against unarmed fleeing felony suspects. The ruling's effects have been negligible.

Although Murphy may have been correct to identify a geographic divide within the IACP, he miscalculated how committed the organization was to garnering widespread political support and rejecting criticism. The battle was not only over how best to spend federal funds; it was over how the police as a unit would be treated. In the past, the thinking was that greater resources would lead to respect for the police. Now the police would wield respect like a pistol in a stickup. The IACP in 1982 used its annual meeting to urge greater federal spending, invoking familiar specters, like communism, and relatively new ones, like drugs. Proudly, one IACP member reflected on changing public perceptions of the profession: "We used to be 'no good, rotten pigs'" (Harris 1982). The new esteem cops garnered was the result of professionalization, but esteem alone was insufficient. They needed money more than legitimacy. Neither protesters in the streets nor longtime members like Murphy could apply derogatory labels by the 1980s, went the thinking, if Reagan would allow more funding to become available. And soon he did. Reagan pushed Congress to pass an extensive new federal crime bill to his liking in 1984, which redesigned the law-enforcement assistance program and included provisions to expand asset forfeiture and standardize sentencing. The former would incentivize a range of law-enforcement activities that had little to do with crime control.

Making Money Moves

By Bill Clinton's presidency (1993–2001), the IACP had overcome some of the rifts among police executives that characterized the preceding two decades. In the 1990s, the IACP mobilized its membership to act in directly political ways. It created a legislation committee to monitor laws that might affect expenditures for law-enforcement agencies and lobby state and federal officials. Further, *The Police Chief* started featuring a monthly "Legislative Alert" section. A "Congressional Update" sometimes accompanied the section, offering a tabular listing of roll-call votes in Congress on legislation of concern to IACP members. This direct monitoring of the voting records of elected officials illustrates a shift: not only was the IACP trying to shape anticrime legislation, it was trying to make elected officials accountable to police, rather than the other way around. IACP president Sylvester Daughtry, Jr. (1994), described his goal as increasing the IACP's visibility. He felt he had been successful, with press appearances and "the presence of the association's leadership at numerous meetings and press conferences" with Clinton, the vice president, the attorney general, and the FBI director. The positions of the IACP and the Clinton administration on crime policy were becoming virtually indistinguishable.

Like Johnson and Reagan, Clinton addressed the IACP's annual meeting to speak about his signature anticrime push. Yet the two prior presidents came to the IACP seeking support for their efforts. The timing of the 1994 Violent Crime Control and Law Enforcement Act differed. Clinton addressed the IACP immediately after its passage, discussing how funds were already being disbursed within two weeks of the beginning of the fiscal year. He informed the assembled chiefs of the benefits they would reap from the new legislation. Clinton departed the meeting with an IACP baseball jacket emblazoned with the words "America's Chief" on the back, unthinkable for Lyndon Johnson, who painstakingly avoided the appearance of federal control over local police. Three decades of federal efforts, however, had allayed police chiefs' and doctrinaire conservatives' fears that federal funding would come with strings attached. By 1994, the legislation provided $8.8 billion for hiring new cops, an entailment all the prior crime bills avoided. In fact, municipalities with populations under fifty thousand, once the most reluctant to back federal expenditures because of worries about loss of prerogative, would now receive fast-tracked funding through a simplified application process that did not require a trained grant writer (Kime 1994; Kenworthy 1994). The legislation created its own constituency whose thirst for resources would be difficult to slake.

Conclusion

Historians and political scientists have recently demonstrated the importance of the federal government in fostering aggressive and expansive policing and incarceration in the United States since the 1960s (Hinton 2016; Murakawa 2014). But lower-scale police were not simply recipients of imperatives from Washington. They also became active and self-interested agents of their own destiny by organizing and reorganizing. This article has described the federal relationship with lower-scale governing units as mediated by organizations that allow extrajurisdictional cohesion and political power, particularly the IACP. It has also argued that this mediation has itself transformed in purpose over time. Without this perspective, it becomes impossible to explain how the two greatest crises involving police in the past half-century—the "civil disorders" of the 1960s and Black Lives Matter— led to such divergent outcomes, with professionalization efforts in the past and their repudiation in the present.

To assume that the federal government could transmit its dictates to the local level without passing through a mediating institution is to revert to an unsupportable view of law enforcement as neutral and inert. Instead, law enforcement, and particularly policing, as this article demonstrates, is a polyglot institution that has a specific materiality and identifiable interests—and cleavages around those interests. These interests have been mutable, relationally shifting in response to exogenous transformations and propelling endogenous transformations. Among the exogenous transformations has been the availability of funding from the federal government, which spurred the increase of available funding from state governments. Since the 1990s, police have been remarkably successful in promoting an exception to fiscal austerity. This position was not inherent but had to be developed through intensive efforts to organize police politically into an institution with leverage. Elected officials hailed police as political actors by answering political support with fiscal outlays. But now elected officials are increasingly beholden to police, who make demands that have little to do with their working conditions or the reality of the crime or terrorism they are called on to fight. Strangely, the only restraint on the political power of police today seems to be the growing divergence between police executives, who typically serve at the pleasure of elected officials and thus are responsible for producing measurable results, and the rank and file, who answer to no one but themselves. As one result, US citizens have little official information on the numbers of people police kill. Rather than submitting to oversight, what police seek is the continual endowment of their sector with resources. It is a profiteering outlook, attached to a capacity for organization, that deserves its own analytic attention, separate from the way police protect and serve social conditions amenable to capital accumulation. A critique of policing that fails to address this specific institutional materiality is destined to fail politically in its quest to shrink the power of police.

References

Abbott, Andrew. 1988. *The System of Professions: An Essay on the Division of Expert Labor.* Chicago: University of Chicago Press.

ACIR (Advisory Committee on Intergovernmental Relations). 1977. *Safe Streets Reconsidered: The Block Grant Experience 1968–1975.* Washington, DC: ACIR.

Armenta, Amada. 2017. *Protect, Serve, and Deport: The Rise of Policing as Immigration Enforcement.* Oakland: University of California Press.

Bittner, Egon. 1978. "The Rise and Fall of the Thin Blue Line." *Reviews in American History* 6, no. 3: 421–28.

Brenner, Neil. 2009a. "Open Questions on State Rescaling." *Cambridge Journal of Regions, Economy and Society* 2, no. 1: 123–39.

Brenner, Neil. 2009b. "A Thousand Leaves: Notes on the Geographies of Uneven Spatial Development." In *Leviathan Undone? Towards a Political Economy of Scale*, edited by Roger Keil and Rianne Mahon, 27–49. Vancouver: University of British Columbia Press.

Brown, Michael K. 1988. *Working the Street: Police Discretion and the Dilemmas of Reform*. New York: Russell Sage.

Caplan, Gerald. 1973. "Reflections on the Nationalization of Crime, 1964–1968." *Law and the Social Order* 3: 583–635.

Cox, Kevin R. 2009. "'Rescaling the State' in Question." *Cambridge Journal of Regions, Economy and Society* 2, no. 1: 107–21.

Daughtry, Sylvester Jr. 1994. "The Year in Review." *The Police Chief*, October. 6.

Detroit Tribune. 1964. "Efforts to Improve Criminal Justice at the Starting Point." July 11.

Fassin, Didier. 2013. *Enforcing Order: An Ethnography of Urban Policing*. Malden, MA: Polity.

Fogelson, Robert. 1977. *Big-City Police*. Cambridge, MA: Harvard University Press.

Ford Foundation. 1964. *Annual Report: October 1, 1963 to September 30, 1964*. New York: Ford Foundation.

Gentel, William D., and Martha L. Handman. 1980. *Police Strikes: Causes and Prevention*. Washington, DC: Government Printing Office.

Harring, Sidney L. 1983. *Policing a Class Society: The Experience of American Cities, 1865–1915*. New Brunswick, NJ: Rutgers University Press.

Harris, Art. 1982. "Lack of Crime-War Funds Deplored." *Washington Post*, November 19.

Harvey, David. 1989. "From Managerialism to Entrepreneurialism: The Transformation in Urban Governance in Late Capitalism." *Geografiska Annaler B* 71, no. 1: 3–17.

Henry, Neil. 1978. "Police Unit Head Blasts Rival Group." *Washington Post*, November 8.

Herbers, John. 1982. "Murphy Assailed by Police Chiefs." *New York Times*, July 8.

Herbert, Steve. 1996. *Policing Space: Territoriality and the Los Angeles Police Department*. Minneapolis: University of Minnesota.

Hinton, Elizabeth. 2016. *From the War on Poverty to the War on Crime: The*

Making of Mass Incarceration in America. Cambridge, MA: Harvard University Press.

Kelling, George L., and Robert B. Kliesmet. 1971. "Resistance to the Professionalization of the Police." *The Police Chief*, May, 30–39.

Kenworthy, Tom. 1994. "Clinton Crime Speech Gets Warm Greeting." *Washington Post*, October 18.

Kime, Roy Caldwell. 1994. "Distribution of COPS Monies Well Underway." *The Police Chief*, December. 8–9.

LEAA (Law Enforcement Assistance Administration). 1973. *1973: LEAA Activities July 1, 1912 to June 30, 1973*. Washington, DC: LEAA.

Lewis, Alfred E. 1965. "Top Police Aide Assails Civil Rights Disorders." *Washington Post*, October 8.

Miller, Byron. 2009. "Is Scale a Chaotic Concept? Notes on Processes of Scale Production." In *Leviathan Undone? Towards a Political Economy of Scale*, edited by Roger Keil and Rianne Mahon, 50–66. Vancouver: University of British Columbia Press.

Murakawa, Naomi. 2014. *The First Civil Right: How Liberals Built Prison America*. New York: Oxford University Press.

Murdy, Ralph G. 1965. "Is There a Board in Your Future?" *The Police Chief*, June. 10–12.

New York Times. 1966. "Legion Is Warned of 'War' in the Streets." August 28.

Peck, Jamie. 2012. "Austerity Urbanism." *City: Analysis of Urban Trends, Culture, Theory, Policy, Action* 16, no. 6: 626–55.

Peirson, Gwynne Walker. 1977. "An Introductory Study of Institutional Racism in Police Law Enforcement." PhD diss., University of California, Berkeley.

The Police Chief. 1963a. "Southern Police Institute Holds Conference for Southern Chiefs." June, 10–11.

The Police Chief. 1963b. "They Spoke to the Mayors." August. 18–22.

The Police Chief. 1964. "The Civil Rights Act of 1964—Implications for Law Enforcement." September. 8–9.

Poulantzas, Nicos. (1978) 2000. *State, Power, Socialism*, translated by Patrick Camiller. New York: Verso.

President's Task Force on Twenty-First-Century Policing. 2015. *Final Report of the President's Task Force on Twenty-First-Century Policing*. Washington, DC: Office of Community Oriented Policing Services.

Schrader, Stuart. 2017. "More than Cosmetic Changes: The Challenges of Experiments with Police Demilitarization in the 1960s and 1970s." *Journal of Urban History*. doi.org/10.1177/0096144217705523.

Schrader, Stuart. 2019. *Badges without Borders: How Global Counterinsurgency Transformed American Policing*. Oakland: University of California Press.

Spitzer, Steven. 1993. "The Political Economy of Policing." In *Crime and Capitalism: Readings in Marxist Criminology*, edited by David Greenberg, 568–94. Philadelphia: Temple University Press.

Tafoya, William L. 1990. "The Virtuosos of Policing." *American Journal of Criminal Justice* 14, no. 2: 205–27.

UPI (United Press International). 1982. "The International Association of Chiefs of Police." July 8.

Walker, Samuel. 1977. *A Critical History of Police Reform: The Emergence of Professionalism*. Lexington, MA: Lexington Books.

Wilson, James Q., and George L. Kelling. 1982. "Broken Windows: The Police and Neighborhood Safety." *Atlantic Monthly*, March. 29–38.

. . . .

Stuart Schrader teaches Africana studies and sociology at Johns Hopkins University. He is the author of *Badges without Borders: How Global Counterinsurgency Transformed American Policing* (2019), and his writing has also appeared in *Humanity, Journal of Urban History,* and *NACLA Report on the Americas,* among other venues.

Bodycams and Gender Equity: Watching Men, Ignoring Justice

Kim Shayo Buchanan and Phillip Atiba Goff

The widespread adoption of body-worn cameras by police departments across the country promises outcomes that appeal to a broad spectrum of stakeholders, ranging from Black Lives Matter and the American Civil Liberties Union (ACLU) to the International Association of Chiefs of Police and the Police Executive Research Forum. They hope that the presence of body-worn cameras ("bodycams") will improve the behavior of police officers and of people who interact with them. The idea is that the routine recording of police-citizen interactions will encourage compliance with departmental rules and policies, reduce misconduct and unnecessary use of force, ensure accountability, facilitate criminal and disciplinary investigations, and advance racial justice. These hopes are based on the expectation that officers will behave better when they know that they are being watched (see, e.g., Stanley 2015; Katz 2015; Yokum, Ravishankar, and Coppock 2017).

Images can catalyze change. Since 2014, a series of high-profile videos and livestreams of killings and other troubling police-citizen interactions have drawn unprecedented public and governmental attention to racial profiling and police brutality—long-standing systemic problems that Black, Indigenous, and other non-White communities have protested for decades. At the same time, community hopes that images of police misconduct might lead to meaningful accountability have not generally been realized. Whether videos are taken by citizen witnesses or police dashcams or bodycams, footage showing unlawful police behavior has rarely resulted in criminal conviction. In 2018, though, for the first time in more than fifty years, a Chicago police officer was convicted of murder for an on-duty killing—largely because police dashcam videos belied the story told by police officers who had witnessed the killing (Crepeau et al. 2018).

Public Culture 31:3   DOI 10.1215/08992363-7532739
Copyright 2019 by Duke University Press

Racial justice has been central to discourse about the costs and benefits of bodycams, as it has been to other conversations about police reform. Gender, however, has been largely overlooked. In this essay, we reconsider bodycam policy through an intersectionally gendered lens, asking: What might we learn about bodycam policy, if gender were taken into account? And what might a gendered view of bodycam policy reveal about the promise and limitations of police reform more generally? The first part of this essay shows that existing bodycam policies and best-practice recommendations ensure that cameras will often be turned off when the person interacting with the police officer is a non-White woman or a gender-nonconforming person. The second part notes that the situations in which bodycams are likely to be turned off are notorious sites of gender bias in policing: investigations of domestic violence; sexual assault and abuse; and sex work or sex trafficking. The third part uses the limitations of bodycam policy reform to illuminate broader challenges to the project of policing reform. The gender biases that plague such investigations could not be solved by simply requiring that cameras be activated in these situations: routine video recording of such interactions might be both impractical and undesirable. The deeper challenge is that many of these abusive or unjust policing practices are functionally permitted. Where the officer behaviors being recorded are allowed by law or authorized by departmental policy or custom, video recording is unlikely to result in meaningful accountability. The gendered injustices revealed in this essay, like the racial injustice that has more typically been the focus of conversations about policing reform, will require a more systemic and institutional response.

While the parameters of these more fundamental institutional and law reforms lie beyond the scope of this essay, we conclude with a few recommendations about how best to alleviate the immediate gender justice concerns we raise about bodycam surveillance. To mitigate the harms and inequities of current bodycam policies, police departments could and should design or amend their bodycam policies in consultation with the groups most affected by the gendered limitations of bodycam surveillance: sex workers, survivors of sexual and domestic violence, and gender-nonconforming people. Police departments should solicit direct community input on their bodycam policies through public meetings, private submissions, and/or community surveys about the situations in which bodycams should and should not be activated. Furthermore, police departments could share bodycam footage with independent auditors to examine their own policing practices for fairness, courtesy, procedural justice, and compliance with criminal laws, antidiscrimination rules, and departmental policies. As with all other criminal justice reforms, the effects of bodycam policy on vulnerable stakeholders must be taken into account if bodycams are to fulfil their promise to advance civil rights through accountability.

The limitations of bodycams identified in this essay may well generalize to the racial injustice that has been a central focus of police reform. Gender and masculinities interact with racial bias in policing in ways that academics in many fields are only beginning to unpack (see, e.g., Harris 2010; Poteat, Kimmel, and Wilchins 2011). By offering a critical, intersectional gender perspective on the design and effects of bodycam policy, this essay offers two contributions to the broader discourse on police accountability. First, it illuminates important ways that women and gender-nonconforming people (who are likely to be non-White) have been overlooked in the design and implementation of bodycam policies specifically, and in discourses of police reform more generally. Second, it illuminates systemic barriers to the accountability that bodycam advocates hope for, suggesting that bodycams may produce accountability only where they are accompanied by an institutional commitment to racial and gender equity in policing practice. These insights, in turn, might guide subsequent research and action regarding how best to create the circumstances in which police accountability mechanisms could be expected to advance public safety and equal justice.

Gendered Crime and Bodycam Rules

Police leaders, policing organizations, and civil liberties advocates who hope for the investigative, accountability, and fairness benefits of bodycams nonetheless acknowledge that indiscriminate recording of police-citizen interactions might jeopardize legitimate privacy interests of police officers, criminal suspects, and civilians such as victims or witnesses. As a result, guidelines issued by police and civil liberties organizations, as well as bodycam policies adopted by individual police departments, typically require or permit that bodycams be turned off in the following three situations (among others): in private homes; when interacting with minors or other victims of crime; and while officers are undercover or are interacting with a confidential informant (see, e.g., LAPD 2015; Chicago PD 2018; Miller, Toliver, and PERF 2014; ACLU 2015; IACP 2014; Fan 2016). These are all circumstances in which police officers are more likely to interact with those who are marginalized by gender inequality and gender violence: women, gender-nonconforming people, and/or sex workers.

Most people arrested by police are male (e.g., in 2015, about 73 percent of all

627

arrests involved men or boys[1]), but interactions with women, children, and gender-nonconforming people are also quite common. More than one quarter of all adults arrested every year are women. Girls make up more than 29 percent of those who are arrested at age seventeen or younger (FBI 2015). Over one million girls and women are arrested each year in the United States.

Moreover, men and women are arrested for distinct kinds of offenses, implicating distinct policy considerations. For most criminal offenses, a majority of persons arrested are men or boys. The only exception is prostitution, for which a majority of persons arrested—at least 60 percent—are women or girls (FBI 2015).[2] Many of the men and boys who are arrested for prostitution are gender-nonconforming or are perceived to be gender-nonconforming (James et al. 2016).

Police officers interact with women and gender-nonconforming people not only as suspects, but also as victims or witnesses. While victimization rates for violent crimes are roughly equal for men and women, a majority of victims of domestic or intimate partner violence, sexual victimization, and sex trafficking are women or girls (Truman and Morgan 2015: 13; Catalano et al. 2009; Rieger 2007).

Most violent and property crimes fit the male-perpetrator, male-victim pattern, and are likely to be influenced by conventional expectations of masculine gender performance (Poteat, Kimmel, and Wilchins 2011; Harris 2000). The crimes that diverge from this pattern are the ones that are most often subjected to critical gender analysis. This essay will use *gendered crimes* as a shorthand for crimes related to domestic violence, sexual victimization, and prostitution, even as its authors recognize that gender-role expectations probably affect practically all criminal behaviors, as well as criminal justice responses to them.

When bodycam rules or guidelines allow or require cameras to be turned off inside private homes or when dealing with minors, they trace the privacy interests in home and family that have traditionally been recognized in criminal and family law. Feminist theorists have long critiqued the gendered construction of privacy, noting that legal recognition of privacy interests in the home and family has tended systematically to insulate cisgender men against accountability for violence against women and children (see, e.g., Siegel 1996; Suk 2006). For example,

---

1. These gender classifications are reported by police departments and may not necessarily reflect the gender identities of persons who are arrested.

2. To the extent that transgender women who are arrested for sex work may be logged by police as male, the proportion of female-identified persons arrested for prostitution offenses may be higher. A 2015 survey of transgender persons found that two-thirds of transgender women who were stopped by police officers who thought they were sex workers were not actually involved in sex work (James 2016: 184).

men's expectations of privacy in the home and family formed the basis for statutes and judge-made rules that blocked criminal and civil accountability for men's violence against their partners and children, and for marital rape (Siegel 1996).

Along the same lines, bodycam rules accommodate privacy interests in the home and family, as well as the investigative demands of undercover work, in ways that will predictably result in cameras being turned off while officers are investigating domestic violence or sexual victimization, or are interacting with sex workers. Such protections as bodycams might offer, then, are likely to bypass many of the situations in which women, children, and gender-nonconforming people are most vulnerable to gendered violence.

Moreover, while gender injustice is less salient in contemporary political conversations about policing than racial injustice is, they are not independent concerns. Racism intersects with heterosexism and gender inequality in ways that can structure the vulnerability of children, women, and gender-nonconforming people to violence. Because many groups of non-White women are exposed to gendered crimes at higher rates than Whites (Breiding et al. 2014; Human Rights Campaign 2019),[3] the people whose interactions with police go unrecorded will disproportionately be women, children, and gender-nonconforming persons who are non-White.

Although the adoption of bodycams is designed to promote racial justice, it does not seem that bodycam rules and best practices have been designed to account for the ways that conventional gendered understandings of privacy can impede investigation and accountability for gendered crimes. The bodycam rules are not designed to create impunity for gender violence, and it is not necessarily clear that the rules themselves should be changed. For instance, it is quite reasonable that undercover officers should not wear bodycams that would betray their identity. We do not recommend, either, that bodycams be used indiscriminately to record investigations of domestic violence, sexual assault, prostitution, or sex trafficking. It seems very likely that many victims, witnesses, and persons suspected of such crimes might prefer not to be recorded, and might feel exposed or traumatized by being recorded against their will.[4] Many bodycam policies permit

3. Lifetime prevalence of sexual violence, stalking, and victimization among Black women is slightly higher than for White women. For Indigenous and multiracial-identified women, lifetime prevalence for each of these types of gendered crimes is about 50 percent higher than for White women. For each of these groups of crimes, lifetime prevalence for Latinas is somewhat lower than for White and Black women (Breiding 2014). Of twenty-six transgender people whose killings were recorded in 2018, at least twenty-three were non-White (Human Rights Campaign 2019).

4. The ACLU (2015: 5) has documented a number of incidents in which bodycam footage of police-citizen encounters was inappropriately released to the public, in ways that humiliated the citizens shown in the videos.

or require officers to deactivate video recording on the request of a victim or a person present in a private home (Chicago Police Department, Los Angeles Police Department). Considerations of justice and transparency might operate differently with respect to the privacy interests of suspected perpetrators and those of victims (although, in practice, the distinction between these two roles may not be immediately obvious to officers attending on a domestic violence call: Coker 2001). Furthermore, the interests and priorities of victims of domestic violence do not necessarily align with those of police and prosecutors (Coker 2001; Nash 2005; Suk 2006). For example, routine video recording of domestic violence calls, which was supported by more than three quarters of officers in a recent survey (Newell and Greidanus 2017: 19), could be used as evidence to continue a prosecution when a victim does not believe that prosecution will enhance her safety.

As they stand, though, bodycam rules and best practices that accommodate legitimate investigative demands and broadly held cultural notions about privacy in the home, family, and body will functionally exempt investigations of gendered crimes from otherwise-mandatory video surveillance. This exemption warrants particular concern because such investigations are notorious sites of gender disparity and discrimination in policing (USDOJ 2016; PERF 2012). In other words, to the degree that bodycams can alleviate racial injustice, they will exclude women and gender-nonconforming people from those protections. Policy neglect of these considerations reveals the marginality of women and gender-nonconforming people in the broader conversation about police reform. The following section identifies a few ways in which police responses to gendered crimes have been shown to exacerbate gender inequality—highlighting the fact that it is no small oversight to ignore the potential for gendered abuses by police.

Gendered Injustice in Policing: Domestic Violence, Sexual Assault, and Sex Work

Gender bias and discrimination permeate the policing of gendered crimes in the United States. As recently as 2016, the US Department of Justice (USDOJ 2016: 3) identified a number of ways that gender bias could influence police investigations, including "misclassifying or underreporting sexual assault or domestic violence cases, or inappropriately concluding that sexual assault cases are unfounded; failing to test sexual assault kits; interrogating rather than interviewing victims and witnesses; treating domestic violence as a family matter rather than a crime; failing to enforce protection orders; or failing to treat same-sex domestic violence as a crime."

When responding to domestic violence calls, gender biases can result in officers accepting the reassurances of male abusers that there is no problem despite the pleas and physical injuries of their victims, and failing to press charges despite evidence of physical violence against the abusers' wives and children (Coker 2001; Suk 2006). Too frequently, police officers are reported to have urged women to reconcile with their abusers rather than facilitating arrests and charges at the request of the abused (Goodmark 2011; Schneider 2000; Sack 2004; Siegel 1996).

In response to a well-publicized 1992 experiment that found a decrease in homicides when police made an arrest in response to domestic violence calls for service (Sherman et al. 1992), many states and police departments introduced mandatory arrest policies requiring that officers must make an arrest every time they find evidence that domestic violence may have occurred. Mandatory arrest policies are designed to protect public safety by initiating criminal proceedings regardless of the victim's wishes, to prevent the abuser from intimidating the victim into recanting. While this may be a laudable goal, such policies can also compromise the autonomy of a victim who perceives no further danger from the partner, who wants to end the abuse while continuing the relationship, or who believes that further criminal justice involvement will increase the danger (Coker 2001; Suk 2006). Furthermore, mandatory arrest policies may be associated with increased arrests of women who are victims of domestic violence (Coker 2001; Miller 2001; Rajan and McCloskey 2007). Moreover, because arrests for domestic violence are more common in low-income non-White families, victims who interact with police are disproportionately non-White (Suk 2009: 45). The consequences of mandatory arrest policies may be borne disproportionately by African American women, who are likely to be viewed as more masculine and less worthy of protection, compared to white women (Goff, Thomas, and Jackson: 2008). Black women may also be more likely to fight back when beaten by a partner, and are more likely to be arrested for doing so (West 2007). Transgender people may face particular danger from police responses to domestic violence: of three trans people who were killed by police officers in 2017, two were shot during domestic disturbance calls (Human Rights Campaign 2017; Deppen 2017; Lohr 2017). To the extent that bodycams are turned off when officers respond to domestic or intimate partner violence calls, the circumstances of those calls will go unrecorded, and the potential evidentiary value of such recordings will be lost.

Along the same lines, police departments in the United States have been criticized for systemic and institutional failure to respond adequately to allegations of sexual assault. Many policing agencies acknowledge that—as antirape advocates contend—gender bias in sexual assault investigations remains widespread (see, e.g., USDOJ 2016; PERF 2012; IACP 2011), and can contribute to the failure to report these assaults to the police. According to the US Department of Justice, sexual assault is the violent crime least likely to be reported to police, with 65 percent of sexual assaults in the United States going unreported (Langton and Berzofsky 2012: 4). In the United States, Black and Indigenous people experience sexual victimization at higher rates than Whites, but are less likely to report them (Catalano et al. 2009: 5; Planty et al. 2013: 3, 13). Transgender survivors of sexual violence are especially unlikely to report violent or sexual victimization to police. Most transgender people say they feel "somewhat" or "very" uncomfortable asking police to help (James et al. 2016: 184). This further endangers non-White and gender-nonconforming people, since victims of violence who do not report their victimization face an elevated risk of being victimized again (Ranapurwala, Berg, and Casteel 2016).

When asked why they did not contact the police, one common reason given by sexual assault survivors is that they fear that police officers would not or could not help (Planty et al. 2013). When women (or other survivors of sexual violence) report a sexual offense to the police, they often feel revictimized by the investigative response. Survivors of sexual assault often encounter investigators who accuse them of lying about their victimization. Federal legislation, DOJ guidance, and consent decrees have had to direct police departments to stop routinely subjecting survivors to polygraph tests when they report sexual assault (see USDOJ 2016; IACP 2018: 5).[5]

It is also quite common for investigators to suggest that a survivor might have invited a sexual assault by the way they dressed, or because they had been drinking or taking drugs, were transgender or nonstraight, were unchaste, or knew the person who assaulted them (see, e.g., USDOJ 2016; Crenshaw 1991; Estrich 1986). The practice of "unfounding" a report of sexual assault—declaring it to be false or baseless—is also more common than it should be (USDOJ 2016; Spohn, White, and Tellis 2014). There is evidence that sexual assault allegations by sex workers, LGBTQ people, or Black or Indigenous women are more likely to be dismissed as "unfounded" solely because of those identities (USDOJ 2016; Pokorak 2006). Worse, in many jurisdictions, victims of sex trafficking, including children and youth, have been prosecuted for their involvement in the sex trade (US Department of State 2015: 352). These disparities are consistent with the common beliefs that such victims do not deserve to be taken seriously or that men who assault them should not be punished as criminals (Tuerkheimer 2016). To the extent that

5. See also the Violence against Women Act, 42 U.S.C. §3796gg-8, "Polygraph Testing Prohibition."

bodycams are turned off during investigations and interviews with victims of sexual victimization, such interactions will go unrecorded, leaving officers' behavior undocumented.

Gender disparities in law enforcement outcomes are particularly acute with respect to sex workers. In the United States, the adults and children who are involved in sex work and sex trafficking are disproportionately non-White—Black, Asian American, Latinx, and Indigenous (Fitzgerald, Patterson, and Hickey 2015). Because they face pervasive discrimination in legitimate employment, transgender people are overrepresented in sex work (James et al. 2016). Sex workers, of any race or gender, face a very high likelihood of sexual victimization and intimate partner violence, whether on the job or in their private lives (USDOJ 2016: 11). Nonetheless, there is a marked pattern of "unfounding" or refusal to investigate reports of gender violence against sex workers in the United States (USDOJ 2016). This practice is so emblematic that the DOJ uses it as an exemplar of the kind of biased investigation that police departments ought to guard against:

> Example: A woman who has been known to engage in prostitution flags down a police officer who frequently patrols her neighborhood. She reports to the officer that she was just raped. The police officer on duty writes down her statement, but, when he returns to the police station, he immediately classifies the complaint as "unfounded," and takes no further action, because of the woman's sexual and criminal history. (11)

As one sex-worker advocate puts it, "The police and criminal justice systems treat sex workers as though rape were a mere 'occupational hazard' of their work—an accusation that would never be thrown at a bank teller who survived a robbery" (Keenan 2014).

Not only has the police response to crimes against sex workers been less than vigorous—unfortunately, it is not unusual that some police officers themselves victimize sex workers and adults and children who have been trafficked. Non-White women and trans people who are suspected of involvement in the sex or drug trade, who are under investigation or arrest, or who are otherwise vulnerable are especially likely targets (Blades 2017; Ritchie 2017). Police officers in multiple jurisdictions have conducted vaginal searches of non-White women, in full view of the public, at traffic stops and in airports (Ritchie 2017). Physical and sexual abuse by police officers is widespread enough that the International Association of Chiefs of Police has issued guidelines to departments on how to prevent it[6] (IACP 2011).

6. But "no evidence-based strategies for prevention [of sexual misconduct] are available for use by police departments" (Reingle Gonzalez, Bishopp, and Jetelina 2016: 614).

Sex workers are especially vulnerable to sexual exploitation and physical violence at the hands of law enforcement. A recent study of the National Blacklist, a website used by sex workers to warn each other about dangerous men, found that 10 percent of postings on the site dealt with police officers (Clark-Flory, Gilat, and Cuen 2015). A 2002 study of sex workers in Chicago found that 20 to 24 percent of street-based sex workers and 30 percent of exotic dancers who had been sexually assaulted said that the perpetrator was a police officer (Raphael and Shapiro 2002). This study also found that 25 percent of escorts had been robbed by a police officer (Raphael and Shapiro 2002). A 2005 study of indoor sex workers in New York City found that 14 percent of them reported sexual violence at the hands of police officers, while 16 percent reported having been "involved in sexual situations" with police officers (Thakral, Ditmore, and Murphy 2005: 11). Sex workers in Alaska report that they have been "threatened into sexual favors by members of Alaska's law enforcement, or finding themselves in legal trouble after providing sexual favors to a man presumed to be a client, but who is actually a cop" (Hatch 2017).

Trans people who work in the sex trade—or who are assumed by police to be sex workers—indicate very high rates of harassment and abuse at the hands of police. The National Transgender Survey found that, among trans people who had interacted with officers who thought they were sex workers, nearly all—86 percent—reported some kind of mistreatment, whether verbal harassment, physical violence, or sexual assault (James et al. 2016: 158). When officers are undercover, though, such interactions will almost certainly go unrecorded.

Policy Implications: When Will Bodycams Help?

A gendered look at the limitations of bodycam policy highlights that many of the most harmful instances of gender bias may be lawful, consistent with departmental policy, or may in practice be institutionally tolerated. Bodycam recording is unlikely to impose accountability or improve behavior when the conduct shown on tape is effectively allowed. With respect to domestic violence, for example, one particularly egregious practice that has been repeatedly documented is police failure to respond to a report that an abuser has breached a restraining order that requires that they stay away from their ex-partner and children (Suk 2006). Where a police department does not vigorously enforce restraining orders, bodycams are unlikely to help. No video recording will occur unless the officer wearing a bodycam attends in response to the call.

Furthermore, where a department has a policy of refusing to enforce restraining orders, the beneficiary of the order (i.e., the victim) cannot sue the department or its officers for that failure, even if they or their child is injured or killed. Police departments are judicially immunized against lawsuits for failure to protect, removing one incentive that might otherwise motivate them to more vigorously protect women, children, and others against domestic violence.[7] Where enforcement is not required by law, and civil lawsuits are foreclosed, it is unclear how video recording might be expected to serve as an accountability mechanism except perhaps where departmental policy requires vigorous enforcement of restraining orders.

Furthermore, police officers enjoy considerable discretion as to how they go about investigating sexual assault or any other crime. An officer's determination of whether an allegation is credible and offers probable cause to make an arrest may fall squarely within the officer's investigative discretion. Even where probable cause exists, an officer does not have to make an arrest (unless a mandatory charging policy or other rule removes that discretion). If an officer believes that an allegation is false or that no serious crime has occurred, it is probably not misconduct for the officer to exercise his or her discretion not to charge anyone, even if the officer's judgment may have been shaped by unconscious gender bias. Similarly, if a mandatory charging policy requires an officer to press assault charges against a survivor who defended themself against an abuser, such an arrest does not reflect misconduct by the individual officer. Video of such interactions would not likely facilitate accountability, since the source of the problem is the institutional rule, not misconduct by an individual officer.

Similarly, in sexual assault investigations (like other criminal investigations), neither the tone nor the content of the questioning is ordinarily prescribed or prohibited by law or departmental policy. It is not unlawful to ask a complainant difficult questions, or to disbelieve him or her—even if those actions stem from sexist rape myths. Unless departmental policy explicitly requires police officers to disregard the fact that a complainant is a sex worker, the decision to unfound an allegation on that basis may also fall within the scope of each officer's discretion.

Even the most egregious of systematic gendered abuses in policing, such as sexual exploitation, may not necessarily contravene criminal law or departmental policy. About thirty-one states, as well as many police departments, lack any law or rule that explicitly forbids police officers to have sex with people in detention

---

7. See Castle Rock v. Gonzales, 545 U.S. 748 (2005); DeShaney v. Winnebago Cty. Dept. of Social Services, 489 U.S. 189 (1989).

or under investigation (Ducharme 2018; Ritchie 2017).[8] In such jurisdictions, an officer who has sex with a detainee, even one who is in handcuffs, can argue that the sex was consensual (see, e.g., Samaha 2018). It is unclear how video recording might help reduce or deter such abuse. Where officer-detainee sex is prohibited, it seems likely that an officer who has sex while on duty would turn off the body-cam. In jurisdictions where officer-detainee sex is not categorically banned, a video recording might be of little help: lack of overt resistance by a person who submits out of fear, or hopes for leniency, could be taken as evidence of consent.

Some police departments permit or even encourage officers to engage in sexual contact with a person under investigation, if the person is a sex worker (Walters 2011; Hatch 2017; Ritchie 2017). Most police departments lack any policy expressly forbidding such conduct (Ritchie 2017). A spokesperson for an Alaska police department recently defended the "right" of police officers to have sexual contact with sex workers they are investigating on the basis that such touching may help thwart sex worker tactics aimed at ascertaining whether a new potential client is a cop (Hatch 2017). A lawyer for the state, likewise, argued that officers must be allowed to have sexual contact with people suspected of sex work so that "prostitutes do not have a bright line test" by which they could ask a would-be client to prove he is not a cop by touching them.

Sexual touching and physical assault of sex workers are not consistent with best practices for the investigation of prostitution-related crimes (Walters 2011; USDOJ 2016), but departments are not legally required to adopt best practices that have been identified by policing or advocacy organizations. Most state courts that have considered the question found no constitutional prohibition on sexual touching of a person the officer is investigating for sex work.[9] Even if an officer who inter-acts with a sex worker is not undercover and is wearing a camera, officers enjoy wide (though not unlimited) discretion to use force on criminal suspects.[10] Where sexual touching by police officers is consistent with state law and departmental policy, it is unclear how a recording of permissible conduct would result in discipline or any other form of censure.

8. In recent months, several jurisdictions have introduced legislation recognizing that sex between a police officer and someone being interviewed, investigated, or detained is not consensual (see, e.g., Ducharme 2018; Lefler 2018; Sanchez 2018).

9. See, e.g., United States v. Cuervelo, 949 F.2d 559, 567 (2d Cir. 1991); United States v. Nolan-Cooper, 155 F.3d 221, 233 (3d Cir. 1998); Municipality of Anchorage v. Flanagan, 649 P.2d 957, 959 (Alaska Ct. App. 1982); and State v. Thoreson, No. A06-454, 2007 Minn. App. LEXIS 310 (Minn. Ct. App. Apr. 10, 2007).

10. See Graham v. Connor, 490 U.S. 386 (1989).

The most important limitation of the bodycam as accountability mechanism, then, is that it can be expected to influence behaviors only where a recording shows individual officers behaving in a way that is effectively prohibited by departmental policy or legal rules. It does not seem likely that this limitation would be confined to gendered crimes. As has been seen with high-profile videos of severe and lethal use of force by police in other contexts, the fact that misconduct is captured on camera does not mean that an officer will face disciplinary or criminal sanctions—even where, as in the cases of Tamir Rice, Terence Crutcher, and Philando Castile, the video shows use of force that appears to contravene criminal law and departmental policy and resulted in civilian death (see, e.g., Associated Press 2017; Moye 2017; Halpern 2015).

The hope that bodycams will improve safety and fairness rests on the premise that the behavior being recorded would violate criminal laws or departmental norms. To the extent that gendered and racial disparities arise from institutional rules rather than individual wrongdoing, bodycams are unlikely to help. Bodycams can alleviate racialized and gendered injustice only where they are accompanied by a systematic institutional commitment to just and ethical policing so that departmental expectations and legal rules are meaningfully enforced.

Directions for Bodycam Policy Reform

An intersectional, gendered perspective on bodycam policy and practice reveals systemic limitations on the promise of bodycams to bring transparency and accountability. Many of these limitations would require systematic institutional and criminal law reforms that might constrain abusive or unjust policing practices that are currently allowed. We hope that these insights might inspire further research and advocacy about how to create circumstances in which police accountability for gender and racial injustices could be realized. Meanwhile, in this section, we briefly consider directions for bodycam policy reform that might help to alleviate the gendered gaps and injustices we have identified.

As shown above, the solution to these difficulties cannot be the indiscriminate recording of every police-citizen interaction. Gender-nonconforming people, cisgender women, and sex workers, like all other people, have privacy and dignity interests that should preclude such practices. Moreover, it is not clear that video recording affects police-citizen interactions in the way that bodycam proponents hope it will (see Yokum, Ravishankar, and Coppock 2017; Cubitt et al. 2017; Lum et al. 2015; Ariel, Farrar, and Sutherland 2015; Miller, Toliver, and PERF 2014). To the extent that bodycams improve police behavior, the existing research has yet to identify the mechanism of such desirable effects, or the circumstances that yield them. But, most importantly, bodycams can advance accountability only when they are accompanied by an institutional commitment to racial and gender equity inscribed in policy and the disciplinary culture of the jurisdiction.

Bodycam policy, like any other policing policy, should account for the interests and perspectives of vulnerable persons at the intersection of gender, race, and criminal justice. As discussed above, the safety and dignity interests of sex workers and survivors of gendered violence cannot be assumed to align seamlessly with the evidentiary priorities of law enforcement. Rather, a well-designed bodycam policy (like any other well-designed policing policy) will reflect the needs and realities of law enforcement alongside the well-being of the communities they aim to protect. Bodycam policy, then, must be designed in consultation with advocacy groups for survivors and sex workers. Consultations between these groups and police would involve speaking and listening on both sides to identify common interests as well as points of divergence. Community surveys, conducted by social scientists on departments' behalf, could also be used to ascertain whether and how bodycams might be deployed to promote the safety, dignity, and equality interests of the most vulnerable members of the communities that officers protect.

Conclusion

By questioning the consensus that bodycams will mitigate racial disparity by promoting accountability, this essay demonstrates that intersectional thinking must be central, not peripheral, to policing reforms. Thoughtful attention to the dynamics of gender and sexual orientation alongside racial justice can illuminate the benefits and limitations of policing interventions that are designed to benefit everyone. Bodycams are likely to be turned off in contexts where women and trans people are especially vulnerable to discrimination and abuse, missing the unique harms that women and gender-nonconforming individuals may suffer at the hands of police. Our intersectional view of the promise and limitations of bodycams reveals limitations of the premise that videography will help hold police officers accountable. Instead, it seems that bodycams will promote accountability only where they are accompanied by an institutional commitment to fair and professional policing.

This essay offers an opportunity to reflect on our national theory of change in policing. By centering the experiences of non-White women, sex workers, and trans people, our analysis disrupts a theory of police accountability that assumes that existing policy reforms are already aligned with racial or gender justice. The limitations of bodycams exposed in this essay may identify crucial opportunities for police-community consultation as well as for broader institutional and criminal justice reforms. We must confront the effects of policing practices on our most vulnerable populations if police reform is to promote public safety for everyone.

References

Ariel, Barak, William Farrar, and Alex Sutherland. 2015. "The Effect of Police Body-Worn Cameras on Use of Force and Citizens' Complaints against the Police: A Randomized Controlled Trial." *Quant. Criminology* 31, no. 3: 509–35.

Associated Press. 2017. "Police Officer Who Shot Dead Philando Castile Acquitted of All Charges." *Guardian*, June 16.

Blades, Lincoln Anthony. 2017. "Police and Sexual Assault: When Officers Are Perpetrators." *Teen Vogue*, November 22.

Breiding, Matthew J., Sharon G. Smith, Kathleen C. Basile, Mikel L. Walters, Jieru Chen, and Meslissa T. Merrick. 2014. "Prevalence and Characteristics of Sexual Violence, Stalking, and Intimate Partner Violence Victimization—National Intimate Partner and Sexual Violence Survey, United States, 2011." *Mortality and Morbidity Weekly Report* 63 (SS08): 1–18.

Catalano, Shannon, Erica Smith, Howard Snyder, and Michael Rand. 2009. *Female Victims of Violence*. Washington, DC: US Department of Justice Office of Justice Programs, Bureau of Justice Statistics. www.bjs.gov/content /pub/pdf/fvv.pdf.

Chicago PD (Police Department). 2018. *Body-Worn Cameras*. Special Order S03-14. Chicago PD, April 30. directives.chicagopolice.org/directives/data /a7a57b38-151f3872-56415-1f38-89ce6c22d026d090.html.

Clark-Flory, Tracy, Matan Gilat, and Leigh Cuen. 2015. "Sex Workers More Worried about Cops than Dangerous Johns." *Vocativ*, October 23. www.vocativ .com/239316/national-blacklist-for-sex-workers/index.html.

Coker, Donna. 2001. "Crime Control and Feminist Law Reform in Domestic Violence Law: A Critical Review." *Buffalo Criminal Law Review* 4, no. 2: 801–60.

Crenshaw, Kimberlé. 1991. "Mapping the Margins: Intersectionality, Identity Politics, and Violence against Women of Color." *Stanford Law Review* 43, no. 6: 1241–99.

Crepeau, Megan, Christy Gutowski, Jason Meisner, and Stacy St. Clair. 2018. "A Historic Murder Conviction of a Chicago Cop—and a City's Sigh of Relief." *Chicago Tribune*, October 6.

Cubitt, T. I., R. Lesic, G. L. Myers, and R. Corry. 2017. "Body-Worn Video: A Systematic Review of Literature." *Australian and New Zealand Journal of Criminology* 50, no. 3: 379–96.

Deppen, Colin. 2017. "Domestic Disturbance Call Ends with Twenty-Three-Year-Old Fatally Shot by Police." *Penn Live*, January 10. www.pennlive.com /news/2017/01/domestic_disturbance_call_ends.html.

Ducharme, Jamie. 2018. "New Bill Would Prohibit Federal Law Enforcement Officials from Having Sex with People in Custody." *Time*, July 28.

Estrich, Susan. 1986. "Rape." *Yale Law Journal* 95: 1087–184.

Fan, Mary D. 2016. "Privacy, Public Disclosure, Police Body Cameras: Policy Splits." *Alabama Law Review* 68: 395.

FBI (Federal Bureau of Investigation). 2015. *Uniform Crime Reports, 2015.* "Table 35, Five-Year Arrest Trends by Sex, 2011–2015." ucr.fbi.gov/crime -in-the-u.s/2015/crime-in-the-u.s.-2015/tables/table-35.

Fitzgerald, Erin, Sarah Elspeth Patterson, and Darby Hickey. 2015. *Meaningful Work: Transgender Experiences in the Sex Trade.* National Center for Transgender Equality. www.transequality.org/sites/default/files/Meaningful%20 Work-Full%20Report_FINAL_3.pdf.

Goff, P. A., M. A. Thomas, and M. C. Jackson. 2008. "'Ain't I a Woman?': Towards an Intersectional Approach to Person Perception and Group-Based Harms." *Sex Roles* 59, nos. 5–6: 392–403.

Goodmark, Leigh. 2011. *A Troubled Marriage: Domestic Violence and the Legal System.* New York: NYU Press.

Halpern, Jake. 2015. "The Cop." *New Yorker*, August 10 and 17.

Harris, Angela P. 2000. "Gender, Violence, Race, and Criminal Justice." *Stanford Law Review* 52, no. 4: 777–807.

Hatch, Jenavieve. 2017. "Sex Workers in Alaska Say Cops Are Abusing Their Power to Solicit Sexual Acts." *Huffington Post*, August 17. www.huffington post.com/entry/sex-workers-in-alaska-say-cops-are-abusing-their-power-to -solicit-sex_us_596e1d26e4b010d77673e488.

Human Rights Campaign. 2018. *Violence against the Transgender Community in 2017.* www.hrc.org/resources/violence-against-the-transgender-community -in-2017.

Human Rights Campaign. 2019. *Violence against the Transgender Community in 2018.* https://www.hrc.org/resources/violence-against-the-transgender -community-in-2018.

IACP (International Association of Chiefs of Police. 2011. *Addressing Sexual Offenses and Misconduct by Law Enforcement: Executive Guide*: www.theiacp

.org/resources/document/addressing-sexual-offenses-and-misconduct-by-law
-enforcement-executive-guide.

IACP (International Association of Chiefs of Police. 2014. *Body-Worn Cameras: Model Policy.* www.theiacp.org/model-policy/wp-content/uploads/sites
/6/2017/07/BodyWornCamerasPolicy.pdf.

IACP (International Association of Chiefs of Police). 2018. *Sexual Assault Incident Reports: Investigative Strategies.* www.theiacp.org/portals/0/pdfs/Sexual
AssaultGuidelines.pdf.

James, S. E., J. L. Herman, S. Rankin, M. Keisling, L. Mottet, and M. Anafi.
2016). *The Report of the 2015 U.S. Transgender Survey.* Washington, DC:
National Center for Transgender Equality. www.transequality.org/sites/default
/files/docs/usts/USTS%20Full%20Report%20-%20FINAL%201.6.17.pdf.

Katz, Charles M. 2015. "Phoenix, Arizona Smart Policing Initiative: Evaluating
the Impact of Officer Body-Worn Cameras." www.utility.com/perch/resources
/phoenix-smart-policing-study-sept-2015.pdf.

Keenan, Jillian. 2014. "Sex Workers Don't Deserve to Be Raped." *Daily Beast*,
September, 274. www.thedailybeast.com/sex-workers-dont-deserve-to-be
-raped.

Langton, Lynn, and Marcus Berzofsky. 2012. *Victimizations Not Reported to the
Police, 2006–2010.* Washington, DC: United States Department of Justice
Department of Justice Programs, Bureau of Justice Statistics. www.bjs.gov
/content/pub/pdf/vnrp0610.pdf.

LAPD (Los Angeles Police Department). 2015. Special Order No. 12, s.VI. LAPD,
April 28. assets.lapdonline.org/assets/pdf/body%20worn%20camera.pdf.

Lefler, Dion. 2018. "New Law: Kansas Cops Can't Have Sex during Traffic
Stops." *Wichita Eagle*, May 10.

Lohr, David. 2017. "Transgender Woman Killed by Police Was 'Harassed and
Executed,' Relative Says." *Huffington Post*, August 24. www.huffingtonpost
.com/entry/transgender-woman-police-killing-stlouis_us_599df3f7e4b05710
aa599d34.

Lum, Cynthia, Christopher Koper, Linda Merola, Amber Scherer, and Amanda
Reioux. 2015. *Existing and Ongoing Body Worn Camera Research: Knowledge Gaps and Opportunities.* Fairfax, VA: George Mason University. cebcp.
org/wp-content/technology/BodyWornCameraResearch.pdf.

Miller, Lindsay, Jessica Toliver, and PERF (Police Executive Research Forum).
2014. *Implementing a Body-Worn Camera Program: Recommendations and
Lessons Learned.* Washington, DC: Office of Community Oriented Policing
Services.

Miller, S. L. 2001. "The Paradox of Women Arrested for Domestic Violence: Criminal Justice Professionals and Service Providers Respond." *Violence against Women* 7, no. 12, 1339–76.

Morin, Rich, and Renée Stepler. 2016. *The Racial Confidence Gap in Police Performance.* Pew Research Center, September 29. www.pewsocialtrends.org/2016/09/29/the-racial-confidence-gap-in-police-performance/.

Moye, David. 2017. "Police Officer Who Killed Terence Crutcher Has Manslaughter Charge Expunged from Record." *Huffington Post*, October 27.

Nash, Jennifer C. 2005. "From Lavender to Purple: Privacy, Black Women, and Feminist Legal Theory." *Cardozo Women's Law Journal* 11: 303–30.

Newell, Bryce Clayton, and Ruben Greidanus. 2018. "Officer Discretion and the Choice to Record: Officer Attitudes towards Body-Worn Camera Activation." *North Carolina Law Review* 96: 1525–78.

PERF (Police Executive Research Forum). 2012. *Improving the Police Response to Sexual Assault.* www.policeforum.org/assets/docs/Critical_Issues_Series/improving%20the%20police%20response%20to%20sexual%20assault%202012.pdf.

Planty, Michael, Lynn Langton, Christoher Krebs, Marcus Berzofsky, and Hope Smiley-McDonald. 2013. *Female Victims of Sexual Violence, 1994–2010.* Washington, DC: U.S. Department of Justice Office of Justice Programs, Bureau of Justice Statistics.

Pokorak, Jeffrey J. 2006. "Rape as a Badge of Slavery: The Legal History of, and Remedies for, Prosecutorial Race-of-Victim Charging Disparities." *Nevada Law Journal* 7, no. 1, art. 2.

Poteat, V. Paul, Michael Kimmel, and Riki Wilchins. 2011. "The Moderating Effects of Support for Violence Beliefs on Masculine Norms, Aggression, and Homophobic Behavior during Adolescence." *Journal of Research on Adolescence* 21, no. 2: 434–47.

Rajan, M., and K. A. McCloskey. 2007. "Victims of Intimate Partner Violence: Arrest Rates across Recent Studies." *Journal of Aggression, Maltreatment & Trauma*, 15, nos. 3–4: 27–52.

Ranapurwala, Shabbar I., Mark T. Berg, and Carri Casteel. 2016. "Reporting Crime Victimizations to Police and the Incidence of Future Victimizations: A Longitudinal Study." *PLoS One* 11, no. 7: e0160072.

Raphael, Jody, and Deborah L. Shapiro. 2002. *Sisters Speak Out: The Lives and Needs of Prostituted Women in Chicago: A Research Study.* http://www.healthtrust.net/sites/default/files/publications/sistersspeakout.pdf.

Reingle Gonzalez, Jennifer M., Stephen A. Bishopp, and Katelyn K. Jetelina. 2016. "Rethinking Police Training Policies: Large Class Sizes Increase Risk of Police Sexual Misconduct." *Journal of Public Health* 38, no. 3: 614–20.

Rieger, April. 2007. "Missing the Mark: Why the Trafficking Victims Protection Act Fails to Protect Sex Trafficking Victims in the United States." *Harvard Journal of Law and Gender* 30: 231–56.

Ritchie, Andrea J. 2017. "A Warrant to Search Your Vagina." *New York Times*, July 21.

Sack, Emily J. 2004. "Battered Women and the State: The Struggle for Future of Domestic Violence Policy." *Wisconsin Law Review.* 2004: 1657–1740.

Samaha, Albert. 2018. "An Eighteen-Year-Old Said She Was Raped while in Police Custody: The Officers Say She Consented." *Buzzfeed*, February 7. www .buzzfeednews.com/article/albertsamaha/this-teenager-accused-two-on-duty -cops-of-rape-she-had-no#.gfDeq4WJY.

Sanchez, Luis. 2018. "New York Lawmakers Pass Bill Banning Police from Having Sex with People in Custody." *Hill*, March 31.

Schneider, Elizabeth M. (2000). *Battered Women and Feminist Lawmaking.*

Sherman, Lawrence, Janell D. Schmidt, Dennis P. Rogan, and Douglas A. Smith. 1992. *The Variable Effects of Arrest on Criminal Careers: The Milwaukee Domestic Violence Experiment. J. Crim. L. & Criminology* 83, no. 1: 137–69.

Siegel, Reva B. 1996. "'The Rule of Love': Wife Beating as Prerogative and Privacy." *Yale Law Journal* 105: 2117–207.

Spohn, Cassia, Clair White, and Katharine Tellis. 2014. "Unfounding Sexual Assault: Examining the Decision to Unfound and Identifying False Reports." *Law and Society Review* 48, no. 1: 161–92.

Stanley, Jay. 2015. *Police Body-Mounted Cameras: With Right Policies in Place, a Win for All.* Version 2.0. American Civil Liberties Union, March. www.aclu .org/sites/default/files/assets/police_body-mounted_cameras-v2.pdf.

Suk, Jeannie. 2006. "Criminal Law Comes Home." *Yale Law Journal* 116, no. 1: 2–70.

Suk, Jeannie. 2009. *At Home in the Law: How the Domestic Violence Revolution Is Transforming Privacy.* New Haven, CT: Yale University Press.

Thakral, Juhu, Melissa Ditmore, and Alexandra Murphy. 2005. *Behind Closed Doors: An Analysis of Indoor Sex Work in New York City.* New York: Urban Justice Center Sex Workers Project. sexworkersproject.org/downloads/Behind ClosedDoors.pdf.

Truman, Jennifer L., and Rachel E. Morgan. 2015. *Criminal Victimization, 2015.*

Washington, DC: U.S. Department of Justice Office of Justice Programs, Bureau of Justice Statistics. www.bjs.gov/content/pub/pdf/cv15.pdf.

Tuerkheimer, Deborah. 2016. "Underenforcement as Unequal Protection." *Boston College Law Review* 57: 1287–1335.

United States Department of State. 2015. *Trafficking in Persons Report 2015.* www.state.gov/documents/organization/245365.pdf.

USDOJ (United States Department of Justice). 2016. *Identifying and Preventing Gender Bias in Law Enforcement Response to Sexual Assault and Domestic Violence.* Washington, DC: USDOJ. www.justice.gov/opa/file/799366/.

Walters, Philip. 2011. "'Would a Cop Do This?' Ending the Practice of Sexual Sampling in Prostitution Stings." *Law & Inequality* 29, no. 2: 451–76.

West, Carolyn M. 2007. "'Sorry, We Have to Take You In:' Black Battered Women Arrested for Intimate Partner Violence." *J. Aggression, Maltreatment & Trauma* 15, nos. 3–4: 95–121.

Yokum, David, Anita Ravishankar, and Alexander Coppock. 2017. "Evaluating the Effects of Police Body-Worn Cameras: A Randomized Controlled Trial." Working paper. Washington, DC: The Lab @ DC. bwc.thelab.dc.gov /TheLabDC_MPD_BWC_Working_Paper_10.20.17.pdf.

Kim Shayo Buchanan is Senior Legal Scholar at the Center for Policing Equity. Her scholarship analyzes the intersections of race, gender, and sexuality in criminal justice.

Phillip Atiba Goff is the president of the Center for Policing Equity and the inaugural Franklin A. Thomas Professor in Policing Equity at John Jay College of Criminal Justice at City University of New York. He is an expert in contemporary forms of racial bias and discrimination, as well as on the intersections of race and gender.

The Exceptional Prison

Samira Bueno and Graham Denyer Willis

We walk through an arched pergola draped with passion-fruit vines. "Everything happens for a reason," says Luis,[1] the military police officer walking with the two of us. In the distance, gunfire crackles in occasional bursts from a training ground behind a grove of citrus trees. "He killed eight people . . . all while off duty." Luis is speaking of someone who has turned his life around. He's been rehabilitated. "He isn't one of those people, you know, the corrupt kind . . . he was taking justice into his own hands, you know?" His eyes seek recognition. Pedro is a good person now, *right?*

Pedro, a convicted mass murder and also a military police officer, later shows us around the apiary. "I got lost in the emotion," he says. Pedro goes on to tell us, again, about how he ended up here twelve years ago. Sentenced to more than one hundred years in prison, he had gone on a killing spree. Off the job, and over the course of a year, he "cleaned" a poor neighborhood on the north side of a major city. Unable to control the thrill of killing, he mis-stepped, getting in trouble for such extreme violence.

"Try my honey," he says. "Everything in it is natural. The sugar for the hives comes from cane. The starter beeswax I order. The pollen . . . is pollen." The honey is really good, and Pedro is very personable. As he shows us a dead queen bee with its wing squeezed delicately between tweezers, and later stings himself

The authors extend gracious thanks to participants in the *Public Culture* workshop at Columbia University in October 2018 and to Niyousha Bastani, Maximilian Curtis, Shreyashi Dasgupta, Alejandro Lerch, Amy Jaffa, Josh Platzky Miller, Carly Rodgers, Andrés Sevilla-Gaitán, and Caroline de Souza for conversation and comments on key ideas. This work was made possible in part thanks to the Centre of Latin American Studies at the University of Cambridge, which hosted Samira Bueno as a Visiting Researcher. We also send our thanks to the prison administration for granting access to this space.

1. All names are pseudonyms. We have altered some details and made use of composites in ways that do not impact the analysis.

Public Culture 31:3   DOI 10.1215/08992363-7532775

Copyright 2019 by Duke University Press

twice with bees to explain that doing so, regularly, strengthens the immune system, one can't help but feel disarmed—especially in a prison environment like this, adjacent to a pond full of tilapia, a greenhouse with rows of lettuce, and groves of tangerine trees.

We're interrupted. Two kids run up, panting from running freely around the lush grounds. "Do you have honey?" they ask Pedro, between gasps. "In the jar and the basin, guys," he says, pointing to the shed. "And close the door behind you." Luis interjects, seeing the incredulity that must be displayed on at least one of our faces, "They are the boss's kids." We are in a Latin American prison. But it seems like nothing of the sort. This is a prison solely for "wayward" police officers, one of only a few in the world.

The starting point of this article is, What constitutes "wayward"? Prisons are widely understood to be exceptionally punitive and foreclosed spaces, the outcome of the deployment of the heavily punitive carceral condition in the contemporary historical moment. From this counterintuitive location we ask, What might an exceptional prison such as this tell us about who and what is contained, and who and what is not? Or, of what violence is wayward? This space defies what is well known about neoliberal penality, punitive containment, and mass incarceration. Moreover, it defies how prisons are meant to operate as a technique of social, political, and racial order across the Americas. Or does it? In fact, almost no one in this prison is here because they were found guilty for lethal violence on the job. We propose, as a result, that this case, this space, provides a novel and complementary window on the mundane; of how law, policing, and prison operate within the logic of political will. While the scholarship on prisons overwhelmingly examines the carceral spaces of the criminalized subjects of law—obviously, and for good reason—this rare case affords a very different opportunity: to scrutinize what a prison for people working for the maintenance of liberal capitalist power looks like, empirically.

We consider the narratives of sixteen in-depth interviews with police prisoners, all of whom are men sentenced for murder,[2] and describe a counterintuitive finding: only one was sentenced for on-the-job violence. In a state where police have killed 16,816 citizens since 1990[3], these police speak openly about violence

2. This article is substantiated and informed by our respective ethnographic research (Bueno 2018; Denyer Willis 2015, 2017). The interviews for this article were carried out largely by the first author, who was given access via a judicial decision, over a six-month period. The second author has carried out extensive multiyear ethnographic research on police violence, homicide, and disappearances in Brazilian cities. At the time of our research there was only one female prisoner.

3. According to the statistics of the state Public Security Secretary.

in policing. That violence isn't why they are here. These prisoners are wayward because they have committed other kinds of murder. While around half of the prison population has been sentenced or charged with murder, only around 10 percent of those being held for murder in this prison are here because they have been found guilty for doing so on the job. Almost every prisoner is here because, like Pedro, they deviated from "acceptable" killing. And they know why. They talk about it: They killed off the job. They killed too many. They killed intimate partners or family members. They took money to "clean up the streets." Ending up in this prison, in other words, is refracted through other "deviations."

We ask how police that have been punished make sense of the logics and value systems of everyday policing. These conversations shed light on how they came to transgress the rules and norms that matter in practice. This helps show why they, and not others, are in this prison. Prisoners discuss how it matters that violent killings are a constitutive part of policing, being "normal cases" (Sudnow 1965) that happen, on average 2.34 times per day. Or, as one former officer puts it, of what it looks like when "death is like a family custom."

Our argument, then, is twofold: first, that the punishment of lethal police violence is not apparent in this prison, the only place where institutional punishment of lethal police violence could materially exist; and second, that the reasons that police who are here reveal what kinds of violence is acceptable by virtue of how it sits structurally outside the symbolic and material space of institutional punishment. Seen from the egregious racial and violence inequality of Brazil, policing and its management are not particularly concerned with limiting police violence. The implication is this: to speak of impunity for lethal police violence on the job is to dramatically misunderstand the work of policing.

Three parts follow: (1) "The Exceptional Prison" describes how this case is exceptional and why it matters for rigorous reflection; (2) "What Abides" considers wayward violence through what exists within the walls of this prison; (3) "Beyond Containment" shows how it matters that some kinds of violence are contained here, but on the job police violence is not.

The Exceptional Prison

Few prisons anywhere are like this one. In almost every way, the global prison literature couldn't illustrate a more dramatically different space, logic, and moral economy of commonplace prison conditions under neoliberal governance (e.g., Gilmore 1999; Pettit and Western 2004; Simon 2007; Comfort 2009; Rios 2011; McKittrick 2011; for a counterpoint see Johnsen, Granheim, and Helgesen 2011).

This is even more so in Latin America. As J. Amparo Alves (2018: 149) writes of a pretrial jail in São Paulo, "A small curtain made up of old clothes covered what was supposed to be a bathroom: just a hole in the wall through which a trickle of cold water ran constantly, with a dirty broken toilet bowl and a small water tap. The temperature in the cell was around forty degrees Celsius and there was an unbearably strong, nauseating smell in the air."

A growing body of work on Latin American prisons laments the bleak—sexual violence, massacres, and fires that consume hundreds of lives. Prisons are sites of acute degradation, overcrowding, and extensive violence, strongly evoking a presence of political will through the absence of attention (Salvatore and Aguirre 2010; Garces 2010; Lemgruber and Paiva 2010; Drybread 2009, 2014, 2016; Alves 2016; Godoi 2016; O'Neill and Fontes 2016; Weegels 2016). A remarkable and similarly contrasting pattern has emerged across the region. Many prisons are regularly "self-governed" as a result. Behind the walls built evermore by states, prison groups of different varieties manage everything from distribution of food, rooms, and beds; security; and cleaning (Godoi 2010; Macaulay 2013; Darke and Garces 2017; King and Valensia 2014). Under the mitigated authority of a handful of guards who rarely enter, rich and complex political economies drive patterns of survival and meaning (Biondi 2017; for the United States, see Skarbek 2011; for elsewhere, Symkovych 2017). As Jon Carter (2014: 475–76) argues, such spaces become "gothic," structured by a kind of absent power that is nonetheless "haunted by crypts of its own lawlessness."[4]

None of these problems and practices is present in the police prison. There are no "gangs," and there is no substantive sexual or other violence. The prisoners don't carry out their own tribunals and in-house executions. There is no concern for high walls and fortifications. Guards walk the grounds, strolling with prisoners. Administrators walk unaccompanied. And on the weekends or on special occasions, so do their children. This prison is widely celebrated as a model. Unlike any other prison in Latin America, its managers commemorate and invest in its distinction. The International Standards Association, a global reference for quality management, has certified this prison. This is for maintaining key principles like "customer focus," "leadership," "evidence-based decision making," and "relationship management," for a "quality that is consistently improved."

4. This has allowed for all sorts of peculiar and transcendental practices to emerge or become fortified, including urban extortion (Fontes 2016), a transnational and heavily gendered drug trade (Gay 2012; Giacomello 2014), global tourism (Whitfield 2016), and practices of social order that have led to widespread homicide declines in cities (Dias 2010; Denyer Willis 2015; Lessing and Denyer Willis 2019).

It is hard to imagine a more distinctive and stiff departure from the global carceral condition. What, then, can such an incongruent case tell us that might actually matter? Our conceptual departure point is that some kinds of "exceptional cases" have important analytic and "disruptive" normative and scholarly potential. This can be because they evoke something about systemic political and legal practice (Schmitt 1985; Benjamin 1996; Das 2004), because their "spectacularity" helps isolate new categories (Larkins 2015), or because they allow for heuristic interpolation of well-entrenched patterns and assumptions (Ermakoff 2014). Exceptional cases are important, too, because they stand at odds with some general model of causal relations (Seawright and Gerring 2008). And while identifying what constitutes an exceptional case can be treacherous, their significance is established in their conspicuous contrast with existing theories and affirmations.

Why this prison exists is a puzzle of its own. One reason might be that the scarcity of police prisons obscures them from view, both mitigating an interest in them and constraining access to researchers. Only in a country like Brazil are police so violent and "extralegal" as to require a prison of their own. A second possibility is that there is really no good reason for such a unique prison to exist; wayward police would typically be placed in a prison for the general population, perhaps in a particular wing. In other words, there may be peculiar institutional and historical reasons such a prison should exist at all. A third explanation might be that such as an instance isn't really exceptional at all, being, instead, the product of different "cultures" or moments of punishment in which Brazil sees punishment of police as a kind of cultural imperative, or a product of a distinctive political or government crackdown on police violence.

We surmise that it is odd that this prison, as an identifiable space, exists at all. It is exceptional for institutional reasons. In Brazil, everyday "beat cops," who are the most numerous, most public, and most central, interface with citizens on the street and operate under a separate system of justice administered through a military hierarchy. Any street-level police officer is a military police officer and a reservist in the national military. They are not subject to ordinary legal procedures but instead to military jurisprudence. Other, smaller, and more institutionally distinct police institutions, civil ones, do indeed send their wayward police through "normal" penal channels. When convicted, these civilian police end up in the regular prison system, albeit, usually in a small wing specifically maintained for police, the university educated, and politicians.

The distinctive condition of the exceptional prison can operate as an abnormal but complementary window on what prisons routinely imply in their slimmest function, to contain violence and violent individuals. The difference between the exceptional and the mundane prison perhaps lies most acutely in a consideration of law in practice. Prisons are for populations that are the subject of law. The exceptional prison is for something contrasting: for those who deploy the law, working on behalf of it, toward the reproduction of the former. And so the question becomes, amid the arbitrariness of law (Comaroff and Comaroff 2004), when does law actually govern the people who work on behalf of power?

This spatial confluence contains analytical possibility as a peculiar empirical location where the unvarnished outcomes and logics of law and institutional justice have been filtered and made material. Most acutely, we think, is how this prison offers a spatial condition revelatory of what kinds of violence are actually subject to state punishment. Who is actually punished, and why, is spatially sorted here. This sorting strips the foils of power that cloud critical inference of the structural logics of policing.

What Abides

The handheld video that had flashed across the evening news was deeply incriminating. After a police chase, a police officer corners a suspected thief above a precipice. The suspect lies flat on his stomach and raises his hands above his head, a gun pointed at his head. He's placed in handcuffs. But as the police officer raises the man to his feet and moves toward the edge, he shoves the man over. He falls to an unseen ground, leaving the camera frame in the process. Seconds later, two gunshots echo. The man is declared dead at the hospital with gunshot wounds.

Six police officers from this case subsequently arrived at the prison. They were arrested, given red badges as recent arrivals, and placed in a particular wing for pretrial detainees. For around eighteen months the six made this prison their home. Some time later, all six were declared to have acted in self-defense. They walked free, returning to their job.

Carlos was a long-serving police officer. He and the others are interested in this previous case and the ways that the police were publicly chastised. Carlos was involved in one of the largest prison massacres in the history of the country. Shortly after he entered a prison alongside his colleagues to quell a riot, more than one hundred inmates lay dead. Carlos likes to talk about what the public knows of policing. There is an important distinction to be made between what is presented to the public, he says, and what occurs on an everyday basis. To be a police officer is to know and act in a different reality: "When a guy enters the police force, he comes to live in a fictional world emulating a stage of war. The people around him induce him to think that he is in a war and that this war is legitimate. This is not 'the police' but some of the important people who represent the institution."

Carlos's analysis distinguishes between "the police" as a formal entity and the shared sensibility that exists, as a set of assumptions and practices, within it. While police trumpet and publicly perform respect for human rights, the everyday understanding of police work, behind the stage, is much different; it is a "stage of war," of violence. For Carlos the idea of being a soldier in the war is a feeling present throughout life as a police person. Far from diminishing this desire, police work condenses and legitimates this logic. For Carlos, until the early 1990s, "the death of bandits was a practice institutionalized by the police, with the understanding of all." If an incident "really happened" in the course of a criminal act, or if it was contrived—*forjado*—after the fact, it didn't really matter. No one would have understood it any differently; "what mattered," he says, "was the end result." Carlos believes things are no longer this way.

But Carlos didn't end up in prison for any of this kind of violence, for his association with this massacre, or for on-the-job violence that he speaks of openly. Carlos is in prison for something much different, despite his nostalgia for a kind of police work that he believed existed, that could openly exalt lethality. He has been convicted, twice, of murdering transgendered sex workers off the job, targeting them as a category threatening his heteronormativity.

If there is a divergence between how Carlos talks about the violence that courses through policing and what makes him a resident of this prison, he is not alone. Prisoners routinely speak of what they idealize about policing. And as in Carlos's case, the values of policing emerge in stark relief to the actual historical and legal condition of their containment.

Luis claims that the police have always supported the use of lethal force, as long as it was done in a "slow way." A former beat cop, he speaks of having "snapped" following a personal experience with crime: the sound of his car being stolen outside his house. After this episode, he recalled, he decided that he was OK with this prison being his future home. As he put it, he "started to go crazy off duty . . . and suddenly had eighteen police reports on my back." This new killing spree was off duty but targeted the same kinds of people that he'd already been killing on the job. He recalls blithely that after finishing his shifts he used to pick up his car and go out "hunting" in the neighborhood where he lived, picking up clues and tips from local merchants. He sums it up in his own terms: "I only killed delinquents."

Until nearly the year 2000, police officers commonly and publicly received medals after what are known as "resisting arrest followed by death" cases. These "death medals" operated as an archetypal and public benchmark for the success of an officer's career. The linear and public relationship between death and commendation has been pushed underground.[5] But the symbolism of such medals and commendation now has a front stage and a back stage; what they mean to a police officer is different than how they are presented to the public. Crucially, receiving a medal was an affirmation of leadership and bravery. Even today it allows a police person to claim an esteemed social category—"the Billy,"—a brave, effective, and deadly efficient police officer (Bueno, 2018). Today medals are divided into five grades. The first three are given by a local commander, and the next is given by a regional commander. The highest degree is bestowed by the commander general of the military police. It is very difficult for a police officer to receive all five commendations.

José, the eldest of the police officers interviewed, boasted that he had received the five medals, describing in detail the "white medal"—a first-degree honor given to him after a killing. For José, medals were official commemorations of valued everyday police practices. The most common of these was to mark the butt of the service weapon with white paint for each killing—an informal commemoration. "The more stripes, the more Billy," said José, who could not disguise his pride of having a "zebra gun." José speaks openly of killing sixteen people throughout his career as a police officer. He was, though, convicted of the murder of his ex-wife and of three attempted homicides, one of which was against a girlfriend.

Younger police officers complained that today no medals or public commendations are awarded after killings, nor do they get away with dressing up an execution. "There is no honor in death," said Paulo, evoking the disappearance of public exaltation. He was frustrated that he'd not won a medal when he broke up a bank robbery and killed two criminals. Before ending up in prison for what he called "high-risk incidents," Paulo was a police officer in a regional tactical unit akin to a low-level SWAT squad.

Paulo served for eight years in one of these specialized units before being arrested for killing a man in a shopping mall, whose death he says was paid for by a foreign mafia. As Paulo tells it, "I had already snapped at that point." Being violent on the job wasn't enough. He'd been killing for years "without any financial benefit, just out of job satisfaction." He decided to make a living, taking money from others to go on doing what he'd been doing on the job anyway. Paulo sees his own baptism and "Billy status" clearly: "The tactical unit man is baptized and no longer an ordinary man. He feels different, he's different, he's not a regular cop or

5. The practice of public commemoration has started to reemerge under President Jair Bolsonaro, who took power in 2019.

an ordinary human being." For Paulo there is a key distinction in being *the* police and being *of* a particular unit—placed systemically above all others.

This concern with hierarchies in policing closely follows the ways that police talk about their fondness for on-the-job violence and the sought-after social categories that operate within it. Where elite units are professionally sought after, more well-resourced and enabled to carry out violence with impunity, incentive structures and desirability follow. Policing is a collective enterprise, with police advancing, every day, a set of assumptions about how to protect "good" populations from those who would do them harm. *Tirocínio* is understood as the heightened cognitive ability to differentiate between these two, to be followed with violence to reassert the difference.

The same logic appears in José's words when he speaks of the killings he carried out: "For us police officers you feel satisfaction, you feel more satisfaction than when you arrest. For some cops killing becomes an addiction, when you cannot kill you feel like your service has not been done properly. You feel that you can solve the problems of society, and you want at any cost to do it." But transgressing these limits creates practical political problems for others, who are otherwise on side. Being a Billy with *tirocínio* means being a sentient, controlled killer who understands the boundaries between acceptable and unacceptable violence—between how violence is now carried out and celebrated quietly, mundanely accepted, as long as it does not transgress mutually observed norms and larger social assumptions.

Such violence has a distinctive and clear history in Brazil, with some individuals gaining public and unabashed fame in the national press for "cleaning the streets" (Manso 2016). While this violence was more transparent in a different historical moment, for which these police have nostalgia, they describe how this violence remains but in transformed ways. What matters now is that it needs to be maintained in more secretive ways. It wears a shroud. Luis's explanation mixes personal satisfaction with professional recognition. According to him, the reason he ended up in prison is that he took it too far. As he put it, "That [killing] was ostentatiousness, I was feeling like superman, being recognized on the side of good . . . everyone knew, my superiors knew, my colleagues knew. . . . Although I did harm to many, I did very well for others."

"In my view I was doing the right thing," a prisoner named Joseph recalled. Joseph was convicted for killing sixteen people off the job. "By eliminating the enemy and protecting good people; society wants you to do this, but it crucifies you when you do." Indeed, the process of being remanded, publicly shredded, and held in this prison feels like punishment for police like Joseph. They have a sense of being thrown under the bus.

Victor sighs before discussing a cornerstone of his past, and of fitting in. He describes having killed at least thirty people as a police officer. "What the police taught me," he says, "is that I was different. I am a born follower. I've always wanted this, to do it perfectly. There is no way to take the blame and be caught out, you just have to assume who you are and do it exactly like everyone else." Victor was eventually caught after veering into different territory. He killed a man, in the midst of a fight, that he alleges had murdered a friend of his.

Not all the police that are here see the wrongs of their violence directly or indirectly in opposition to the violence they carried out on the job. Around five years ago, Jorge was a police officer working the day shift in the prison. It was a Sunday, and he had worked all day tending to prisoners and other duties. He left the prison and went home. Arriving there, his wife confronted him. She wanted a separation. She had cheated on him previously, and he had forgiven her. But this time, she seemed to be laughing in his face. He felt hurt, his honor deflated, a "lesser man." He wouldn't accept a separation. Jorge shot and killed her. She should have known the risk this time, he said. Jorge spent the rest of that night in the same prison that he had guarded that workday. Jorge has been in this same prison ever since and has twenty years left to serve.

Jorge's case is symptomatic in other regards. First, the egregious murder of his wife is what police describe as a "crime of passion"—a gendered sociolegal category of violence that typically involves men murdering women. And while the category itself contains a mechanism for normatively diminishing or justifying the act—passion—new laws for batterers and discussion of femicide have raised public scrutiny. According to administrators, 18 percent of the population is held for "crimes of passion."[6] Jorge's act, which he proudly and unrepentantly owns as the result of an affront to his masculinity, is the subject of new public concerns.

Second, like every other police officer we've introduced, Jorge is now posttrial. He is a convicted murderer serving out his sentence, following the letter of the law, as laid down by a judge. He spends his days in the general population. Much of his time is spent circulating around the prison and its lush green grounds. Not all prisoners live together, however. This is defining in other ways: convicted rapists are held in their cells, though administrators deny this is a formal practice. Convicted thieves and those found guilty of corruption are not seen outside their

---

6. In 2015 this type of crime became codified as femicide (*feminicidio*) in the Brazilian penal code, recognizing gender relations as an aggravating factor in many homicides.

quarters either. Those that killed off duty walk the grounds. And those that killed on duty are, simply, not here for that reason.

Beyond Containment

You're ridding the community of bad little fruit. And if you spare the wolf today, you condemn the sheep to die tomorrow.
—Victor

Marcos swears he didn't do it. Not this time, he says. He was found guilty for participating in a twilight mass murder—*chacina*—of seven men. Two months earlier he'd been caught on camera with others by a resident who filmed him and other police extorting and harassing neighborhood residents. The mass killing was pinned on him, Marcos believes, because of the public nature of the video and the widely assumed logic of the crime—police seeking to eliminate witnesses that might testify. Marcos swears on being a just and honest person who has become the subject of a politicized injustice as a result. "This world is hypocritical, capitalist, no one cares about their neighbor. If I had just looked the other way I'd have been fine."

He was too good, he believes. "The guy that worked with me didn't know the limits, I did. I was always methodical and empirical, but what is the method of the institution? Beatings, bludgeoning, and bombs. Study doesn't matter. The police wants you to be a hunting dog, but they sell another story [to the public]." Marcos, who speaks of having killed on the job, leaves the paradox of injustice hanging: "Before they arrested me I was in a really good group, and it is even because of this that I was arrested, we were so great. Even me, an old guy, I felt young again."

The exceptional prison can tell us crucial things about policing and the use of violence. Three are preeminent. First, even in a city where at least 25 percent of all formally registered violent deaths are committed by on-duty military police, virtually none of it is punished. In this place, one in four violent deaths is the result of police action. This won't come as much surprise to those who study Brazil. After all, between 2013 and 2016, in one city alone, police killed nearly thirty-five hundred people—66.5 percent of whom were black.[7] Much work attests to the feeble or nonexistent judicial responses to police violence in Brazil that result in few police being arrested, brought to trial, or found guilty (Caldeira 2002; Zaccone 2015; Misse et al. 2013). Policing is, after all, about order maintenance (Ericson 1982; Fassin 2013; Steinberg 2014).

7. This despite the black population being, officially, only 37 percent of the population

Particularly striking, given the racial inequality of Brazil and the patterns evident in the statistics of police violence, is that race appears only as a pseudonym. In the version of liberal capitalism practiced in this country, a country that solicited and received the most chattel slaves from the transatlantic trade, order maintenance and threat are centrally about race. But under democracy, such an enemy is rarely explicitly defined as the young black or ethnic man—although this is a category well shaped in assumption and police practice. Our interviewees almost never used racial terminologies to locate their violence. Instead, they used myriad color-blind synonyms: *wolf, bad people, thugs (bandidos), prey, delinquents, fringe elements*, or *bad fruit*. These constructs, under symbol and pseudonym, produce and rely on wider assumptions of an "evil" and threatening figure that must be combatted at all costs and with all available means (Misse 2010). In Brazil, as elsewhere (Yahmatta Taylor 2016), color-blind and "racial democracy" narratives have been fastened together in the years since the end of the Cold War. Implied in these whitening euphemisms is what Alves (2018) calls the blackpolis—the city built on policing black life.

In the deeply racialized topography of the postcolonial Brazilian city, the real or implied black body is a particular target (Vargas and Alves 2010). Rich ethnographic work details how this violence is felt by its subject population, experienced affectively and through resurgent and recurrent trauma for black Brazilians (Smith 2013, 2015; Alves 2014). Several studies of police violence in Brazil demonstrate how racial bias and selectivity in police actions that result in heavily racialized police deaths (Cano 2014; Sinhoretto et al. 2014). A recent study by Michel Misse et al. (2013) found that public prosecutors archived 99.2 percent of all cases of lethal police violence in one city over a ten-year period. Under these conditions, historically heavy-handed approaches to address "fear of crime" haven't led to only stop and frisk, "three strikes," or the privatization of the prison system. In substantive addition, control takes place through mundane categories of police work, known variously around the country as "resisting arrest followed by death," "death resulting from police intervention," or "resistance cases" (Cano and Massini 1997). Such a condition is in keeping with how P. S. Pinheiro (1997) sees police action, as an expression of a system of domination under which law is precarious, enabling a kind of "socially implanted authoritarianism" (47).

Second, there are mechanisms for obscuring how unhindered this violence actually is. In an era of democratic accountability, rights, and the rhetoric of justice reform, the political sphere must defend itself. "Participatory security," citizen engagement, and public oversight are some of the ways. This prison is a foil, casting a façade of police accountability through a peculiar performance and pageantry of punishment. Many police arrive in this prison, but few become long-term residents. They are held for the duration of their trial and judgment before being released. Only one prisoner that we spoke with, a man named Francisco, was in this prison after being found guilty for killing a young black man on the job in a city *favela*. (Francisco also describes police officers as specially trained "hunting dogs" that need to go through a "beefing up process.") Under these conditions, this prison operates as a kind of temporary insulation from public scrutiny, evoked in new reports after spectacular and egregious events, effectively deflecting criticism under the hopefulness of justice in process. Politicians can claim that accountability and oversight is coming. It is about iterative gains, a long arc of justice and citizenship. But, inevitably, public outrage blows over, consumed by the next case, unable to sustain its attention to individual cases in the flood of others. Years on, news quietly leaks out that police have been *inocentado* for their killing, and by now, they are flying well below the public-outrage radar.

Third, this institutional aberration reveals the dissonance between law on the books and law in practice. These walls serve a logic of containment different from what is widely surmised of prisons. To speak of police violence as "unjust" doesn't make sense if law is the reference point; it flows through the law. Each of the police officers interviewed participated in many "resistance killings," but they were never held responsible for them. Rather, they were arrested for crossing the fungible but observable line between what is constructed as permissible and not. What emerges from the evidence is that police who fail to kill in the appropriate manner, to kill the right people, to kill with the approved justifications and with appropriate self-control are subject to punishment. Don't be wayward. You can't kill your wife and not repent. Don't take money to kill. Don't kill too many people too quickly. Don't kill again after you've been punished. A contrast emerges: learn to kill on the job.

The exceptional prison shows how violence carried out by police is not about individuals or deviation from occupational roles. At least not in the ways we expected. Violence (or, if you will, "force") is an inalienable part of policing. Of that there is broad agreement. The debate about the adequate, controlled, slowly escalated or measured use of force is not trivial. It consumes large parts of criminology as a field of inquiry, with the distinctions and variations between "the use of legitimate and necessary force" and "police violence" the subject of worldwide studies (Skolnick and Fyfe 1993; Chevigny 1995; Klockars 1996; Bittner 2003). Not only so, it drives foundational scholarly and policy considerations about civilian control, accountability, and public service. For many, the meaningful boundary between the use of "legitimate force" (which can result in death) and the "abuse of force" varies substantially according to the regime of government, cultural, and social context, and the relevant legislation of different countries and jurisdictions. In Brazil, police are legally justified to use lethal violence, but only in cases of extreme necessity and in the strict fulfillment of duty or in self-defense. Police officers in this prison never used the verb *matar*—to kill—with us, even in the face of visceral descriptions. Such violence is understood as legitimate. Why call it "killing"? There is, it seems, virtually no such thing as abusive force on the job, that is, in terms of who is actually punished.

This makes sense relative to previous research. Police violence has become so institutionally normal that those responsible for investigating police violence turn, pedagogically, toward making it less emotionally problematic for those involved. In 2015, during previous work, one of the authors observed homicide detectives—who are responsible for investigating lethal police violence—instructing police, after a case, to "be calm" and "aim for the center of the body . . . next time" (Denyer Willis 2015: 84).

The exceptional prison and the problem of police violence is not just about Brazil. The debate about measured use of force requires holistic interrogations of its basic assumptions. The world over (see also Jauregui 2015), there is little evidence that police are actually held to account for lethal violence. In the United States, the visibility of such violence has come with recent technological advances, and the use of body cameras was widely hoped to limit police use of force (there is substantive evidence to the contrary; see Ariel et. al 2016). To reiterate: the debate about the adequate, controlled, slowly escalated or measured use of force is not trivial; it is misguided.

This all raises key questions about the relationship between political will, violence, and policing. One school of thought, political liberalism, holds that contestation, mobilization, and the evocation of rights through citizenship allows for vital iterative gains. Democracy, via the state, allows for progress toward emancipation. Slow gains reshape injustice, beat back structural violence, and allow—demand—substantive institutional reforms. Iterative gains move toward a horizon of justice, on an unknown time line but with an ultimate (but undefined) promise. This body of thought has a long and prominent history in scholarship on Brazil and Latin America—often brought by scholars from a Northern elsewhere. But if this school and its political practice are correct, their successes are not evident in the exceptional prison and police violence. Indeed, if police continue to kill with abandon, not much has changed since Brazil's redemocratization in 1985—or, indeed, over the last several hundred years (Holloway 1993). This political prescription has perhaps made it necessary for violence to be less public, requiring the political sphere to develop techniques of obscurity and opacity. The ramification of making police violence less visible (to some) is the possibility of misguided hope. The horizon of justice is a mirage.

Another body of thought makes much more sense. "Instead of considering reason as the truth of the subject," writes Achille Mbembe (2003: 14), "we can look to other foundational categories that are less abstract and more tactile, such as life and death." Both Mbembe and Carlos speak of police work as "a stage of war" and as "war by other means." This prison and the life and death that it contains (and doesn't contain) says invaluable things about politics in this regard. In having a prison like this, the politics of life and death, of sovereignty, of politics as ongoing war, shows its hand. This allows a glimpse at who can kill, under what conditions and how, on behalf of power—the emperor without his clothes. The implication, in the meantime, we leave to a prisoner named Pingo. "There is no way to fight what is done by police on the street," he says, gesturing to himself as though on the street. "I will teach you the good, the bad, and what is possible, and you'll need to walk among it."

References

Alves, Jaime Amparo. 2014. "Neither Humans nor Rights: Some Notes on the Double Negation of Black Life in Brazil." *Journal of Black Studies* 45, no. 2: 143–62.

Alves, Jaime Amparo. 2016. "'Blood in Reasoning': State Violence, Contested Territories, and Black Criminal Agency in Urban Brazil." *Journal of Latin American Studies* 48, no. 1: 61–87.

Alves, Jaime Amparo. 2018. *The Anti-Black City: Police Terror and Black Urban Life in Brazil*. Minneapolis: University of Minnesota Press.

Ariel, B., A. Sutherland, D. Henstock, J. Young, P. Drover, J. Sykes, S. Megicks, and R. Henderson. 2016. "Wearing Body Cameras Increases Assaults Against Officers and Does Not Reduce Police Use of Force: Results from a Global Multi-Site Experiment." *European Journal of Criminology* 13, no. 6: 744–55.

Benjamin, W. 1996. "Critique of Violence." In *Selected Writings, Vol. 1*, edited by M. Bullock and M. W. Jennings, 236–54.

Biondi, K. 2017. *Sharing This Walk: An Ethnography of Prison Life and the PCC in Brazil*. Chapel Hill: University of North Carolina Press.

Bittner, E. 2003. Aspectos do trabalho policial. Tradução: Ana Luísa Amêndola Pinheiro. São Paulo: Edusp.

Bueno, S. 2018. Trabalho sujo ou missão de vida? Persistência, reprodução e legitimidade da letalidade na ação da PMESP. Tese de doutorado em Administração Pública, São Paulo, FGV.

Caldeira, T. P. 2002. "The Paradox of Police Violence in Democratic Brazil." *Ethnography* 3, no. 3: 235–63.

Cano, I., and N. Massini. 1997. *Letalidade da ação policial no Rio de Janeiro.* Rio de Janeiro: Iser.

Cano, I. 2014. Viés racial no uso da força letal pela polícia no Brasil. MPMG Jurídico 1: 17–25.

Carter, J. 2014. "Gothic Sovereignty: Gangs and Criminal Community in a Honduran Prison." *South Atlantic Quarterly* 113, no. 3: 475–502.

Chevigny, P. 1995. *Edge of the Knife: Police Violence in the Americas.* New York: New Press.

Comfort, M. 2009. *Doing Time Together: Love and Family in the Shadow of the Prison.* Chicago: University of Chicago Press.

Comaroff, Jean, and John Comaroff. 2004. "Criminal Obsessions, after Foucault: Postcoloniality, Policing, and the Metaphysics of Disorder." *Critical Inquiry* 30, no. 4: 800–24.

Darke, S., and C. Garces. 2017. "Informal Dynamics of Survival in Latin American Prisons." Special issue, *Prison Service Journal* 229.

Das, V. 2004. "The Signature of the State: The Paradox of Illegibility." In *Anthropology in the Margins of the State*, edited by V. Das and Deborah Poole, 225–52. Sante Fe, NM: School of American Research Press.

Denyer Willis, Graham. 2015. *The Killing Consensus: Police, Organized Crime, and the Regulation of Life and Death in Urban Brazil.* Oakland: University of California Press.

Drybread, K. 2009. "Sleeping with One Eye Open." In *Violence: Ethnographic Encounters*, edited by Parvis Gassem-Fachandi, 79–96. New York: Berg.

Drybread, K. 2014. "Murder and the Making of Man-Subjects in a Brazilian Juvenile Prison." *American Anthropologist* 116, no. 4: 752–64.

Drybread, K. 2016. "Documents of Indiscipline and Indifference: The Violence of Bureaucracy in a Brazilian Juvenile Prison." *American Ethnologist* 43, no. 3: 411–23.

Ericson, R. V. 1982. *Reproducing Order: A Study of Police Patrol Work.* Toronto: University of Toronto Press.

Ermakoff, I. 2014. "Exceptional cases: Epistemic Contributions and Normative Expectations." *European Journal of Sociology/Archives Européennes de Sociologie* 55, no. 2: 223–43.

Fassin, D. 2013. *Enforcing Order: An Ethnography of Urban Policing.* Cambridge: Polity.

Fontes, A. W. 2016. "Extorted Life: Protection Rackets in Guatemala City." *Public Culture* 28, no. 3: 593–616.

Garces, C. 2010. "The Cross Politics of Ecuador's Penal State." *Cultural Anthropology* 25, no. 3: 459–96.

Gay, R. 2012. *Lucia: Testimonies of a Brazilian Drug Dealer's Woman*. Philadelphia: Temple University Press.

Giacomello, C. 2014. "How the Drug Trade Criminalizes Women Disproportionately." *NACLA Report on the Americas* 47, no. 2: 38–41.

Gilmore, R. W. 1999. "Globalisation and US Prison Growth: From Military Keynesianism to Post-Keynesian Militarism." *Race & Class* 40, nos. 2–3: 171–88.

Godoi, R. 2010. *Ao redor e através da prisão: Cartografias do dispositivo carcerário contemporâneo*. Doctoral diss., Universidade de São Paulo.

Godoi, R. 2016. "Intimacy and Power: Body Searches and Intimate Visits in the Prison System of São Paulo, Brazil." *Champ pénal/Penal field* 13. https://journals.openedition.org/champpenal/9386.

Holloway, T. 1993. *Policing Rio de Janeiro: Repression and Resistance in a Nineteenth-Century City*. Stanford, CA: Stanford University Press.

Jauregui, B. 2015. "Just War: The Metaphysics of Police Vigilantism in India." *Conflict and Society* 1, no. 1: 41–59.

Johnsen, B., P. K. Granheim, and J. Helgesen. 2011. "Exceptional Prison Conditions and the Quality of Prison Life: Prison Size and Prison Culture in Norwegian Closed Prisons." *European Journal of Criminology* 8, no. 6: 515–29.

King, R. D., and B. Valensia. 2014. "Power, Control, and Symbiosis in Brazilian Prisons." *South Atlantic Quarterly* 113, no. 3: 503–28.

Klockars, C. B. 1996. "A Theory of Excessive Force and its Control." In *Police Violence: Understanding and Controlling Police Abuse of Force*, edited by William A. Geller and Hans Toch, 1–22. New Haven: Yale University Press.

Larkins, E. R. 2015. *The Spectacular Favela: Violence in Modern Brazil*. Oakland: University of California Press.

Lemgruber, J., and A. Paiva. 2010. *A dona das chaves: Uma mulher no comando das prisões do Rio de Janeiro*. Rio de Janeiro: Editora Record.

Lessing, B., and G. Denyer Willis. 2019. "Legitimacy in Criminal Governance: Managing a Drug Empire from Behind Bars." *American Political Science Review* 113, no. 2: 584–606.

Macaulay, F. 2013. "Modes of Prison Administration, Control, and Governmentality in Latin America: Adoption, Adaptation, and Hybridity." *Conflict, Security & Development* 13, no. 4: 361–92.

Manso, B. P. 2016. "Homicidal Military Police." In *Homicide in São Paulo*, 45–65. Cham, Switzerland: Springer.

Mbembe, Achille. 2003. "Necropolitics." *Public Culture* 15, no. 1: 11–40.

McKittrick, K. 2011. "On Plantations, Prisons, and a Black Sense of Place." *Social & Cultural Geography* 12, no. 8: 947–63.

Misse, M. 2010. "Crime, sujeito e sujeição criminal: Aspectos de uma contribuição analítica sobre a categoria 'bandido.'" *Lua nova* 79: 15–38.

Misse, M., C. C. Grillo, C. P. Teixeira, and N. E. Neri. 2013. *Quando a polícia mata: Homicídios por "autos de resistência" no Rio de Janeiro (2001–2011)*. Vol. 1. Rio de Janeiro: Booklink.

O'Neill, K. L., and A. W. Fontes. 2017. "Making Do: The Practice of Imprisonment in Postwar Guatemala." *Journal of Latin American Geography* 16, no. 2: 31–48.

Pettit, B., and B. Western. 2004. "Mass Imprisonment and the Life Course: Race and Class Inequality in US Incarceration." *American Sociological Review* 69, no. 2: 151–69.

Pinheiro, P. S. 1997. "Violência, crime e sistemas policiais em países de novas democracias." *Tempo Social*, 9, no. 1: 43–52.

Rios, V. M. 2011. *Punished: Policing the Lives of Black and Latino Boys*. New York: NYU Press.

Salvatore, R. D., and C. Aguirre, eds. 2010. *The Birth of the Penitentiary in Latin America: Essays on Criminology, Prison Reform, and Social Control, 1830–1940*. Austin: University of Texas Press.

Schmitt, C. 1985. *Political Theology*. Cambridge, MA: MIT Press.

Seawright, J., and J. Gerring. 2008. "Case Selection Techniques in Case Study Research: A Menu of Qualitative and Quantitative Options." *Political Research Quarterly* 61, no. 2: 294–308.

Skarbek, D. 2011. "Governance and Prison Gangs. *American Political Science Review* 105, no. 4: 702–16.

Simon, J. 2007. *Governing through Crime: How the War on Crime Transformed American Democracy and Created a Culture of Fear*. New York: Oxford University Press.

Sinhoretto, Jacqueline, Eduardo Batitucci, Fábio Reis Mota, Maria Carolina Schlittler, Giane Silvestre, Danilo de Souza Morais, Letícia Godinho de Souza, Rosânia Rodrigues de Sousa, Sabrina Souza da Silva, Luiza Aragon Ovalle, Paulo César Ramos, Fabrício Bonecini de Almeida, and Welliton Caixeta Maciel. "A filtragem racial na seleção policial de suspeitos: segurança pública e relações raciais." In *Segurança pública e direitos humanos: temas transversais*. Coleção Pensando a Segurança Pública, v. 5. Brasília: Ministério da Justiça; Secretaria Nacional de Segurança Pública.

Skolnick, J. H.; and J. Fyfe. 1993. *Above the Law: Police and the Excessive Use of Force*. New York: Free Press.

Smith, C. A. 2013. "Strange Fruit: Brazil, Necropolitics, and the Transnational Resonance of Torture and Death." *Souls* 15, no. 3: 177–98.

Smith, C. A. 2015. "Blackness, Citizenship, and the Transnational Vertigo of Violence in the Americas." *American Anthropologist* 117: 384–87.

Steinberg, J. 2014. "Policing, State Power, and the Transition from Apartheid to Democracy: A New Perspective." *African Affairs* 113, no. 451: 173–91.

Sudnow, D. 1965. "Normal Crimes: Sociological Features of the Penal Code in a Public Defender Office." *Social Problems* 12, no. 3: 255–76.

Symkovych, A. 2017. "The 'Inmate Code' in Flux: A Normative System and Extralegal Governance in a Ukrainian Prison." *Current Sociology*. doi.org/ 10 .1177/0011392117744596.

Vargas, J. C., and J. Amparo Alves. 2010. "Geographies of Death: An Intersectional Analysis of Police Lethality and the Racialized Regimes of Citizenship in São Paulo. *Ethnic and Racial Studies* 33, no. 4: 611–36.

Weegels, J. 2016. "The Prisoner's Body: Violence, Desire and Masculinities in a Nicaraguan Prison Theatre Group." In *Gender and Conflict*, 151–73. Routledge.

Whitfield, J. 2016. "Other Neoliberal Penalities: Marching Powder and Prison Tourism in La Paz. *Theoretical Criminology* 20, no. 3: 358–75.

Yahmatta Taylor, K. 2016. *From #BlackLivesMatter to Black Liberation*. Chicago: Haymarket Books.

Zaccone, O. 2015. *Indignos de vida: a forma jurídica da política de extermínio de inimigos na cidade do Rio de Janeiro*. Rio de Janeiro: Revan.

Samira Bueno holds a PhD in public administration and government from the Getulio Vargas Foundation and is the executive director of the Brazilian Forum on Public Safety. Her research and publication interests include criminal justice policies, human rights, public security and violence, police practices, and police-citizen contact.

Graham Denyer Willis is a senior lecturer in development and Latin American studies in the Department of Politics and International Studies at the University of Cambridge. His ethnographic work examines questions of lived politics, violence, policing, and the political conditions of death and disappearance. His first book, *The Killing Consensus*, was published in 2015.

See inside front cover for ordering information.

Keep up to date on new scholarship

Issue alerts are a great way to stay current on all the cutting-edge scholarship from your favorite Duke University Press journals. This free service delivers tables of contents directly to your inbox, informing you of the latest groundbreaking work as soon as it is published.

To sign up for issue alerts:

1. Visit **dukeu.press/register** and register for an account. You do not need to provide a customer number.

2. After registering, visit **dukeu.press/alerts**.

3. Go to "Latest Issue Alerts" and click on "Add Alerts."

4. Select as many publications as you would like from the pop-up window and click "Add Alerts."

read.dukeupress.edu/journals

JMEWS ◊ Journal of Middle East Women's Studies

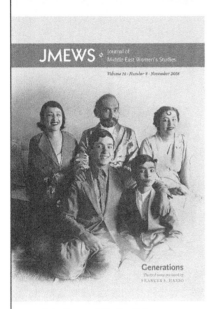

Soha Bayoumi, Sherine Hafez,
and Ellen McLarney, editors

*The official journal of
the Association for Middle East
Women's Studies*

This interdisciplinary journal
advances the fields of Middle East
gender, sexuality, and women's
studies through the contributions
of academics, artists, and activists
from around the globe in the
interpretive social sciences and
humanities. *JMEWS* publishes
area-specific research informed by
transnational feminist, sexuality,
masculinity, and cultural theories
and scholarship.

Sign up for new issue alerts
at **dukeu.press/alerts**.

Subscribe today.
Three issues annually
Subscription includes membership in the Association for Middle East Women's Studies.

Individuals
print and electronic, $75
electronic only, $55

Students and activists
print and electronic, $35
electronic only, $15

**Retirees, independent scholars, and
individuals in low-income nations**
print and electronic, $50
electronic only, $30

dukeupress.edu/jmews

ENGLISH LANGUAGE NOTES

A respected forum of criticism and scholarship in literary and cultural studies since 1962, *English Language Notes* (*ELN*) is dedicated to pushing the edge of scholarship in literature and related fields in new directions. Broadening its reach geographically and transhistorically, *ELN* opens new lines of inquiry and widens emerging fields.

Sign up for new issue alerts at **dukeu.press/alerts**.

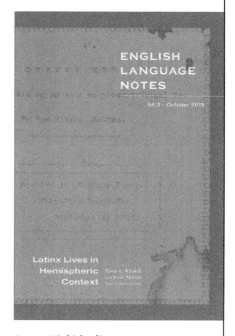

Laura Winkiel, editor

subscribe today
Two issues annually

Individuals · $40
Students · $25

dukeupress.edu/english-language-notes

Printed and bound by CPI Group (UK) Ltd, Croydon, CR0 4YY

13/04/2025

14656479-0001